STARDANCE - Flow with Energy
Shine like a star… the aloha way

STARDANCE

Flow with Energy
Shine like a star…the aloha way

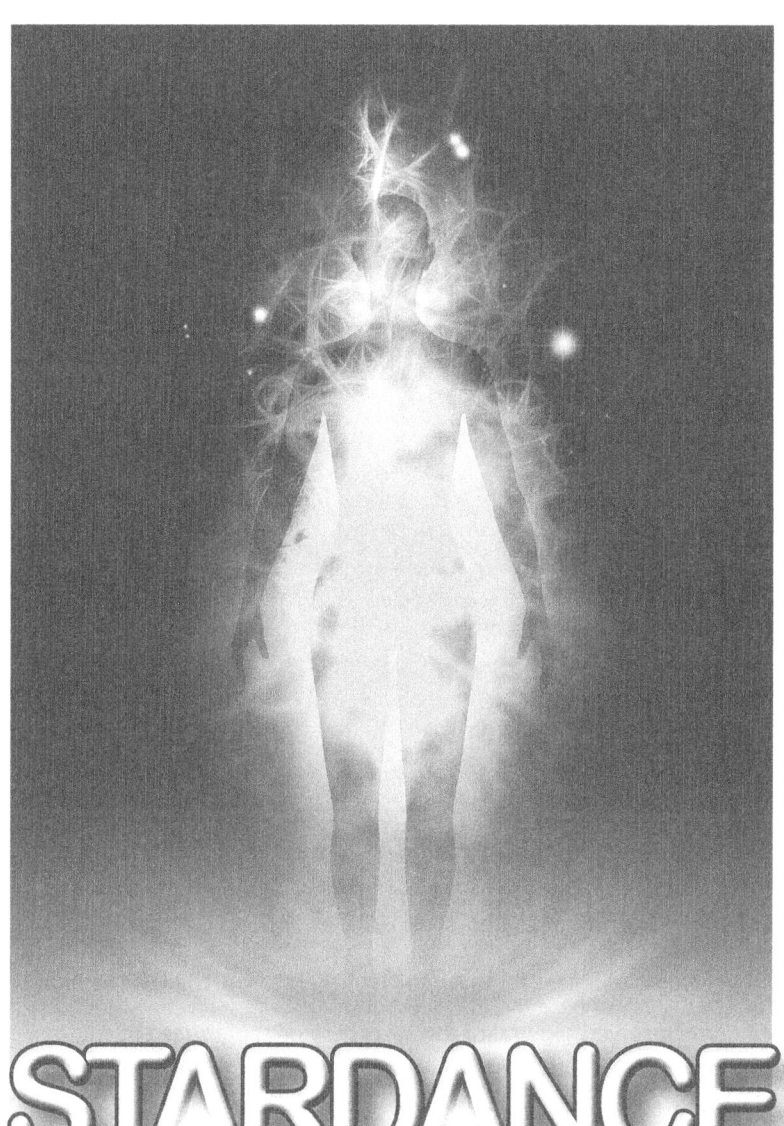

KEVIN ENGLAND D.C., D.D.

STARDANCE - Flow with Energy
Shine like a star… the aloha way

First published in 2015 by
Panoma Press Ltd
48 St Vincent Drive, St Albans, Herts, AL1 5SJ UK
info@panomapress.com
www.panomapress.com

Cover design by Michael Inns
Artwork by Karen Gladwell

ISBN 978-1-909623-75-0

The rights of Kevin England to be identified as the author of this work has been asserted in accordance with sections 77 and 78 of the Copyright Designs and Patents Act 1988.

A CIP catalogue record for this book is available from the British Library.

All rights reserved. No part of this work may be reproduced in any material form (including photocopying or storing in any medium by electronic means and whether or not transiently or incidentally to some other use of this publication) without the written permission of the copyright holder except in accordance with the provisions of the Copyright, Designs and Patents Act 1988. Applications for the copyright holder's written permission to reproduce any part of this publication should be addressed to the publishers.

This book is available online and in all good bookstores.

Copyright © 2014 Kevin England

Contents

| | About the Author | ix |
| | Acknowledgements | xi |

Part One

	Kamalamalama	3
	Stardance	4
	Who are we?	5
	Time to get wise	6
1:1	Introduction	8
1:2	A new dawn	9
1:3	Dare to dream	10
1:4	Keiki wisdom	11
1:5	Meeting Honu	13
1:6	Island rules	24
1:7	Isle de la azura	25
1:8	Aloha & Welcome	29
1:9	Soul retrieval	32
1:10	Dark side of the moon	35
1:11	Rosa	38
1:12	Sandy	40
1:13	Ha-Wai-i	41
1:14	Fear of the ocean	42
1:15	Hawaiian good luck sign	46
1:16	50th State	48

1:17	Chief Seattle	50
1:18	Ring of Fire	55
1:19	When in a hole	55
1:20	Neuro-science	57
1:21	Conscious creation	58
1:22	Life is a gift	61
1:23	Law of Attraction	62
1:24	Picture book	70
1:25	Quantum vision	72
1:26	Desiderata	77
1:27	Tallulah	79
1:28	Beautiful You	86
1:29	The Aloha Spirit	88
1:30	Act of kindness	93
1:31	Happy and sad	95
1:32	Stop negative thoughts	98
1:33	Cock-a-doodle-do!	105
1:34	Bowl of light	106
1:35	Flick the switch	106
1:36	Act as if	107
1:37	Learn to accept and love yourself	109
1:38	Compliments	111
1:39	Saturation praise	114
1:40	Inner beauty	120
1:41	Charisma	123
1:42	All day energy	127
1:43	Breaking bad habits	130
1:44	Way of learning	133
1:45	Developing new habits	134
1:46	Developing a skill	137
1:47	The man who thinks he can	141
1:48	Web of light	142
1:49	The zone	143
1:50	The flow	145

1:51	What is the secret?	**147**
1:52	In this moment	**153**
1:53	Love is the secret of healing	**155**
1:54	Cosmo-human body	**156**
1:55	To be a star	**158**
1:56	Solar and lunar	**162**
1:57	Betwixt and between	**164**
1:58	The science of spirituality	**165**
1:59	Stargate	**170**
1:60	Animal Laulima	**173**
1:61	Lomilomi	**177**
1:62	Hoku	**185**
1:63	Ho'oponopono	**187**
1:64	Piko-piko	**189**
1:65	Dynamind	**196**
1:66	Hula for Health	**200**
1:67	Emotions and bones	**201**
1:68	We do not diagnose	**203**
1:69	Rainbow energy	**204**
1:70	Spectrum Energy Technique	**209**
1:71	Starlite bodywork update	**211**

Part Two

2:72	Aloha philosophy	**223**
2:73	Aloha values	**224**
2:74	Crossroads	**226**
2:75	Aloha diet	**231**
2:76	Stardust	**271**
2:77	Turning dreams into reality	**314**
2:78	Faith, trust and stardust	**317**
2:79	If only…	**318**
2:80	Starlite is	**319**
2:81	Mahalo	**320**
	Testimonials	**321**
	Bibliography	**323**

ALOHA
& Welcome

In Hawaii we greet friends, loved ones and strangers with aloha, which means with love.

Aloha is the key word to the universal spirit of real hospitality, which makes Hawaii renowned as the world's center of understanding and fellowship.

Try meeting or leaving people with aloha.

You'll be surprised by their reaction.

I believe it and it is my creed.

Aloha: to you.

Duke Paoa Kahanamoku 1890-1968

About the author

Kevin England D.C., D.D.

Kevin's career in the healing arts spans five decades: he has served as a physiotherapist and chiropractor to a diverse range of people from professional sportsmen, Olympians, celebrities and actors, to HIV patients, midwives, babies and mothers suffering from birth trauma.

He is the world's foremost authority on the art of Hoku body alignment, the most technically advanced lomilomi bodywork on the planet.

Chiropractor* Teacher* Author* Businessman* Philanthropist* Presenter* Speaker*

Kevin teaches Chirapisa a metaphysical form of bodywork that embraces the embodiment of love, compassion and kindness on the mind, body and soul.

His mission is to share the aloha spirit by introducing others to the empowering and transformational Star-lite Universe-ity.

He has a heart-centered approach and down to earth style of helping, healing and empowering others.

"I am a guy who likes to share what I know, not because I am a master of technique or information, but simply because by sharing, it empowers others and deepens my own learning into a totally integrated and balanced experience."

He is the founder of azura, a body of energy, aloha in action, sharing knowledge and inspiring growth.

For many years he has been an active fundraiser for charities supporting children's hospices and dedicated to bringing smiles and laughter to seriously and terminally ill children, an interest activated by the infant death of his firstborn.

He is an inspirational speaker for the Blue Cross animal hospital charity and is an integral part of their educational program. He has recently set up Paws pet rescue service in association with the Blue Cross.

www.kevinengland.london

Acknowledgements

I would like to extend a big Mahalo (thank you) to everyone who has encouraged me to write this book which completes my transformation from mudlark to beachcomber.

I dedicate this book to my beautiful granddaughters Abigail, Isabelle and Imogen.

To everyone at Panoma Press who has made this possible, especially Mindy, Emma, and the talented Michael and Karen.

To all my students, clients, friends and family – and my expanded O'Hana.

O'Hana is family; it includes those we have always known as our family, surrounding us with love at the time of our birth.

O'Hana includes those we choose to call our family, for the connection we share with them enriches our life.

O'Hana becomes a sacred form for sharing our lives with aloha, for it gives us unconditional gifts of love, understanding, forgiving and acceptance.

O'Hana is the most secure and comfort-filled support we have for facing truth, for it never loses hope.

O'Hana has strong, supple bonds; they flex with giving and with the love and acceptance of aloha, yet they are made rigidly secure by those same supports. These bonds may be tested, but they cannot be broken.

O'Hana is a human circle of complete aloha.
–Rosa Say

May the spirit of aloha bless your lives with awe and wonder.

Aloha, a hui hou.

Kevin

(Dove Cottage, West Sussex, 2014)

Part One

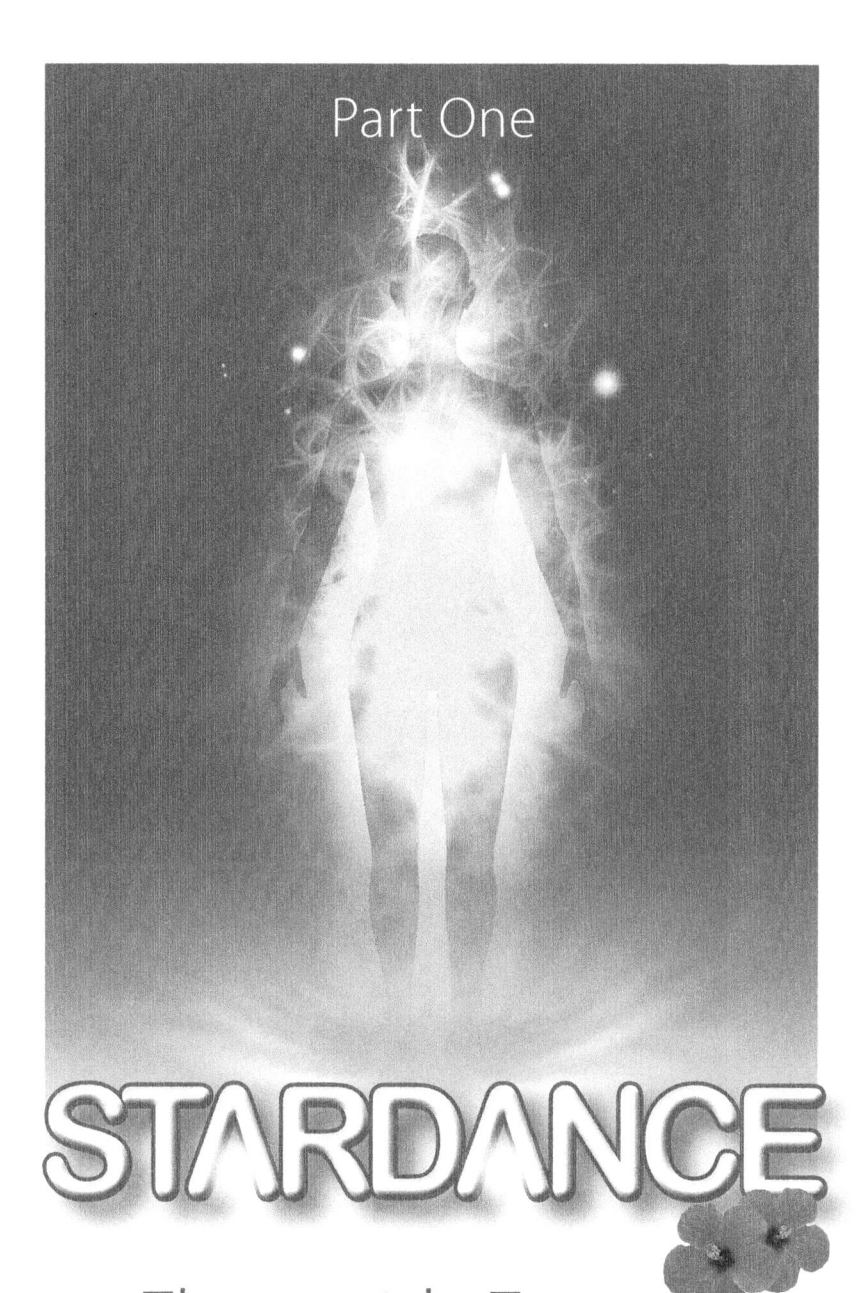

STARDANCE

Flow with Energy
Shine like a star … the aloha way

Part One

Kamalamalama

> ### The Light of Knowledge
>
> *Kamalamalama or the light of knowledge is a story of my introduction into traditional and contemporary understanding of a Hawaiian way to learn: a Hawaiian way to knowledge, truth and enlightenment.*
>
> *Aloha is generally interpreted around the world as love. The simplicity of the meaning of love as aloha is not in the definition of the words, but in living it. By demonstrating the Hawaiian way to love we can understand the Hawaiian way of aloha.*
>
> *This is a philosophical approach to a Hawaiian way of observing and relating to nature and man, Kahunaism. This concept is based on the ability of using the power of the total mind.*
>
> Patrick Ka'ano'i

These inspirational and profound words belong to Patrick Ka'ano'i, but they also reflect perfectly every life-giving word and thought found within these pages that bring with them the creative energy of the aloha spirit.

Stardance

> *A Dancing Mind is one of continuously new and exciting physical, mental and spiritual beginnings and lifelong positive change. By shifting your attitudes and beliefs about what is possible in your world, you will be able to redefine your potential, which is really unlimited, and unlock the extraordinary powers of your mind.*
>
> Chungliang Al Huang

Stardance is a cosmic entanglement of physical and metaphysical energy, riding on a wave of super consciousness. Vibrating, resonating and radiating to the tune of the universe. Creating a galaxy of wonder where dreams are made and wishes are granted.

Every thought and feeling is the drum beat that regulates a neurohormonal hula within and among us as we dance through life.

Paul Pearsall

I start this adventure with alacrity... (joyful enthusiasm)... and offer a diet of aloha, the Polynesian recipe for a daily dose of love, laughter and joy. Polynesia is a collection of islands scattered across thousands of miles in the Pacific Ocean, therefore the traditions and cultures referred to in this book are known as Oceanic.

> **The stars of heaven descended from the infinite soul of the Supreme Being. They were distributed from the almighty flame of creation through "the eye" of the infinite.**
>
> **The Pleiades made their entrance in a cluster, glided through space to find their allotted place. Came the first child of spirit, came the last child of spirit who belonged to this group.**
>
> –Tumuripo (the Hawaiian chant of creation)

Who are we?

At a quantum level you are nothing but love.
Bruce Lipton

The Hawaiians say that we are spirit beings, beings of light here to have the human experience. Spiritual just means the opposite to material.

Scientists can now confirm that we are not solid matter, but continually moving waves of energy. We are concentrated vibrated energy.

Through my experience of "this time around" I can confirm the following:

We arrive as a spiritual "spark of light," a twinkle of the divine matrix – consciousness of thought in creation.

> **Our "spark of light" is our spirit which in turn is the essence of consciousness, the energy of the universe that creates all things. Each one of us is a part of that spirit – a divine entity.**
> –Shakti Gawain

We take up an embodiment, often within the same ancestral line, especially if our work was not completed the last time around. If a whole new experience is required we can become embodied into any culture, creed, time or indeed any animal or physical being.

When we take up residence in a newborn embodiment, we know who we are; we know why we have chosen to come here at that given time, we know our mission and the difficulties that lie ahead.

We are a body of light comprising two parts: spirit and soul. The spirit is our divine essence and will act as an observer during this experience; it is also the source to our true nature should we need to call upon it. The soul is the recorder of our life's journey; its job is to record events experienced through the language that it understands: feeling and emotion.

Our physical embodiment consists of two parts: body and mind. The body is the mobile home, a suit of flesh and bone that will enable us to truly experience life on earth. The mind is a software program to the body's computer, the brain, which operates the mobile home and interacts with all elements within the physical dimension. It has the ability to grow and expand within the limits it sets itself. It also has the ability to interact with the soul and spirit of our light body if it learns to expand and express itself with unlimited love and enlightenment.

When our body of light embodies into the physical it sends an aka cord (energy cord) to the mind of our physical embodiment, through which feeling and emotion can travel to be recorded and eventually downloaded at the end of life, and into the consciousness of creation.

However, no matter how good our intentions, the reality of survival of our physical being takes precedence, and as we concentrate on the daily activity of learning, in order to communicate for food, comfort and security, we start to forget who we really are (you become what you concentrate on). This process is natural and necessary for our experience of this dimension to be authentic, and without the security of knowing your greatness, the safety net of knowing that you will return from whence you came into the arms of loving consciousness.

This temporary (lifetime) memory removal is also one of the biggest hurdles for us to overcome as humans as we struggle through life trying to "find ourselves" and understand our purpose. How we sail the sea of life and ride the storms we face depends not only upon the knowledge and skills gained as we grow, but also the faith we have that the stars will guide us home.

When it is time to leave our temporary home (of mind and body), once again our soul-spirit is set free – free to ride a cosmic wave of light back to eternity.

Time to get wise

We need a new vision, a new world view, and a new paradigm. We only see what we believe is possible, we have to go beyond our senses to experience that which is and always has been.

Two millennia ago, the wise people of Polynesia anticipated the miraculous discoveries we are just making now in modern physics, psychology and medicine. They were the ultimate scientists, reading the ocean waves and understanding the stars and planets. They knew the sacred secrets of a blissfully connected life and practiced them every day. –Paul Pearsall

We now have a science of spirituality that is fully verifiable and objective.

–Amit Goswami, PhD

Time before Time

*Out of the mist came the light
The light burned hot
The mist arose
Baring a blue oven below
Out of the mist came the earth
The ocean swelled around her
The sea became fruitful with fish
The sky became heavy
With clouds of rain
An arch of many colors, raised
To unite the sky and the sea
Thus, these lands were born.*

*The earth shook and quivered
Mountains arose from the depths
From the sky came flocks of birds
Soaring above the mountain peaks
They nested, filling the air with song
The earth grew and flourished
Then from the ocean, came man.*

–Island chant

The ancients have stolen all our best ideas.

–Mark Twain

*Part One - **Shine like a star**... the aloha way*

1:1 Introduction

Everyone who is seriously involved in the pursuit of science becomes convinced that a spirit is manifest in the laws of the universe – a spirit vastly superior to that of man.

–Albert Einstein.

Anyone who has been practicing complementary therapy for a few years will have experienced the aggressive, closed-minded and bigoted views of the so-called intelligent classes.

The medical doctor who walked out of a chiropractic conference shouting, "Bones don't move," as he went. The scientist who stated that complementary therapy was "quasi healing and all in the mind." The BBC radio presenter who stated that healing with energy was not real scientific healing but some "floaty, pseudo spiritual claptrap." In the last 44 years I've heard it all, time and time again; the very people who limit their own beliefs and what they expect from life try to impose their narrow view of reality on others, often with aggressive tendency. Just remember that they are only opinions based on a belief formed with limited knowledge; it doesn't make them real or true. When you open up a belief, its true nature can be revealed… be- lie- f. We really have no conception of the limits we place on our perceptions.

I decided long ago that it was not my job, not my calling, to try to convert or convince the skeptics that a bigger reality existed in an ever-expanding magical universe. I would spend the next four decades practicing the healing arts with spirit, energy and compassion. It was my hope that someday science would eventually catch up with these ancient practices and be able to engage with human consciousness and universal intelligence with an open mind. This is happening now.

> *Give up your powerful attachment to conventional reality. Life is nothing like what we pretend it is. Newton's world view has absolutely no bearing on the way the world works at its core.* –Pam Grout

This is not a New Age gobbledygook book filled with empty promises. It is a reflection and dissection of life experiences, being shared for the empowerment of others. Everything in this book is real, the lessons and advice are down to earth and geared for modern living, but the encouraged expansion of the mind and personal energy is restricted only by your own beliefs.

I am so grateful to those noetic scientists who in the last 20 years or so have broken through the self-imposed walls of limited belief, have embraced the mind/body connection and human consciousness challenge with vigor. Because of them the chronic battle between science and spirit, material and metaphysical, is coming to a positive resolution. All it will take for a quantum leap in human evolution to occur is for mankind to open up their minds, become enlightened and aware of their true potential.

Come and explore the Science of Spirituality in our Star-lit, Universe-ity of life.

This is a pragmatic approach to learning and using the power of your mind to influence **your** world and change **your** life; by experiencing and understanding how universal energies work, you can shine your light. This book is dedicated to that intent.

> *Open your mind and clear it of all thoughts that would deceive.*
> -A course in miracles

1:2 A new dawn

> *Ka la hiki ola ~ means a new dawn is upon us. With that sunrise we get another chance to be all we can possibly be. The sun comes with a fresh new start, and the gift of more time.*
> –Rosa Say

Regardless of our religious, spiritual, philosophical, and/or intellectual inclinations, we are innately plugged into the nebulous realm of our will's inexplicable driven impulse to continually "wish upon a star." To ride this wave of truth is in my humble opinion to be connected – intimately, existentially and profoundly in a deep way as a celestial child of the universe. –Barbara Chang

The first part of this book is a continuation of my first book *Starlite ~ The Secret Lomi* and concentrates on understanding how your body, mind, spirit and soul work in unison with cosmic energy to produce personal growth, health and happiness. The final section consists of two 30-day empowerment courses and you are encouraged to choose the one that meets your personal requirements. The challenge now is to totally surrender to the flow of universal energy and enjoy the ride.

I believe that even those who have not experienced the magic of aloha can hear its distant music, and feel its ancient call.

If you want to experience a beautiful wondrous life, you had better start believing in a magical Star~lit universe because… you're in one.

And so it begins…

1:3 Dare to dream

In the shining spectrum of our universe, something truly amazing is occurring on this planet.

For the first time in thousands of years, we have a real chance of a New Dawn.

A window of opportunity has opened ~ now you have a choice: stick with the old or embrace a new future.

Dare to Dream ~ your most incredible dream

For anything is possible

> *The state of aloha can be created in an instant. It is a decision to behave with kindness, with generosity, wanting to give joy to another.*
>
> Auntie Irmgard Farden Aluli

1:4 Keiki wisdom

Wordsworth said that children come into this world "trailing clouds of glory" and it's virtually impossible to stay depressed for long when there are little children in the room.
–Alan Loy McGinnis

- *Keiki is the Hawaiian word for children.*
- *I love the Keiki wisdom that reminds me the spirit of aloha is reborn every day in the face of a child.* –Genie Joseph
- *One day if you swallow a rainbow then you let some drip out of your mouth when you smile, that's what aloha is.* –Hana, age 6
- *Aloha is like when a puppy licks your face, only it's not so sticky.* –Olan, age 5
- *Aloha is when you have to say goodbye, but you want to leave a piece of you behind because now you have to go home.* –Sera, age 7
- *Even though some people live in big fancy houses with lots of toys, aloha makes us all the same.* –Rafelyn, age 6
- *Aloha is my favorite word because when you say it, it makes you smile.* –Makoa, age 5
- *Aloha means we're friends forever – especially if you're invisible.* –Shai, age 6
- *Aloha is what dolphins whisper to each other and to you when they pass you under the ocean.* –Nikko, age 6
- *It should be a flavor of ice cream because it's that good.* –Ivoreen, age 5

Part One - **Shine like a star**... the aloha way

- *Aloha is all the good feelings like love and missing someone, but it isn't so mushy. –Nick, age 6*
- *Aloha is when there is a room with a million strangers and then they say aloha and then they are not strangers anymore. –Makana, age 7*
- *Aloha was my goldfish's name but then he died, but it is like he is still alive because whenever anybody says aloha I remember him and other kids probably have things like that too. –Kailey, age 6*
- *Aloha means I remember you even though I haven't met you before. –Taytalaasa, age 7*
- *Aloha is one of the words that mean everything good, which is good because everything would need a lot of words otherwise. –Devin, age 7*
- *Aloha means you treat everyone nice even if you don't like the way they smell. –Tufaga, age 5*
- *My tutu says aloha is the old way, the way people used to be. And also aloha is the way it is today, because it's how the old ways are still alive if the very, very, very old people are gone. –Ikaika, age 7*
- *Aloha is the way we live.* **–Miss Na'a** *(kindergarten teacher)*

Kids will be kids…

The temperature was over 80 degrees, I was exhausted, breathing deeply and perspiring like a rainman. We had just finished a three-hour martial art training session and were standing in rows waiting to be dismissed. He had been staring intently at me for around 20 minutes, sitting in the front of the spectator seats; the five-year-old boy now turned to his mom and said, "Mom! That man is… melting."

After a great family afternoon, filled with fun and laughter, my granddaughter Abi, aged six, sat lovingly on my lap looking at my face with some concern. She stroked her index finger gently down my laughter line, then she looked into my eyes and said, "Granddad, are you cracking up?"

> 🎵 *Come with me into the mystic.*
> *Come with me into the night.* 🎵
> *We can live forever- skinwalker.*
>
> Robbie Robertson

The Wise Man believes profoundly in silence – the sign of a perfect equilibrium. Silence is the absolute poise or balance of body, mind and spirit. – Ohiyesa (Santee Sioux)

1:5 Meeting Honu

I sat in silence listening to the night song; the moonlit musical playing out around the woodland clearing that contained the spirit house.

A year had passed since I had received the blessing of the aumakua guardian spirits to name their advance bodywork system Hoku, a unique blend of advanced Pacific island healing art techniques. It was never my intention to teach lomilomi massage for there are many good teachers doing good work, but recently that too has been included into the exotic mix of island style massage called Honu and used as a precool to the Hoku treatment.

"Collect Pacific island techniques and blend into one, for they too were from the one original source," said the voice in my head over and over again. Now that I have carried out your wish, what do I call it, this combined massage? Honu- Honu- Honu.

Night after night the name Honu would appear, but unable to trust my inner feelings I asked, "Is this a message from spirit or from my own consciousness?" A month ago I had simply asked the question and let it fly free into the matrix of existence.

As I sat cherishing this peaceful moment my meditation was interrupted by a noise from behind.

I quickly turned around to see an old lady sitting quietly on a rock; she was dressed in khaki which was in complete contrast to the blaze of color of the spirit house. I smiled and said, "Sawatdee Kraup," using the local language for greetings. "Sawatdee Kah," she responded.

"Honu is a Pacific island sea turtle that has been in existence for 180 million years. It is revered as a sacred symbol of life force energy, an embodiment of guardian spirits; bring peace, humility and good luck," said the old sage-like lady.

I was startled!

And I just stared at the old lady and listened, as she spoke in the local language that I heard in my own. "Why do you *still* not trust your own innate spirit? You must learn to have faith for it is tuned into the frequency of creation and speaks with the vibration of life. All you have to do is listen and trust." Feeling stupid, I said, "I know I should, but it is difficult, I guess I am just asking for reassurance that the voice is from spirit and not from my own ego."

"William Clarke, an old friend of mine, once said that faith dares the soul to go further than it can see – faith is about trusting the divine love of pure consciousness working through you and all creation," said the sage. "If it *feels* right, if it brings happiness, love and laughter, if it's for the greater good and you know this 100% in your heart of hearts then it's properly from spirit. Or to put it another way if it looks like a duck, swims like a duck, and quacks like a duck, then it's probably a duck."

I laughed as she humored my appetite for inductive reasoning.

"Who are you, what is your name?" I asked.

"Who am I, who are you?" she replied. "We are all only passing through. I have had many names and lived many lives as an embodied spirit; my recent name was Loy Lom and I have spent over 80 human years on this beach giving and teaching massage, now I suppose you could me a spiritwalker, a connection between the physical and the nonphysical realms. I am a gatekeeper, guardian of the portal; I believe you know my friend azura."

A simple "yes" didn't seem the right response, but it was all I could say, how did she know azura?

"Now go to the beach, there is someone I want you to meet," she said as she smiled and turned away.

"Kop Khun Kraup – thank you," I said.

> **When we understand us, our consciousness, we understand the universe and the separation disappears.**
> –Amit Goswami, physicist

What a beautiful night, the sand was soft between my toes, the gentle breeze embraced my bare chest and the large waves crashed against the shore as they were released from the pull of the full moon. The beach was alive with moonlight, the woodland surrounding it mysterious in moonshadow. I walked gently along the edge of the surf watching the sand crabs run for cover as I approached. I reached a set of rocks, climbed up onto the largest one and sat up on the top watching the waves break on the opposite side – what a beautiful night.

Spiritwalker is a native term for shaman I thought to myself as I contemplated the meeting at the spirit house. Is this a dream or is it real? No it's real, I remember waking up in the hotel room unable to sleep any longer due to jet lag from the recent long-haul flight. I had climbed out of the bed quietly as my wife slept and walked out onto the balcony overlooking the hotel pool. From the pool there was a pathway with little ground lighting leading down the hill toward the beach. It was halfway down this path, between the waterfall and the bridge, that I had found stepping stones leading onto a wooded hillside. I had counted 120 steps from the pathway up the hillside to the spirit house. The spirit house was built at the same time as was the hotel; it allows harmonious living for any spirit occupants of the land on which the hotel was built. Decorated in flowers and set in lush tropical gardens nestled around a tranquil pond, bubbling waterfalls, tinkling wind chimes, the sounds of nature – the spirit house is a delight for all senses. But was the spiritwalker real? I had looked into her dark eyes, eyes that shone with ancient wisdom and the light of a thousand souls; she was clearly more – much, much more than a physical being.

Splash!

"Oh s**t!"

I had just been washed off the rock by a large wave, a wet slap that had left me prostrate in the sand. *Ha! Ha! Ha!* I could hear laughter, looking up from my humble position I could not see anyone.

"Hello, is anyone there?"

"I am here."

"Where are you?"

"I am here; you have been sitting on my back."

"No, I have been sitting on that large rock…"

"Exactly."

"My god, I am talking to a rock." Altered consciousness or insanity – a strange encounter to be sure.

"My name is Honu, I am known locally as the turtle rock, a name which you will understand when you see me by the light of the day."

"Why are you here?"

"I have been resting here on this beach for 18.5 million years and I was one of the original guardians to the starmen from a star cluster in the Pleiades called Honu. There was a migration from the stars – a migration of light souls traveling across the cosmos. We came to this blue planet because there was a primitive life-form ready to receive us. Most high guardians departed when their job was done, but some stayed and are still here."

"But why as a rock?"

"I am waiting until humanity is ready to transcend this physical dimension and ascend as light bodies and travel back across the stars to our true celestial home. A rock is a great way to hibernate as there is little one needs."

"Okay! I know that we are spirit beings embodied to have the human experience. But what you seem to be saying is that through evolutionary growth we can reach the stage where we will no longer embody during each lifetime, but instead we can ascend to a higher level of consciousness."

"That is correct."

"But how do we get to that point?"

"Every thought you contemplate and embrace has a vibratory frequency, which is experienced as feeling and emotion. Experience the higher frequencies of love shared and expressed. Use your thought process to raise the frequency level of body matter into the frequency of light – ascension is simply the means of taking the entirety of your being into another dimension."

"So you say I can keep my current body, but what is the benefit of that if I can simply just embody again for a new life, a new experience?"

> *When you take your body with you, the body can be raised and lowered upon any frequency level you choose. So if you choose to come back into this frequency, you never have to look for another body, with another ego, in order to exist in another life, with another family, in another country. You no longer have to be born again into this plane of limited thinking only to undergo the programing of social consciousness and have to fight for the expression of self in order to regain your knowingness. You do not have to learn all over again that the body can be restored to the purest light-form from which it came. You do not have to learn that this is just an illusion and a game.* –Ramtha

*Part One - **Shine like a star**… the aloha way*

"How do I start to learn this process?"

"You can start by learning to trust your higher self, your spirit body, your aumakua, allow yourself to receive all thought without judgment. You can achieve or become anything through the power of thought; if you can think it you can achieve it. You all have minds capable of accomplishing remarkable things."

> *What you can do, or dream you can, begin it, for boldness has genius, power and magic in it.* –Goethe

"I hope today that you have learned the extended meaning of the word Honu and to trust in the entirety of light that is the real you; it is the bridge between the consciousness of form and the consciousness of formlessness. Know that you are the angels that you are waiting for – cosmic artist creating with thought and deed. You are spirit embodied!"

"But what happens if we don't ascend? Our physical bodies will just die."

"That is correct; then you will ascend as a spirit body."

"Can you please then explain to me what exactly happens at the point of death, the separation process, the travel and the destination?"

"I can, we have been watching your process closely and feel that you are now ready for this information."

I sat on the sand listening intently as yet another ultimate truth was revealed.

Seeing death as the end of life is like seeing the horizon as the end of the ocean.

I will tell you a great truth, and I wish for you never to forget this: life never ends, you are an eternal being. Life on earth is a round trip – you end up where you began.

The life force of all inhabited creatures, human or animals, is the unseen collective of thought and emotion, which is energy, spiritual energy. There is no such thing as either birth or death of spirit. We can mark our bodies as having a birth and a death, but our soul-spirit has never been born and will never die.

Let me tell you what happens to entities that pass from this plane. When the body can no longer be effective, the energy – the soul – is withdrawn by the spirit of the entity. Everything has a soul. Even animals possess a spirit and a soul.

The death of the body is like going into a slumber. Once the spirit calls forth the soul, it travels up through the energy centers in the body. The soul, which is memory – memory of emotion – leaves the cellular mass of the body through the seventh seal called the pituitary gland. That passage is often experienced as traveling through a tunnel, accompanied by the sound of wind. The light that is seen at the end of the tunnel is the light of your being, the spirit of your being. Once the soul leaves the body, the body expires and the entity becomes a free soul-self. It takes but a moment and it is painless.

Accordingly, when we arrive at the preordained moment to release our present life, we lift out of our body, observing ourselves from a vantage point far above ego and human frailty. From this elevated position of purely objective observation, our soul can behold an incredible panorama of spiritual awareness. We are granted a few moments to center ourselves before we are moved beyond this dimension. There are a few moments of detachment spent bathed in an aura of peace. In that time, we become one with the perfection of the universe. Our consciousness instantly perceives the divine order in all things, and we experience no fear in our transition. All life consciousness and, because we are expressing as consciousness, we are able to manifest at different levels. As we die to the consciousness of the physical realm, we translate ourselves into the consciousness of the higher, more expansive realms.

Although there is a small, momentary pause to help us adjust to leaving this life, there is also a very large part of us that is more than eager to be liberated, for we know we are going home. Without any doubt, an aspect of our immortal soul remembers the way and relishes the prospect of returning again. Death is not a finale. It is no more an end to life than a graduation is to your academic career. Both of these promotions are simply new beginnings, moving us into a more advanced and sophisticated learning system. Life energy (consciousness) is eternal. Nothing can destroy it and, by design, it is destined to expand eternally.

At the instant of transition from our physical bodies back into our light bodies, a silver cord attaching us to the third dimension is severed. With the severance of the cord, the soul is released and we are free again. A loving protocol is in place to usher us through the remaining steps of our transition from the here to the hereafter. Lifting out of the body and moving down the tunnel are effortless on our part. At the moment of death, things begin to illuminate and become awesomely bright, for the moment you pass this plane, you go out of the density of matter and back into a light existence. There you are simply powerful mind and emotion, and your body is a body of light, changing in its electrical form according to the thoughts that are accepted through your light-form.

When we arrive at the light at the end of the tunnel, you are overwhelmed with unconditional love, then immersed in a luxurious state of being and sensual euphoria. Now an entirely new game is about to begin.

What we leave in this world is the uniqueness of our divine mark. And what we take with us into the next world is the understanding of how and why this divine mark was our unique destiny. Your level of cosmic karma is determined through a life review. You will literally relive your life in a 360-degree panorama. In astonishing detail, you will see everything that has happened.

You watch your life from a second person's point of view. In our society, we are taught to be sympathetic toward others, but from the second person's point of view, you'll feel empathy, not sympathy. You literally become every person you have ever encountered. You will experience what it felt like to be that person, and you will feel the direct results of the interactions between you. When you have your panoramic life review, you are the one doing the judging. And believe me, you are the toughest judge you will ever have. Once you have experienced the reliving of your life and judge what you think you could have done differently, it's finished. You immediately discard the memory of all guilt, sadness and regret. This judgment has no punishment attached to it, however through cosmic karma a lifetime of selfish acts and power will have an effect on your level of spiritual enlightenment obtained during this period on earth.

Be not deceived... love is the most powerful force in the universe.

Love is a divine living energy of unparalleled might and magnificence. Love is energy so expansive, so omnipotent and omnipresent that it could only be described as a force so powerful and profound that it nearly defies definition.

What matters now is how often you were willing to help others through love, kindness and compassion. The love you gave away and the potential for love that you instilled in others are the uniqueness of your divine mark. Only love is real, both here and in the hereafter. Making a difference in the lives of others is the spiritual foundation of our human existence.

It is only the love that you will bequeath the world with your passing, and it is only the love that you bring home with you, as your contribution to the expansion of divine consciousness that will define your new level of spiritual enlightenment. As we assist in raising the level of divine consciousness, we ourselves rise to higher levels of enlightenment and proceed to the deeper inner levels of spiritual heaven.

Part One - *Shine like a star* ... *the aloha way*

To inspire others to love, to encourage them to dream, and to empower them to keep hope alive are among the most blessed of all achievements. Our simple, spontaneous acts of kindness make the greatest impression on spirit; these are the true marks of compassion in action. Learning to live and love from this place of innocent virtue is a goal we must set for ourselves. As we align our hearts and minds with the energy of selfless giving, we succeed at attaining the ultimate goal, for in so doing we assist in raising the level of divine spiritual consciousness.

The greater the number of spontaneous loving moments we perpetuate here, the higher levels of consciousness we will inhabit when we reach the hereafter. The sole purpose of the life review is to act as an impartial tool to help us measure the spiritual growth that took place in the life we are leaving. And it determines which threshold of consciousness we have achieved as we re-enter the heavens.

From that point you go to one of seven levels of consciousness. Which level you go to is determined by the attitudes that you expressed emotionally upon this plane.

1. **Plane of demonstration and three-dimensional perceptions** – entities can witness in matter their creative power and whatever attitudes they are expressing in emotion.

2. **Second level of consciousness** for experiencing pain, remorse and guilt.

3. **Plane of power.** Trying to control and enslave others through control of their minds. Trying to get everyone to see their point of view.

4. **Plane of love** – for entities who are able to love deeply but, unfortunately, they cannot express that deepness. Thus they live a light-level existence in which they are experiencing great love but without the ability to express that love.

STARDANCE - Flow with Energy

5. **Paradise** – home of the golden light. Where one can breathe sound and live in the light. For those who love and express their love outwardly through words and deeds and actions, and desire for their life to be lived through love. Power to express and manifest your love. This is the highest plane that can be reached from the third dimension and is the door to levels six and seven.

6. **Plane of oneness, contemplation of all things.** To be completely at one with something, yet unique and separate from it.

7. **When one sees only Grace of Divinity** in a oneness and lives in that sphere of oneness, he will become that which he sees and lives with.

Because your higher consciousness has guided you to read this information about cosmic karma and the panoramic life review, you have been given a great gift. You also have a blessed responsibility, for much is expected of those to whom much is given.

Our minds need to be trained to look for opportunities to help others. Our spiritual life is as important as anything we do to physically maintain ourselves and the world we live in. When you help others it will produce a flow of joy and beauty in your life unlike anything you could imagine. The immutable universal laws of attraction and correspondence are active every minute of every day. We are constantly attracting people and circumstances into our personal reality based on the thought forms we project and the loving energy we extend. The same holds true for unloving energy. These energies accumulate over the duration of our lives, so during our transition, the life review brings us face-to-face with the actual effects they produced. Remember, on the other side you will become every person you have ever loved or harmed. Knowing that, how will you change the way you treat the people and animals in your life? –Ramtha & D. Brinkley

*Part One - **Shine like a star**… the aloha way*

> **Advice from a sea turtle**
>
> Swim with the current
> Be a good navigator
> Stay calm under pressure
> Be well traveled
> Think long term
> Age gracefully
> Spend time on the beach

"Wow, you have really given me something to think about."

"I hope that I (universal intelligence) have given you a little bit of knowledge and through that knowledge empowerment."

"Remember that aloha is divine love and a diet of aloha is a love of the divine; use your strength and courage to give love, act as if you are a divine being."

"Now my friend, it is time to go."

With these words the first rays of the morning sun started to dance on the tips of the waves. Honu returned to the physical world of non-solid solids and I returned to my room where my wife was still asleep. –Samui, Thailand

1:6 Island rules

> **Island rules**
>
> Never judge a day by its weather
> The best things in life aren't things
> Tell the truth – there is less to remember

> Speak softly and wear a loud shirt
>
> Goals are deceptive – the unaimed arrow never misses
>
> He who dies with the most toys still dies
>
> Age is relative – when you're over the hill,
> you pick up speed
>
> There are two ways to be rich: make more or desire less
>
> Beauty is internal – looks mean nothing
>
> No rain – no rainbows

> Life shrinks or expands in proportion to one's courage.
>
> -Anais Nin

1:7 Isle de la azura

We come forth not to alter your beliefs or to get you to believe in anything. We come forth to re-acquaint you with the eternal laws of the universe, the wisdom about the reality of nature, the ultimate truth and we are here to express all of that to you, in detail. –Ramatha

Brrrrr, splash! Brrrrr, splash!

The outboard motor of the boat kicked in and out as we endured the roller-coaster of the ride of the waves. After every wet climb came a fleeting moment of freedom as the boat took to the skies, a moment of peace that came with a heavy price, a bone-shaking landing resulting in the four of us getting soaked from head to toe. But we had no option, sundown was just a blink away and as the glowing embers of cosmic fire retreated across the southern sky the safe channel through the treacherous reef would be lost for yet another day.

*Part One - **Shine like a star**... the aloha way*

> ***Sitting low on the horizon below the constellation of steed is the gatekeeper, she is the guardian of the portal between the physical and the spiritual dimensions.*** –The Elder Scrolls.

The mystical Isle de la azura sits in the clear crystal waters of the Pacific Ocean just to the left and slightly behind the mist-covered mountains of Bali Hai. She can be seen briefly at dawn or dusk in the light of moonshadow, floating in a world of blurred colors streaming together creating rivers of silver and skies of gold. Known as the lady of twilight, the mother soul of the Pacific, she is associated with mystery, magic, fate and prophecy.

I could hear them, the drums! As we entered the calm waters inside the reef and cut the motor to a gentle hum, I could hear the drums. Quietly at first, not much louder than the crashing waves breaking on the outer reef, but as we started to round the dark shadow of the headland they got louder and louder, until we could see and hear the party on the beach. There were bonfires and bamboo oil lamps burning in the distance of the now dark night, the bay was alive with color, music and movement. Movement of people dancing on the beach which appeared to be the beating heart of the celebration, a vibration of awe and wonderment engulfed us as we arrived at this place of mystery – half of history away. As Kahali'I eased the old wooden boat onto the soft sand, I took a mental picture of the scene before me; I had traveled a lifetime for this moment and now I was about to set foot on this magical land, tired but alive – more alive than I had ever been.

With the sand in my toes and the sound of the drums still beating in my head I lay down next to the fire completely exhausted; after three hours of eating, drinking, dancing and celebrating our arrival, our new friends were fast asleep, right here on the beach. I started to drift away and slowly closed my eyes on the night sky dreaming of a new morn.

No sooner than I had closed my eyes, I had been pulled up into the sea of stars, feet first like a rocket ship speeding through the galaxy.

I traveled through the creation of time and space at warp speed, through dark tunnels that had circles of colored light osculating around the circumference indicating a side where there wasn't one. As I got faster and faster, the pinprick of starlight had become lines of light heading to who knows where.

I started to slow down; bit by bit my speed decreased until I came to a stop and found myself floating in a soft wispy blue ring of smoke – I was surrounded by many blue smoke clouds. Then my focus was attracted to one ring in particular, a smoke ring that seemed to be moving, changing shape, becoming… a holographic head!

This gigantic head appeared to have no beginning and no end, no in and no out – it was not three-dimensional but was of a dimension not yet numbered.

You have responded to the call of aloha and hence been invited onto the island, here you can look into the eyes of the ancestors, the guardians and see that in their deep peace is reflected the spirit of aloha, the message of love, live by giving joy to others and in this giving there is much contentment and much peace. The image before me was communicating through thought… and feeling, I could feel the intensity of love unconditional.

The human race has now entered the period of time known throughout earth history as the end of days – but do not be concerned, do not be afraid for all is not lost! There is still time for mankind to choose another way and to turn back from the brink of disaster. You are one of a number of spirit warriors, light carriers of aloha, illumined individuals helping to weave a rainbow tapestry of vision, creating the very circumstances that will raise and expand the consciousness of humankind.

It is everyone's own decision where and what he is. What he does and doesn't believe in. However, we are all subject to the eternal laws of the universe, we are all one, each a part of the eternal whole. Beauty and good is a cry woven into the heart. There is no line that divides one from another or those in body from those in spirit. All life was founded on love. There was love of family, love of land, love of sea, and love and respect for you and all around you! All were one!

For the first time in thousands of years, we have a real chance of a new dawn. A window of opportunity has opened, now you have a choice: stick with the old or embrace a new future. Dare to dream your most incredible dream, for anything is possible.

The time to choose... is now!

> *You can't stop the waves, but you can learn how to surf.*
>
> Hawaiian proverb

Deeds of love and kindness and understanding can change the world. Then a great light would come from the east – a new dawn. It will come into the hearts of those who are advanced in dreams and deeds. Love and light, the spirit of aloha will cascade down on all races and all religions, conquering every difficulty with the strength of body, the fire of love and the purity of heart.

This light you must find, this spirit you must seek, this truth you must live, the rainbow is a sign from the source of all when you face the right direction.

The morning call of the conch brought me back to the physical reality of life on earth.

> We all come from the sea,
> But we are not all of the sea,
> Those of us who are, we children of the tides,
> Must return, again and again.
>
> Chasing Mavericks

1:8 Aloha & Welcome

> *Welcome to the island where every leaf, every rock, every person, every waterfall, the waves, the ocean, the beach, the scented trade winds, and all life is a manifestation of divine energy and brimming with aloha.* –Harry Uhane Jim

I was on the north shore of the island watching the local keiki (kids) surfing in the large waves; it is believed that the islanders had mastered the art of standing on a surfboard around 1000 years ago, and now here they are flying through the air as though their heels have wings.

"Once upon a wave," said the voice of azura.

Once upon a wave, you become one moving in unity with energy; you enter the zone of timelessness, of no-thought, no-effort, just balance and harmony working in tune with the musical vibration of the universe, to be in the moment focused on the now as each nanosecond weaves itself into a moment of bliss, now that is the power of the universe.

Azura had just reminded me of the Huna principle that states: "Now is the moment of power" – with focused attention, letting go of our conscious will, our ego, we allow ourselves to (enter the zone) connect to the cosmic wave of universal energy. I am sure that every one of us has experienced a time of "being in the zone."

The first time it happened to me was at school; I must have been in my early teens and was at the time a decent cross-country runner, not the best but good enough to run for Croydon schools. During the winter months we would have a cross-country session once a week running around a three-mile school course. Neville was a great friend, he is of Afro-Caribbean descent and a very fast runner; every week he would win, leaving me to battle out the runner-up slot with another classmate. Our only chance of winning was if Neville was not competing that week.

Then one day it happened: we were lining up for our weekly race and the other two runners were missing, I would win today with no problem. After the first few hundred meters the line was strung out and I was leading – no pressure, I could relax and enjoy the sunshine of the fine spring morning, relax into a nice pace, relax with no heavy breathing, relaxed, meter after meter. I was enjoying the moment by moment experience of gliding along taking in the smell of fresh cut grass, the birds singing in the trees, the sun on my face. In that moment life could not have been better, relax as I re-entered the school grounds, relax there was only 100 meters left. Then the shouting started from the PT master, it broke my moment of no-thought, my consciousness kicked in and I tried to run faster, sprint that last few meters and finished more exhausted from the last 50 meters than from the previous three miles.

It was only then that I realized what the shouting had been about: I had broken a 13-year-old school record, a record that we did not know even existed. How? I could not answer that at the time, what I did know is that I put no effort into the race. Correction: I put no conscious effort into the race, it became a run of fun controlled by the subconscious working efficiently – human machine in harmony with cosmic energy. I held that record for three days – that's right, three days; the following week it was broken by Neville, not once but twice.

However I had experienced life in the "brilliant zone" surfing the cosmic wave.

Azura informed me that the massage/bodywork masters on the island were referred to as waveriders, because just like surfers they understand the complexities, movement and art of riding energy waves in the body. "We call this azurii, the oceanic art of body surfing," said azura.

Among the Waikiki beach boys, it was almost as popular as surfing. David Kahanamoku, one of Duke's brothers and winner of five

Olympic medals for swimming, gave lomi massage all his life.

They had set up several surfboards on sawhorses and were happily bodysurfing – riding waves of flesh, energy and muscle, massaging each other here on a bed of sand right next to their watery playground. There was a time, many waves ago, that the longboards were made of wood and the gray-haired riders were fun-loving hearts and daring spirits. Now the boards are short in length and the riders short in years, but the quality of heart and spirit has not diminished with the passing of the years. The techniques and skills were instantly recognizable, but the language – the new language of this generation of waveriders – introduced me to massage terms such as roller, wave break, curve, choppy, epic and bombora.

Deep breath; steady rhythm, ride and glide was the mantra as one beautiful long stroke was followed by another after another.

As a bodyworker I could only marvel at the skills of these youngsters riding the ocean and body waves with finesse, laughter and joy; I could only smile, a big broad smile as I realized that I was now the oldest surfer on the beach....

> ♪ *There's nothing I want to do, no place I'm trying to reach*
> *Only time is now more precious to the oldest surfer on the beach* ♪
>
> Jimmy Buffet

*Part One - **Shine like a star**... the aloha way*

*You will not be punished for your anger;
you will be punished by your anger.*

-Buddha

1:9 Soul retrieval

Imagine yourself sitting in a circle with members of your community. You have gathered together to support one community member who is suffering from a traumatic experience. You know that if one person is suffering and is ill it affects the entire community. So you have come to help hold the space for healing to happen.

It is dark and the stars are shining bright in the night sky. The air is still. Everyone feels held in the loving arms of the universe and there is no doubt that healing will happen for all gathered here.

The shaman begins to drum and dance calling the power of the universe to her as she puts her egoic self aside and becomes an empty vessel that fills with the help of the spirits.

The client lies quietly in the center breathing deeply to be in a receptive state to receive back his lost soul, his lost vitality.

The shaman sings her journey out loud as she tracks down where the soul has fled. And on finding it returns and blows it deeply into the heart of the client filling the entire body with the light of life.

There is a great joy for all, as one heals all are healed. The community is now whole again and can be in peace and harmony.

The work is done. –Sandra Ingerman

Shamanism is the oldest spiritual practice known to humankind. We know from the archaeological evidence that shamanism was practiced all over the world for at least 40,000 years. However many anthropologists believe that the practice dates back over 100,000 years. Soul retrieval is a part of shamanic practice in which it is believed that whenever we suffer an emotional or physical trauma a part of our soul flees the body in order to survive the experience. In psychology they call this disassociation. But in psychology they don't talk about what disassociates and where that part goes. In shamanism it is understood that a piece of the soul leaves the body and goes to a territory in what shamans call non-ordinary reality where, unable to come back on its own, it waits until someone intervenes in the spiritual realms and facilitates its return.

Although I fully understand the concept of soul lost and disassociation as survival mechanisms, and have personally seen a successful retrieval, I have often struggled to truly understand the details of both concepts. As stated above, psychology leaves me with more questions than answers, as does the shamanic idea that parts of our soul can disappear forever if not retrieved by a shaman.

This was a problem I asked azura to help me understand during a shamanic journey while on the island.

"Join me on this wave," said azura, as we drifted slowly beyond the breakers enjoying the gentle motion of the ocean. "Just let go, relax and let me explain, we all need analogies, images, ideas and stories in order to understand a concept. However, please remember that effectiveness is the measure of truth.

"Let me explain in a way that I hope you will understand," she continued. "As you know you are spirit embodied or, to be more precise, your human embodiment consists of a body and a mind, your spiritual self consists of spirit and soul. The soul is the recorder of your life's experiences – an internet if you like, a library of emotions and feelings. Imagine the soul looking like a jelly fish (a body with thousands of tentacles) which then connects to the human mind by way of thousands of electrical impulses. "Imagine a free-flowing optic fiber cable not unlike a horsetail, translucent, vibrating and glowing with light, at the end of each fiber is a little sucker that can attach or detach from the mind. When attached there is a free flow of information between mind and soul; however if the body/mind suffers from a traumatic experience, one single fiber of the electrical connection between mind and soul can become detached, thus preventing access to the traumatic memory. This happens in order to help the body/mind survive the impact of the trauma. To clarify, part of the soul is not lost to the spirit/soul that you are; the body/mind experiences temporary loss of access to part of the soul's memory, various files have been restricted until such time the body/mind feels capable of confronting the memory of the trauma.

"Disassociation, disconnection to the soul is a survival mechanism for the human mind and body only. The spirit and the soul are an eternal part of universal consciousness and are here to experience the emotion of all things. This emotion, this event, is only registered as trauma to the human body/mind; to the soul it is recorded with unconditional love and without judgment for the continual creation of consciousness. The soul does not need a survival mechanism for it sees no bad, no trauma, it exists far beyond the limitations of the physical dimensions. Thus the observation of "soul loss" is from a human perspective only; it's a loss of connection to the memory. When the human body/mind is ready to face the memory of the trauma, a psychiatrist or shaman may be employed to find the "lost memory/soul part" (via a shamanic soul retrieval exercise) and the "optic fiber" containing the memory can once again be connected for a new energy flow and access into the recordings of time and event."

"Once again, you have made the complicated seem simple – I thank you."

"I think this is my wave," said azura as she rode away… into the blue.

🎵 *Long you live and high you fly
and smiles you'll give and tears you'll cry
And all you touch and all you see
Is all your life will ever be.* 🎵

Pink Floyd

1:10 Dark side of the moon

"Don't be afraid to care," said azura as her image appeared, a dark shadow of smoke illuminated against the face of the full moon.

What am I doing? I am out of my depth, how do I share the essence of this beautiful energy that I have found with a world that lives a million miles away. How do I reach… is it even possible to reach teenagers living in a world of self-hate, and youngsters whose lives revolve around drugs, squats, casual sex and urban survival? 45% of American 8th grade students have experimented with alcohol and 25% with drugs. How can I make the message relevant to a culture of celebrity worshippers, people who desire fame and fortune, and will willingly sell their soul for just a taste of either? I had fallen asleep on the couch with these thoughts running through my head; now it was 2am, there was a buzzing from the TV and the room was alight with the cosmic rays from the full moon.

We all take different paths in life and our views reflect that which we see, from where we stand at any given point in time and space. My path had taken me from a south London tenement to the paradise islands of the Pacific, I had found the "way of aloha" – a way to live that would light up my world. I wanted, no I needed, to share this with others, but the very elements that had attracted me, others would find unacceptable, they simply had a different view from where they stood on their particular path of life.

What is aloha, what was the message I was trying to share? For me aloha represented everything that is good in life. It is love and light, it is caring and sharing, it is smiles and cuddles, and it is about living in a way that reflects paradise on earth. It is about accepting yourself as a divine entity, a being of light that is worthy of and deserves the beauty that this life has to offer. Finding aloha is like finding the magical needle in the haystack – what mystics call the piercing of the veil of illusion.

However, there are many who would reject this view as Disney fantasy for they can't even see the haystack. Some live in a world where the haystack itself is nothing more than fantasy, nothing more than a big pile of animal feed grown in an alien world consisting of heat, sunlight and goodness. For they live in the dark – a world of oppression and depression, desire and greed, a material world riddled with haves and have nots.

"There is another way," said azura.

For you see every positive has a negative, yin has yang, head has tails, and where there is light you can find darkness; don't view either one as right and or wrong for they both exist in synergy with each other, bringing balance and harmony to chaos.

"Come with me, let me show you," said azura.

"Show me what?" I said.

"The dark side of the moon," was the reply.

There is always another side, always another way.

Let me explain, you see aloha as all things beautiful, which it is. However aloha is beyond beauty, it is a limitless energy traveling into forever...

"Aloha is the living *expression* of the divine essence of life force energy," said azura.

Freewill gives you uniqueness – yet a oneness with the universe. It is only each person's attitude toward something that makes it a beautiful or a vile or ugly thing. Do not judge, do not seek to control others' thoughts and opinions, for every entity has the ability to choose and create the life of their desire.

And yet how can they desire that which they know not?

> *Everyone is a moon, and has a dark side which he never shows to anyone.*
>
> –Mark Twain

Remember that the love of the divine has no conditions; if anyone's life path crosses yours, share with them if they too desire the power to change their destiny.

Only by moving fully into the darkness can we move through it into the light.

A little while ago we shared with you the magic of stardust *(see Starlite ~ The Secret Lomi)*, the exquisite tonic containing the essence of love; now share with them the joy, the ecstasy found in *that* drug…

> **In an exuberant state of joy, you are at peace with everything about you. When you are in joy with life, you cannot feel remorseful or insecure, fearful, angry, or lacking. In a state of joy, you are creativity flowing like a mighty river from within your being. In a state of joy, you are inspired to the heights of greatness and the depths of feeling.** –Ramtha

Sprinkle stardust into a diet of aloha and allow each person to taste and experience the joy of the aloha spirit in any way they wish. This unique diet will allow the philosophy, or the concepts of reality, to be experienced and through the manifestation of self-experience to become wisdom and truth.

That is love – that is aloha…

Now is that not a wondrous thing?

1:11 Rosa Hoskins – Lessons from my dad

My darling dad has died *(actor Bob Hoskins died May 2014).*

> *I loved him to the ends of the earth and he loved me back just the same. These are the lessons he taught me, I will keep them close to my heart and remind myself of them whenever I stumble or falter. They are his words, the words spoken so often to encourage, comfort and reassure.*
>
> *I love you, Dad.*

1 *Laugh*

There's humor to be found everywhere, even on your darkest days there's something to have a joke about. Laugh long and loud and make other people laugh. It's good for you.

2 *Be yourself*

If someone doesn't like you they're either stupid, blind, or they've got bad taste. Accept who you are, you've got no one else to be. Don't try to change yourself, there's no point. Don't apologize. Don't make excuses. Be yourself and if anyone else doesn't like it they can f*ck off.

3 *Be flamboyant*

It's who you are and always have been. Be eccentric and unique. Don't try to adapt yourself to someone else's view of normal. That belongs to them, not you. Like yourself as who you are.

4 *Don't worry about other people's opinions*

Everyone's a critic, but ultimately what they say only matters if you let it. Don't believe your own press. People can just as easily sing your praises as they can tear you down. Don't waste your time on things you can't change. Let it slide off you like water off a duck's back.

5 Get angry
It's okay to lose your temper now and then. If anger stays in, it turns to poison and makes you bitter and sad. Get angry, say your piece, then let it go.

6 Whatever you do, always give it a good go
Don't be afraid of failure and disappointment. If you fall flat on your face then get straight back up. You'll always regret not trying. Disappointment is temporary, regret is forever.

7 Be generous and kind because you can't take it with you
When you've got something to give, give it without hesitation.

8 Appreciate beauty, take pictures and make memories
Capture it, you never know when it'll be gone.

9 Don't take yourself too seriously
People who take themselves too seriously are boring.

10 Never, ever, ever, ever give up
Keep on punching no matter what you're up against. You're only defeated if you give up, so don't give up.

11 Love with all your heart
In the end, love is the only thing that matters.

It clearly sounds as though our beloved Bob had found the aloha way, his way.

> *It is said some lives are linked across time*
> *They are connected by an ancient calling…*
> *Destiny*
>
> Disney

1:12 Sandy

"I recognize that writing," said the young bride as she signed the wedding register.

As she placed the two birth certificates together, it became evident that they had indeed been written by the same registrar, although four years separated the date of their births. Both partners of the newly married couple had been born at Annie McCall's maternity home in Clapham, London.

Dr. Annie McCall (1858–1949) was one of the first women to qualify as a doctor in the UK and was deeply concerned about the high death rate of mothers during childbirth. Shortly after qualifying in 1885 she started a school of midwifery in her own home and became a significant contributor to the modern practice of midwifery.

It would be another 15 years of separation before they would meet in the most trying of circumstances. They lived and grew up just a few miles apart in the densely populated Victorian streets of south London. Then within a year or two both families moved to the suburbs, a move designed to escape inner city problems and to enjoy a world of new possibilities. Their brothers had met at a local social club and had become friends, then one day there was a street fight, a fight that resulted in one of the brothers lying in hospital fighting for his life after being stabbed in the stomach. It was this single violent act that had brought the long-haired young man and the silly immature teenage girl face to face for the first time. Although another 18 months would pass before they shared a kiss, a spark had been ignited.

I knew from the moment that I saw her that we would marry, that we were destined to join in heart and spirit. I knew that we had a pre-birth agreement to try and find one another and to spend a life together, to experience the sharing of all things, a oneness, a unity of balance, a family life, the sharing of a deep bond of love, where the happiness of the partner became the happiness of the couple.

To my beautiful wife, partner, best friend, and soul mate, I want you to know one thing: if I were to pass tomorrow, I would consider my life to be a blessing having shared it with you. Love is a circle that surrounds you, one that you share daily with family and friends.

May your light shine into eternity…

> *Look to your dreams*
> -Nana Na Moe

1:13 HA-WAI-I

When the first Haole (slang for Caucasian), no doubt one of Captain Cook's crew, arrived at the island of Hawaii, he came ashore and asked the first Hawaiian he saw, "What's the name of this place? Where do you live?" The Hawaiian answered, "Hawaii."

Then the sailor went to another area of the Big Island and asked the next Hawaiian he saw, "Where do you live?" The second Hawaiian said, "Hawaii," and then a third with the same answer, so the island was named Hawaii. What each Hawaiian meant was: I live in the supreme Mana (energy) that rides on the life's breath.

When the sailor visited the next island, he asked the first Hawaiian he saw, "Where do you live?" This Hawaiian said, "Hawaii." And then another island and another, and still the same answer: "Hawaii." So Captain Cook named all the islands Hawaii.

But Hawaii isn't just a place in the middle of the Pacific, it's a place inside you – a place that wherever you go in the world it is still inside you. You see, what the Hawaiian was saying was: I live in…

*Part One - **Shine like a star**… the aloha way*

Ha: meaning breath, or breath of life

Wai: meaning water, but also a code word for Mana or life force, and

I: meaning supreme

I live in the divine essence of life force energy – I live with aloha!

The missionaries eventually arrived to "civilize" the Hawaiians. Only now, hundreds of years later, are we beginning to understand just how far advanced they were.

> Those who push the limits discover that sometimes the limits push back…

1:14 Fear of the ocean

For ocean read life: for wave, sea or water read challenge.

> **The secret of success is to be in harmony with existence, to be always calm, to let each wave of life wash us a little further up the shore.** –Cyril Connolly

A lot of people suffer from fear of the ocean. It can be hard to surf when you're afraid of the sea! The good news is that your fear can mostly be conquered and turned into healthy respect, which is something that is vitally important when dealing with the ocean. With time and dedication, anyone can turn their fear of the ocean into the pure joy of surfing on four-foot waves and beyond!

My story…

I was terrified of the ocean as a little kid. It might sound a little strange, but because of this hurdle, surfing has become one of the most rewarding experiences of my life.

When I started surfing I had a bigger than normal fear of the ocean. When I was little I had gone to the beach with my summer camp and I was knocked over by a wave. I was dragged a little by the water as it drained back out to sea, and I was convinced I was a goner. Well, I survived that experience, but ever since then I had been quite scared of the ocean.

One summer I lived five minutes from the beach and most people would give their right arm to live in such a great location.

My desire to learn to surf stemmed from a few different things. A few people that I looked up to were surfers and because of my fear of the ocean, I thought surfers were pretty much the bravest people in the world. I remember being a little kid at the beach looking at the surfers floating out beyond the breakers and thinking how can they do that? That's so scary! All of a sudden, I wanted to join them.

The first year I surfed I was terrified by tiny one-foot crumblers. Yes, it's true. I don't like to admit it. It was fear of the ocean to the extreme. However, now that I can routinely surf in four/five-foot surf with confidence I love to look back on those days and see how far I've come.

I had to get over my fear of the ocean gradually. The first time I got tumbled by a small two-foot wave I came up spluttering and thrashing, thinking that it was the most extreme experience in the world. I've since learned that it's not!

If you're not comfortable in the ocean, you might want to take a couple of weeks to acquaint yourself with the waves. Get yourself a bodyboard and go boogie boarding! Have fun messing about in the surf and build confidence. This is an excellent way for people who might be a little nervous in the ocean to get used to it. This was my first step in learning how to surf.

Getting over a fear of the ocean is a gradual experience. Always listen to your gut instincts, too. Believe me, I know how frustrating it is to sit on the shore for hours debating whether or not to get in the water, and then deciding that it's too scary and going home with my tail between my legs. It's demoralizing and embarrassing. But it's also no good to be out in surf that is so terrifying to you that you start to panic. Panic is bad, especially in the ocean.

Sometimes you have to override your self-preservation instincts just a little at first, especially in the beginning when one/two-foot waves are frightening. Eventually, as you conquer the one/two footers it becomes more important to listen to your gut instinct. When the waves get beyond three feet, the power increases exponentially. (So does the fun, but don't worry, you'll get there!)

The right mentality before you enter the water should be a little nervous, but also excited to get out there. It's a nervous excitement where the excitement is just a little bigger than the nerves. If you get out of your car and the conditions inspire flat-out fear and a sinking feeling in the pit of your stomach, you probably shouldn't paddle out. You won't make the right decisions in the water and you'll put yourself and others in danger.

Eventually, after surfing one/two-foot ankle biters, you'll come to the beach on a warm sunny day and see three-foot lines peeling gently across the beach. They look a bit bigger than anything you've surfed before, but you've been working on your duck dives and turtle rolls, and you've learned how to stand up pretty well. You're a little nervous, but after observing the waves and currents for a bit it looks so darn fun that you grab your board and jump in with a big grin!

That's how it works. You'll be surprised at how much you can accomplish.

Getting over your fear of the ocean involves taking small, well-educated risks. If you take the time to learn how to swim properly, observe the ocean and currents, and learn about the other associated risks and dangers, you're probably better off than half the surfers out there who don't think about their safety.

One last word: caution is great when you're surfing, but once you decide to go for a wave – go for it! Injury often comes as a result of not committing to the wave, especially for beginners. It's so easy to decide at the last second to bail out, but this puts you in a precarious position, with the wave about to break on you and the board not under control.

I will admit to chickening out on waves sometimes – especially those late drops – and it's a bad habit I don't like. I think it's especially difficult for people who have a fear of the ocean and get scared of big waves. If you can work on this now, it will be less of an issue in the future.

Steps to get over your fear of the ocean:

1. Learn how to swim.
2. Learn about currents, tides, and waves.
3. Take a bodyboard out and learn how the ocean works first-hand.
4. Start surfing on tiny one/two-foot beachbreak waves near the lifeguards.
5. Go surfing with friends.
6. Learn how to read your fear – is it just nervous excitement or flat-out fear?
7. If you start to get scared out there, smile, and remember that surfing is fun!

> **The tsunami** come in two waves, the first giant wave swept away my childhood friend Ki gasping for air. I struggled in a world of thought, dreams, death and imagination. Then the second wave hit…

In the tip of the wave, as if enclosed in some kind of transparent capsule, floated Ki's body, reclining on its side. But that is not all. Ki was looking straight at me, smiling. There, right in front of me, close enough so that I could have reached out and touched him, was my friend, my friend Ki, who only moments before had been swallowed by the wave. And he was smiling at me. Not with an ordinary smile – it was a big, wide-open grin that literally stretched from ear to ear. His cold, frozen eyes were locked on mine. He was no longer the Ki I knew. And his right arm was stretched out in my direction, as if he were trying to grab my hand and pull me into that other world where he was now. A little closer and his hand would have caught mine. But, having missed, Ki then smiled at me one more time, his grin wider than ever. –Haruki Murakami

Part One - **Shine like a star**… *the aloha way*

> Be the Aloha You Wish To See In the World
>
> -Hawaiian proverb

1:15 Hawaiian good luck sign

My Nana is 88 years old and still drives her own car. She wrote me this letter the other day:

> Dear Granddaughter
>
> The other day I went into our local Christian book store and saw a "Honk if you love Jesus" bumper sticker.
>
> I was feeling particularly sassy that day because I had just come from a thrilling choir performance, followed by a thunderous prayer meeting.
>
> So, I bought the sticker and put it on my bumper.
>
> Boy, am I glad I did; what an uplifting experience that followed.
>
> I stopped at a red light at a busy intersection, just lost in thought about the Lord and how good he is, and I didn't notice that the light had changed.
>
> It is a good thing someone else loves Jesus because if he hadn't honked, I'd never have noticed.
>
> I found that lots of people love Jesus.
>
> While I was sitting there, the guy behind started honking like crazy, and then he screamed, "For the love of God! Go! Go! Go! Jesus Christ, Go!"
>
> What an exuberant cheerleader he was for Jesus!
>
> Everyone started honking!
>
> I just leaned out of my window and started waving and smiling at all those loving people.

STARDANCE - Flow with Energy

I even honked my horn a few times to share the love!

There must have been a man from Florida back there because I heard him yelling something about a sunny beach.

I saw another guy waving in a funny way with only his middle finger stuck up in the air.

I asked the young teenage choir boy in the back seat what it meant.

He said it was a Hawaiian good luck sign or something.

Well, I have never met anyone from Hawaii, so I leaned out of the window and gave him the good luck sign right back.

My passenger burst out laughing.

Why even he was enjoying this religious experience!

A couple of the people were so caught up in the joy of the moment that they got out of their cars and started walking toward me.

I bet they wanted to pray or ask what church I attended, but this is when I noticed the light had changed.

So, grinning, I waved at all my brothers and sisters, and drove on through the intersection.

I noticed that I was the only car that got through the intersection before the light changed again and felt kind of sad that I had to leave them after all the love we had shared.

So I slowed the car down, leaned out the window and gave them all the Hawaiian good luck sign one last time as I drove away. Praise the Lord for such wonderful folks!

Will write again soon.

Love, Nan xxx

*Part One - **Shine like a star**… the aloha way*

♪ *Cry for the gods, cry for the people*
Cry for the land that was taken away
And then yet you'll find, Hawaii ♪

-Israel Kamakawiwo'Ole

1:16 50th State

The overthrow of the Kingdom of Hawaii

On January 17, 1893, the last monarch of the Kingdom of Hawaii, Queen Lili'uokalani, was deposed in a coup d'état led by seven non-native subjects of the Hawaiian Kingdom and supported by American minister to Hawaii John L. Stevens and the invasion of US Marines, who came ashore at the request of the conspirators.

> *I Lili'uokalani, by the Grace of God and under the Constitution of the Hawaiian Kingdom, Queen, do hereby solemnly protest against any and all acts done against myself and the Constitutional Government of the Hawaiian Kingdom by certain persons claiming to have established a Provisional Government of and for this Kingdom.*
>
> *That I yield to the superior force of the United States of America whose Minister Plenipotentiary, His Excellency John L. Stevens, has caused United States troops to be landed at Honolulu and declared that he would support the Provisional Government.*
>
> *Now to avoid any collision of armed forces, and perhaps the loss of life, I do this under protest and impelled by said force yield my authority until such time as the Government of the United States shall, upon facts being presented to it, undo the action of its representatives and reinstate me in the authority which I claim as the Constitutional Sovereign of the Hawaiian Islands.*
>
> –Queen Lili'uokalani

The Republic of Hawaii was declared in 1894 by the same parties which had established the Provisional Government. Sanford Dole (drafter of the Bayonet Constitution) appointed himself President of the forcibly instated Republic on July 4, 1894.

Eligibility to vote was also altered, resulting in disenfranchisement of poor native Hawaiians and other ethnic groups who had previously had the right to vote. Many Americans and wealthy Europeans, in contrast, acquired full voting rights at this time, without the need for Hawaiian citizenship.

> *The military demonstration upon the soil of Honolulu was of itself an act of war, unless made either with the consent of the government of Hawaii or for the bona fide purpose of protecting the imperiled lives and property of citizens of the United States. But there is no pretense of any such consent on the part of the government of the queen… the existing government, instead of requesting the presence of an armed force, protested against it. There is as little basis for the pretense that forces were landed for the security of American life and property. If so, they would have been stationed in the vicinity of such property and so as to protect it, instead of at a distance and so as to command the Hawaiian Government Building and palace… When these armed men were landed, the city of Honolulu was in its customary orderly and peaceful condition…*
>
> –President Grover Cleveland

In 1993, the 100th anniversary of the overthrow of the Kingdom of Hawaii, Congress passed a resolution, which President Clinton signed into law, offering an apology to native Hawaiians on behalf of the United States for its involvement in the overthrow of the Kingdom of Hawaii. This law is known as the Apology Resolution.

Many hundreds of Hawaiians went to their graves with broken spirits, hearts laden with sadness, because of what the puritans obliterated with their black pall. Missionaries taught our people to bow their heads, close their eyes, clasp their hands, and pray to their Lord. While the Hawaiians were busy learning to pray to the Christian god, his children were busy grabbing our land. They didn't let the right hand know what the left hand was doing. They bartered their souls for gold and traded their Lord for Hawaii. Now they have our country and we have Jehovah! –Leinani Melville

When life gives you a hundred reasons to cry
Show life that you have a thousand reasons to smile.

1:17 Chief Seattle

In 1851 Chief Seattle and his people were asked by the US Government under the leadership of President Franklin Pierce to sell two million acres of land in Washington State for $150,000 to the US Government. This is his response, which has been described as a "heartfelt love" for the Creator and the environment. There is a strong message in his powerful words.

The great chief in Washington sends word he wishes to buy our land.

The great chief also sends us words of friendship and good will. This is kind of him, since we know he has little need of our friendship in return.

But we will consider your offer. For we know if we do not sell, the white man may come with guns and take our land.

How can you buy or sell the sky, the warmth of the land? The idea is strange to us. If we do not own the freshness of the air and the sparkle of the water, how can you buy them?

Every part of this earth is sacred to my people. Every shining pine needle, every sandy shore, every mist in the dark woods, every clearing and humming insect is holy in the memory and experience of my people. The sap which courses through the trees carries the memory of the red man.

The white man's dead forget the country of their birth when they go to walk among the stars. Our dead never forget this beautiful earth, for it is the mother of the red man. We are part of the earth and it is part of us.

The perfumed flowers are our sisters; the deer, the horse, the great eagle, these are our brothers. The rocky crests, the juices of the meadows, the body heat of the pony and man – all belong to the same family.

So, when the Great Chief in Washington sends word that he wishes to buy our land, he asks much of us. The Great Chief sends word that he will reserve us a place so that we can live comfortably to ourselves. He will be our father and we will be his children. So we will consider your offer to buy our land. But it will not be easy. For this land is sacred to us.

This shining water that moves in the streams and rivers is not just water but the blood of our ancestors. If we sell you land, you must remember that it is sacred, and you must teach your children that it is sacred and that each ghostly reflection in the clear water of the lakes tells of events and memories in the life of the people. The water's murmur is the voice of my father's father.

The rivers are our brothers, they quench our thirst. The rivers carry our canoes and feed our children. If we sell you our land, you must remember and teach your children that the rivers are our brothers – and yours, and you must give the rivers the kindness you would give any brother.

The red man has always retreated before the advancing white man, as the mist of the mountains runs before the morning sun. But the ashes of our fathers are sacred. Their graves are holy ground, and so these hills, these trees, this portion of the earth is consecrated to us. We know that the white man does not understand our ways. One portion of land is the same to him as the next, for he is a stranger who comes in the night and takes from the land whatever he needs. The earth is not his brother, but his enemy, and when he has conquered it, he moves on. He leaves his fathers' graves behind, and he does not care. His fathers' graves and his children's birthright are forgotten. He treats his mother, the earth and his brother, the sky, as things to be bought, plundered, sold like sheep or bright beads. His appetite will devour the earth and leave behind only a desert.

I do not know. Our ways are different from your ways. The sight of your cities pains the eyes of the red man. But perhaps it is because the red man is a savage and does not understand. There is no quiet place in the white man's cities. No place to hear the unfurling of leaves in spring or the rustle of insect's wings. But perhaps it is because I am a savage and do not understand. The clatter only seems to insult the ears. And what is there to life if a man cannot hear the lonely cry of a whippoorwill or the arguments of the frogs around a pond at night? I am a red man and do not understand. The Indian prefers the soft sound of the wind darting over the face of a pond, and the smell of the wind itself, cleansed by a midday rain or scented with the pinion pine.

The air is precious to the red man, for all things share the same breath – the beast, the tree, the man, they all share the same breath. The white man does not seem to notice the air he breathes. Like a man dying for many days, he is numb to the stench. But if we sell you our land, you must remember that the air is precious to us, that the air shares its spirit with all life it supports. The wind that gave our grandfather his first breath also receives his last sigh. And the wind must also give our children the spirit of life. And if we sell you our land, you must keep it apart and sacred, as a place where even the white man can go to taste the wind that is sweetened by the meadow's flowers.

So we will consider your offer to buy our land. If we decide to accept, I will make one condition: the white man must treat *the beasts of this land as his brothers. I am a savage and I do not understand any other way. I have seen a thousand rotting buffaloes on the prairie, left by the white man who shot them from a passing train. I am a savage and I do not understand how the smoking iron horse can be more important than the buffalo that we kill only to stay alive.*

What is the white man without beasts? If all the beasts were gone, men would die from a great loneliness of spirit. For whatever happens to the beasts soon happens to man. All things are connected.

You must teach your children that the ground beneath their feet is the ashes of our grandfathers. So that they will respect the land, tell your children that the earth is rich with the lives of our kin. Teach your children what we have taught our children: that the earth is our mother. Whatever befalls the earth befalls the sons of the earth. If men spit on the ground, they spit on themselves.

This we know: The earth does not belong to man; man belongs to the earth.

This we know: All things are connected like the blood which unites one family. All things are connected.

Whatever befalls the earth befalls the sons of the earth. Man did not weave the web of life, he is merely a strand in it. Whatever he does to the web, he does to himself.

But we will consider your offer to go to the reservation you have for my people. We will live apart and in peace. It matters little where we spend the rest of our days. Our children have seen their fathers humbled in defeat. Our warriors have felt great shame, and after defeat they turn their days in idleness and contaminate their bodies with sweet foods and strong drink. It matters little where we pass the rest of our days. They are not many. A few more hours, a few more winters, and none of the children of the great tribes that once lived on this earth or that roam now in small bands in the woods will be left to mourn the graves of a people once as powerful and as hopeful as yours. But why should I mourn the passing of my people? Tribes are made of men, nothing more. Men come and go, like waves of the sea.

Even the white man, whose God walks and talks with him as friend to friend, cannot be exempt from the common destiny. We may be brothers after all; we shall see. One thing we know, which the white man may one day discover – our God is the same God. You may think you own Him as you wish to own our land, but you cannot. He is the God of man and His compassion is equal for the red man and the white. This earth is precious to Him and to harm the earth is to heap contempt on its creator. The whites too shall pass – perhaps sooner than all other tribes.

But in your perishing, you will shine brightly, fired by the strength of God who brought you to this land and for some special purpose gave you dominion over this land and over the red man. That destiny is a mystery to us, for we do not understand when all the buffaloes are all slaughtered, the wild horses are tamed, the secret corners of the forest heavy with the scent of many men and the view of the ripe hills blotted by talking wires.

Where is the thicket gone? Where is the eagle gone? And what is it to say goodbye to the swift pony and the hunt? The end of living – and the beginning of survival.

So we will consider your offer to buy our land. If we agree it will be to secure the reservation you have promised. There, perhaps we may live out our brief days as we wish. When the last red man has vanished from this earth, and his memory is only the shadow of a cloud moving across the prairie, these shores and forests will still hold the spirits of my people. For they love this earth as the new-born loves its mother's heartbeat. So we will sell you our land, love it as we've loved it. Care for it as we've cared for it. Hold in your mind the memory of the land as it is when you take it. And with all your heart, preserve it for your children and love it... as God loves us all.

> *One thing we know. Our God is the same God (Grace of Divinity). This earth is precious to Him. Even the white man cannot be exempt from the common destiny. We may be brothers after all. We shall see.*
> — Chief Seattle (1854) Native American leader of the Duwamish/Suquamish Nations

1:18 Ring of Fire

> *After enough people have visited a spot, to stand, to pray, to chant, century upon century, its original impact has been layered and amplified until the ancestral atmosphere around the site – these sacred places – is so rich with what Hawaiians call mana you can feel it like a coating on your skin… And when we hear the song the places sing, we are hearing our own most ancient voices.* –Jim Houston

> *Your thinking got you into this mess*
> *Your thinking will get you out of it...*
> —James Borg

1:19 When in a hole… stop digging

I have been fortunate to work with professional soccer players, Olympians, athletes and sportsmen and sportswomen at every level. Often during a rehab session they would express their frustration of the situation and we would inevitably get into the psychology of the sports mind, which is no different from the mind of anyone else, but it is possibly exposed to a higher intensive period of stress and emotion, in a tighter space of time.

The opposite of being in the zone is to be de-zoned or derailed, which stops the smooth running of the event/day. When this happens, we get frustrated, start blaming others or fate, we see ourselves as victims and reinforce that belief by our negative language and thoughts.

*Part One - **Shine like a star**… the aloha way*

A long time ago, and it seems like another lifetime, I was playing badminton when all of a sudden everything seemed to be going wrong. My normal little drop shots just fell to my side of the net; when I smashed the shuttlecock it missed the white line by a whisker. I got frustrated and tried even harder to hit that winning shot, but a funny thing happened: the harder I tried, the more "unlucky" I became. My mind raced: it's not fair, I should be beating him, I am sooo unlucky today, things are just not working out – and so it went on, and before I knew what had happened I was 9-0 down and going out of the annual cup competition.

And then it hit me! When in a hole, stop digging… if you keep doing the same thing, you will get the same result… I needed to listen to my own advice and then carefully apply it to my own life, and this situation, right now. Stop giving away points (your power), stop trying to force the result by playing winning shots. Stop blaming everyone and everything for my situation and most importantly, stop using negative language and thoughts.

By focusing on my preserved misfortune and bad luck I was attracting more misfortune and bad luck to me. But how do you stop? The negative thoughts had triggered feelings, feelings had produced chemicals, chemicals induced emotion, I was now responding to the chemicals in the blood and not the initial issue – a missed shot.

I needed to refocus, keep it simple, my mind said; go back to basics and stop worrying about the result, concentrate on returning the shuttlecock, playing basic safe shots, stop gambling by taking chances. I had "flicked the switch" of my focus, I no longer worried about the result and just concentrated on doing the basics with good technique. A funny thing happened: the rallies became longer as the concentration of my focus became fixated just on getting the shuttlecock back over the net; I let fate take care of itself. As the rallies became longer, my superior fitness started to tell and my opponent, who was no longer gaining points from my mistakes, started to make his own as he tried to win the match. I slowly gained a few points, but my mind was not focused on catching up, just getting the shuttlecock back. At 9-9 my opponent was red-faced, shouting at himself for being so stupid by losing such a lead. I knew exactly where his mind was; I felt totally confident in my ability and the table had completely turned.

For many years I have used this story to help others change their perspective of a situation:

1. Take a step back and reflect on the (zone) situation.
2. Stop using negative thoughts.
3. Flick the switch.
4. Start using positive thoughts.
5. It is simple, but not easy.

1:20 Neuro-science

Emotions are what shape our actions, behavior and decision making. When we feel positive, happy and content we respond better to the message that follows. Using a method called electroencephalography or EEG, neuro-scientists in the UK have backed up quantum physics and proved that what ancient wisdom keepers have been saying for thousands of years is in fact true: what starts with a thought leads to feeling and emotion, and emotion leads to positive action.

> *Science cannot solve the ultimate mystery of nature. And that is because we ourselves are part of the mystery that we are trying to solve.*
>
> Max Planck (1858-1947), physicist

1:21 Conscious creation

Just as all life is built from the four chemical bases that create our DNA, the universe appears to be founded upon four characteristics of the divine matrix that make things work in the way they do. The key to tapping into the power lies in our ability to embrace the four landmark discoveries that link it to our lives in an unprecedented way:

- *There is a field of energy that connects all creation.*
- *This field plays the role of a container, a bridge, and a mirror for the beliefs within us.*
- *The field is nonlocal and holographic; every part of it is connected to every other, and each piece mirrors the whole on a smaller scale.*
- *We communicate with the field through the language of emotion.*

Keys of conscious creation

1. *The matrix is the container that holds the universe, the bridge between all things, and the mirror that shows us what we have created.*
2. *Everything in our world is connected to everything else.*
3. *To tap the force of the universe itself, we must see ourselves as part of the world rather than separate from it.*
4. *Once something is joined, it is always connected, whether it remains physically linked or not.*
5. *The act of focusing our consciousness is an act of creation. Consciousness creates!*
6. *We have all the power we need to create all the changes we choose!*
7. *The focus of our awareness becomes the reality of our world.*

8   To simply say that we choose a new reality is not enough!

9   Feeling is the language that "speaks" to the divine matrix. Feel as though your goal is accomplished and your prayer is already answered.

10 Not just any feeling will do. The ones that create must be without ego and judgment.

11 We must become in our lives the things that we choose to experience as our world.

12 We are not bound by the laws of physics as we know them today.

13 In a holographic "something" every piece of the something mirrors the whole something.

14 The universally connected consciousness promises that the instant we create our good wishes and prayers, they are already received at their destination.

15 Through the hologram of consciousness, a little change in our lives is mirrored everywhere in our world.

16 The minimum number of people required to jump-start a change in consciousness is the $\sqrt{1\%}$ of a population.

17 The matrix serves as the mirror in our world of the relationships that we create in our beliefs.

18 The root of our negative experiences may be reduced to one of three universal fears (or a combination of them): abandonment, low self-worth, or lack of trust.

19 Our true beliefs are mirrored in our most intimate relationships.

We must become in our lives the very things that we choose to experience in our world.

Almost universally, we share a sense that there's more to us than meets the eye. Somewhere deep within the midst of our ancient memory, we know that we have magical and miraculous powers within us.

Holographic consciousness provides for a change made anywhere in the system becoming a change everywhere In the system.

A powerful metaphor to understanding how the universe appears to work is that of a computer. For all intents and purposes, the operating system of a computer is fixed and doesn't change. In other words, it is what it is. When we want to see our computer do something different, we don't change the operating system, we change the commands that go into it. The reason why this is important is that consciousness appears to work in precisely the same way. If we think of the entire universe as a massive consciousness computer, then consciousness itself is the operating system, and reality is the output. Just as a computer's operating system is fixed and changes must come from the programs that speak to it, in order to change the world, we must alter the programs that make sense to reality: feelings, emotions, prayers, and beliefs.

–Gregg Braden

$$E = mc^2 - r$$

Master formula for maximum effectiveness:

"E" stands for **effectiveness**

"m" stands for **motivation**

"c²" stands for two things: **confidence and concentration**

"r" stands for **resistance**

Written out the formula states: Effectiveness equals motivation multiplied by confidence, multiplied again by concentration, and reduced by resistance. To put it less formally, the way to increase your effectiveness is to increase your motivation, concentration, and confidence, while at the same time eliminating or diminishing the stuff that gets in the way.
–Serge Kahili King

> *The reason why the universe is eternal is that it does not live for itself; it gives life to others as it transforms.*
> Lao Tzu (founder of Taoism)

1:22 Life is a gift

Some people see their life and the people in their lives as a gift. They appreciate all of life's experiences as gifts and express gratitude for them. Kindness leads to gratitude and gratitude leads to kindness, a complete circle of aloha.

Gratitude unlocks the fullness of life. It turns what we have into enough, and more. It turns denial into acceptance, chaos into order, confusion into clarity… it turns problems into gifts, failures into success, the unexpected into perfect timing, and mistakes into important events. Gratitude makes sense of our past, brings peace for today and creates a vision for tomorrow. –Melody Beattie

> *Be careful when speaking*
> *You create the world around you*
> *With your words*
> Navajo

Part One - **Shine like a star**… *the aloha way*

1:23 Law of Attraction

- *Whatever we steadfastly believe, we will convince ourselves that it is true; and whatever we know as a truth will transform itself into a reality. That is how powerful our creativity and our wills are. –Ramtha*

- *Through the reality markers of imagination, expectation, judgment, passion, and prayer, we galvanize each possibility into existence. In our beliefs about who we are, what we have and don't have, and what should and shouldn't be, we breathe life into our greatest joys as well as our darkest moments. –Gregg Branden*

- *We are shaped by our thoughts, the mind is everything. We become what we think, when the mind is pure, joy follows like a shadow that never leaves. –Buddha*

- *Our true might is a tangible aspect of our spiritual reality as created by our thoughts, words, and deeds, for they are destined to become energy solidified and manifested in the physical realm, ready to reveal the invincibility of our divine identities. –Dannion Brinkley*

I am often asked if the law of attraction really works or better still why it doesn't work. If you ask a group of people whether they believe the law of attraction works or not, you usually find that the group is split 50-50. I believe that there is a problem with many people accepting the law of attraction and that may start with the use of the word law and the individual understanding of how the law of attraction *really* works. One high profile motivational speaker, who clearly uses the law of attraction in his work, stated at a recent seminar that the law is not a law but a theory. My theory is that it's a method. A method that if followed can result in you obtaining the object of your desire.

But just like baking a cake, you need the right ingredients, a recipe, and a method. Then you need to practice – practice mixing, practice adding energy (heat source) – then try it; see if the result is what you wanted, if not try again. You will not achieve attracting a cake or anything else simply by looking at a picture of one and dreaming of having it. Why? Because attraction requires action.

Before I share with you the ingredients and the "secret" recipe for the energy of attraction, we need to explore the facts behind the law of attraction.

The definition of law is a statement of fact, deduced from observation, to the effect that a particular natural or scientific phenomenon *always* occurs if certain conditions are present. The principles and regulations of a law would need to have been established by some authority.

The natural or scientific phenomenon must *always* occur; if it doesn't then it cannot by definition be called a law. Now this is where the problems start – what are the conditions, principles and regulations? And who in authority established them? Even that is not clear.

On their website Abraham-Hicks claim that they have the original source material for the current law of attraction wave that is sweeping the world and it is the 21st century inspiration for thousands of books, movies, essays and lectures that are responsible for the current paradigm shift in consciousness. They also claim to be the fountainhead of the information upon which the hit movie *The Secret* was based. However, further investigation and research shows that Thomas Troward, who was a strong influence in the New Thought Movement, claimed in 1890 that thought precedes physical form and "the action of Mind plants that nucleus which, if allowed to grow undisturbed, will eventually attract to itself all the conditions necessary for its manifestation in outward visible form." Then there were James Allen, 1902; William Walker Atkinson, 1906; Bruce MacLelland 1907; and numerous others writing and teaching about the benefits of this law throughout the 20th century.

*Part One - **Shine like a star**... the aloha way*

The law of attraction is the name given to the belief that like attracts like, and by focusing on positive or negative thoughts, one can bring about positive or negative results. This belief is based upon the idea that people and their thoughts are both made from pure energy, and the belief that like energy attracts like energy. Conversely we also know that opposites attract. Modern science states that there is no scientific basis to the law of attraction.

Although there are some cases where positive or negative attitudes can produce corresponding results, principally the placebo and nocebo effects (see *Starlite ~ The Secret Lomi*). In Taoism the concept of yin-yang is used to describe how opposite or contrary forces are interconnected and interdependent in the natural world and how they give rise to each other as they interrelate to one another. This means that the energy of attraction must also be linked with the energy of detraction, so be careful what you wish for, you might just get it. Or better still, be careful what your imagination chooses to believe in, for you might just create it.

In 1937, Napoleon Hill published *Think and Grow Rich*, which went on to become one of the bestselling books of all time, selling over 60 million copies. In this book, Hill insisted on the importance of controlling one's own thoughts in order to achieve success, as well as the energy that thoughts have and their ability to attract other thoughts. In the beginning of the book, Hill mentions a "secret" to success and promises to describe it indirectly at least once in every chapter of the book. It is never named directly, for he says that discovering it on one's own is far more beneficial. Many people have argued over what the secret actually is, some claiming that it is the law of attraction. Hill states the "secret" to which he refers is mentioned no fewer than 100 times, yet reference to "attract" is used fewer than 30 times in the text. Most students of the book claim the secret is hidden in its title: *THINK - thinking the right thoughts*.

Thought comes first; feeling follows right after as long as the thought is more than just a passing one. A feeling will produce a chemical reaction from the pituitary gland to form emotion in order to have a physical experience of the feeling. A thought without a feeling is just a shadow of itself. A thought with direction and purpose (emotion and feeling) equals creation.

> *We aren't the sum total of our thoughts, we are a sum total of our feelings. Our feelings are what is translated through our spirit, and with the law of attraction, the universe gives us what we dwell on, what we feel. It's so very important to always strive for a better thought, a happier thought, until you feel positive thoughts dominating your life. Only then will you live a life of happiness and true abundance.*
> –Neville Goddard

We also find in the principles of the 35,000-year-old Hawaiian philosophy Huna that *energy flows where attention goes*, which is the very basis of the law of attraction. While western science is only beginning to understand what our relationship to time and space mean within the context of connectedness, our indigenous ancestors were already well aware of these relationships. If the secret ingredient missing from the law of attraction is not attraction but thought – thought with direction and purpose (willful, conscious intent) – then no wonder many people are not getting the results they desire, it's like trying to bake a cake without the flour.

The Science

As we change our thoughts our body changes too, at a cellular level. The way it works is that chemicals known as neuropeptides are continually manufactured in an area of the brain known as the hypothalamus. From there, many flow into the pituitary gland and are released into the bloodstream in response to our thoughts.

Part One - Shine like a star... the aloha way

As these "molecules of emotion" circulate the bloodstream, they carry information to different parts of the body. Many of them pass this information into cells by fitting into receptors on the surface of the cells. When the neuropeptide fits into the receptor, information is passed to the cell, entering new instructions into its DNA. Some of this information activates or deactivates genes.

> *In this way, our thoughts, attitudes, beliefs and emotions impact on us at the cellular and genetic level. It's happening constantly, throughout the brain and body. It's actually impossible to disentangle your mind and body. The effects of your thinking and feeling, your loves and fears, your attitudes, behavior and relationships are all felt at the genetic level.*
> –David R. Hamilton

Understanding the Law of Detraction

The law of detraction is often misunderstood and misrepresented. Remember that energy flows where attention goes.

If you place your attention into the wish of your desire and increase the magnetic pull with feelings, emotion, and beliefs you can draw that wish toward you. Conversely, if you concentrate on what you don't want in life you increase the magnetic pull and draw into your life that which you don't desire.

Both of these are examples of the law of attraction, not detraction. Detraction works by ignoring a desire or a wish. Detract means to take away, and taking away the attention of your energy from any object will push that object away whether you want it or not.

> *For you to manifest what you want, it has to come through the darkness. It's behind all the things you don't want.*
> –Connie Rios

Remember the old adage "if you don't use it you lose it." That is the law of detraction. A simple analogy is two flower beds, one with weeds and one with daffodils; whichever bed you water will grow (attract growth) and whichever you neglect will wither and die (detract growth). Concentrate on the blooming flowers in your life and pay no attention to the weeds in your life. Understand and make both attraction and detraction work for you.

> *Our thoughts are energy. As you focus on a particular thought you are literally taking energy from your inner world and creating something in the outer world of reality, based entirely on your thoughts.* –James Borg

Ingredients required for attracting what you want

Although the theory behind the law of attraction is very simple, putting it into practice on a conscious level takes work. Negative and limiting belief systems (detraction) are buried deep inside us. Never feel sorry for yourself. Changing or ridding yourself of ideas and old habits that defeat you at every turn can be done. The creative process as portrayed in the extended version of the movie *The Secret* involves three steps to attracting all your desires.

1. **Ask** – You must know what you want. I mean, really know what you want. The universe can't deliver without first knowing what it is that you want to have manifested into your life.

2. **Believe** – You need to truly believe that what you are asking for will become yours. Doubts need to be pushed away. The idea that failure is a possibility will mess up the delivery.

3. **Receive** – It is important that you become an active player in reaching your goals. When opportunity comes your way you must not hesitate. Grab the brass ring when it appears.

These are the ingredients for the law of attraction. But why are so many getting it so wrong? Why do people give up chasing their dreams? Simple: because they have the ingredients but don't have the recipe!

*Part One - **Shine like a star**... the aloha way*

Each moment we're sending our message of emotion, feeling, prayers (Pule), and belief to the source of consciousness, which translates the code of our message into the daily reality for our bodies, relationships, lives, and world. The question now is less about whether this language exists and more about how intentionally we use it in our lives. If the law of attraction gives us the ingredients, then the Star~lit'e Universe~ity will give us the recipe.

Warning

Your responsibility is to ask the universe for great things for you and your loved ones. If you abuse the universe's powers to create fear and hurt in other people, the universe will give you exactly what you are asking for, but it will happen to you. Every thought directed to the universe should focus strictly on the positive and the effect you want.
–Michael Samuels

Manifestation recipe

1. **Ask** – You must know what you want. I mean, really know what you want. The universe can't deliver without first knowing what it is that you want to have manifested into your life. Your thoughts must be clear, consistent, and to the point. Know what you want and write it down in detail. Make a wish list.

    Make a wish… ask with Pule (focused prayer) applying willful, conscious intent.

2. **Affirm** – The outcome of your desire. Declare it succinctly in positive, pleasurable, emotional language (for example: I am a great massage therapist and I love it).

3. **Believe** – Believe that it will happen. Trouble is when we use the word believe many are left with a subconscious nagging doubt that it might not happen and that there might just be a lie hidden somewhere in that belief: be- lie- ve.

    Trust – Maybe change believe to trust – a strong reliable word that won't let you down, learn to trust the universe in every sense. In the word trust you find "us": an unbreakable bond of universe and spirit.

4   **Assume** – That the final result has already occurred. Imagine yourself vividly in this desired condition. Feel and picture your surroundings while generating strong enthusiasm. Verbalize it for reinforcement. Imagine what it will feel like when you reach that goal or receive the item of your desire.

5   **Act** – Act as if you already have the object of your desire. To anchor this state in your subconscious by symbolism. For example, raise your arms with hands pointing upward to the heavens, the invisible realm. On the count of three, pull your hands down into fists, and imagine bringing your invisible desire into visible, physical reality; while shouting "yes" take appropriate actions in the world to further your desired outcome. Make it important.

6   **Receive** – To receive you have to think and become magnetic. It is important that you become an active player in reaching your goals. When opportunity comes your way you must not hesitate. Grab the opportunity when it appears. The universe will start to send you the items on your wish list when you are ready to receive them.

7   **Bless with Gratitude** – Let gratitude seep from every pore in your body. Express gratitude and give blessings to everything that is related to your desire.

8   **Act with Gratitude** – The universe will not give you something for nothing. It does not show favoritism. You must give every person more in worth than you obtain from them. Become a progressive force that radiates enhancement in people's lives.

–Michael Samuels

You are now armed with both the ingredients and the recipe to create the life that you desire.

The thoughts you think and the feelings that follow them have an electromagnetic reality. The concentration of your attention sets up a vibration of energy in your electromagnetic field, which attracts experiences related to what you concentrate on. It is your beliefs – your thoughts, feelings, attitudes and expectations – that actually draw to you everything you experience in form. An electromagnetic field surrounds you. It also flows through you like an electric current, magnetizing your thoughts and feelings so they attract forms that are like them. Every thought you think goes into this field. If you concentrate on an idea, it becomes magnetized more strongly and thus has more power to attract that idea in form. –Kala H. Kos

> Take a breath of the new dawn
> And make it part of you.
> It will give you strength.
>
> – Hopi

1:24 Picture book

Create a manifestation picture book/scrap book

The act of creating a scrapbook or vision board helps to imprint the images of what you want on your subconscious mind and, in this way, helps your subconscious mind to work on manifesting what you want.

A scrapbook works in the same way as a vision board where you collate images that are representative of your dreams and goals. It doesn't have to be about one theme. In fact, it is best if the scrapbook or vision board is a balanced representation of all the key areas of your life – home, finance, relationships, health, personal development, spirituality, career, etc. However, a word of caution: be meticulous in selecting your images otherwise you could end up manifesting or attracting things into your life that you don't want.

Imagine in great detail (not just the outer shell) how your ideal would be inside and out. Then focus on these images, ultimately transforming them from concept to reality.

Here's the deal: whenever you see a photo of something you want, cut out the picture and stick it in your scrapbook. Make sure you pick only photos that inspire you and make you want your goal even more!

The more desire and excitement your scrapbook causes in you when you view it, the more energy you are giving to the creative process of manifestation. Sit for a few minutes every day and review your scrapbook, visualizing yourself as though you had already attained all of the things you have catalogued. Feel the excitement and freedom of the life you would be living if you already had these things. Get excited about it, feel great about it!

Once again, we are triggering the subconscious in a repeated manner to accept that which it sees as reality. Once your subconscious begins to accept and conform to the pictures in your scrapbook, you will find your desires suddenly popping into your life.

Finally, when your goals arrive, take the photo from your scrapbook that caused the manifestation and place it in a second scrapbook. Call this one your Completed Desires scrapbook. The more you look back on this and realize how many of your desires manifested in your life, the more your faith in the process will grow. And as your faith in the process grows, so will your manifestations appear more quickly in your life. This will create a spiral that will cause your life to begin shaping itself to your desires more and more quickly, until you finally find yourself living the dream life you always wanted. When your second scrapbook is fuller than your first, you will know that you are creating your own reality moment by moment. –Jonpeeoh

> *Acting virtuous will make one virtuous.*
>
> —Aristotle

1:25 Quantum vision

Quantum vision is a visualization process where you use your mind to see into a parallel dimension, and gain creativity, knowledge, wisdom, skills and inspiration by seeing-feeling-experiencing alternate versions of yourself.

This happens through a phenomenon known as thought transference. You see, although the solidity of our world seems indisputable, quantum theory suggests that our physical reality is nothing but a very elaborate mirage. A matrix – a super hologram of information and energy.

All physical matter is the result of particles vibrating at a certain frequency – a frequency that if you alter, change or amplify in any way, you change your physical and current reality.

We all know from physics class that if you increase the vibrational frequency of water particles through heat energy, you create steam, and if you slow them down by removing heat energy, you create ice. And just like heat, our thoughts too are energy.

Do you know the true power of your thoughts? The truth is stunning.

> *All matter originates and exists only by virtue of a force which brings the particles of an atom to a vibration which holds the atom together. We must assume behind this force is the existence of a conscious and intelligent mind. This mind is the matrix of all matter.*
>
> —Max Planck, a founding father of quantum physics

If you are to act as if you have already achieved something then you need to have a vision of how to act, how to look-feel-speak-touch. Quantum vision allows you to explore and experience this through a visualization meditation.

Visualization meditation

Before you start to think about what you want to experience, how you would like to see yourself, what would you be doing? What skills do you have? (Maybe you want to learn to play an instrument.)

Now get a piece of paper and without removing the pen/pencil, draw a stick figure of yourself as the vision you want to visit (example: playing the instrument). The trick here is to feel your way as you draw the stick figure; it's okay to do loops and squiggles, only remove the pen/pencil when you are finished.

- *Now relax and make yourself comfortable.*
- *Imagine yourself to be sitting relaxed in a round bamboo hut on the edge of a Pacific island beach. There are streaks of light coming in through the walls and you can hear the waves as they gently caress the golden sand.*
- *We are going to do three deep breaths.*
- *Take in a deep breath through your nose, with your concentration placed firmly on your navel. Breathe out through your mouth (with a loud haa sound) while placing your attention on your head.*
- *This is a cleansing breath.*
- *Now think of a ball of light just above your head, feel it, touch it.*
- *Take in a deep breath through your nose, with your concentration placed firmly on your navel. Breathe out through your mouth (with a loud haa sound) while placing your attention on your head.*
- *This is a connecting breath.*
- *Now think of a ball of light just above your head.*
- *Take in a deep breath through your nose, visualizing the light entering your body, with your concentration placed firmly on your navel. Breathe out through your mouth (with a loud haa sound) while placing your attention on your head.*

- *This is an energizing breath.*
- *Reduce your breathing down to a comfortable, relaxed state.*
- *See yourself (in your vision) relaxed, feel yourself as relaxed.*
- *Concentrate on your stomach area as you gently breathe in golden light.*
- *Mentally say to yourself: my body rests and refreshes itself when I am relaxed.*
- *Mentally say to yourself: every day my image of myself gets better. I can do anything I have a desire to do. I am a wonderful human being; there is no one else on earth exactly like me. Every day I grow stronger knowing that I can: I can think; I can create; I can do. I can do anything I have a desire to do.*
- *Relax, concentrate on the image of you relaxed and at ease. Get a sense of yourself, sitting comfortably, eyes closed.*
  - *Imagine the streaks of light coming into the hut joining together, humming, vibrating, and osculating around the walls until there is no wall, only light. In the light you can see a door – a portal to another dimension. A dimension where your twin image is waiting, a twin image that is already successful in your desire, they are already living the dream (example: playing an instrument).*
  - *Think of this twin, and how successful they are. Contemplate for a moment how their life would be, their upbringing, their education, their family, their home, their job, see them doing (example: playing an instrument) that which you desire, this twin of yours.*
  - *Know with certainty that this twin is an image of you in another possibility. Another dimension that already exists.*
  - *Think to yourself what you would say, what you would ask your counterpart when you meet. What advice would you want? Make this very specific.*

- *Take in a deep breath through your nose, visualizing the light surrounding the door entering your body, with your concentration placed firmly on your navel. Breathe out through your mouth (with a loud haa sound) while placing your attention on your breath of light leaving your body and going back into the doorway.*
- *As you breathe out count 3, 2, 1.*
- *When you get to 1, the door will open for a second and you will leap through it to visit your twin image.*

◆ *Take your time when you get there.*

◆ *Take a deep breath.*

◆ *Then ask your question. Mentally hear yourself articulate the question of your desire. Hear yourself clearly repeat it a word at a time.*

◆ *The more you focus on a thought, the more you concentrate your attention, the more you express your conscious intent, the more successful you'll be.*

◆ *Your intent will take you to the right thoughts and feelings.*

◆ *Then wait…*

◆ *The answer will come to you, as a gift, from your successful twin image.*

◆ *Give them a cuddle and say thank you, and wish them well. Until we meet again – aloha!*

- *Take in a deep breath through your nose, visualizing the light surrounding the door entering your body, with your concentration placed firmly on your navel. Breathe out through your mouth (with a loud haa sound) while placing your attention on your breath of light leaving your body and going back into the doorway of the hut.*
- *As you breathe out count 3, 2, 1.*

- *When you get to 1, the door will open for a second and you will leap through it back into the hut.*
- *When you get back, take a deep cleansing breath, feel the light retreat back into the gaps of the bamboo walls.*
- *Know that you have returned with a little bit of the energy of a successful you.*
- *Take one final breath of gratitude, open your eyes and smile.*

Someday, after mastering the winds, the waves, the tides and gravity, we shall harness for good the energies of love, and then, for a second time in the history of the world, man will have discovered fire.

–Pierre Teilhard de Chardin

The Enchanted Wish

The creation of change: *If you want to change your life, you have to change your life* is a powerful concept.

Abracadabra is an Aramaic word that means I will create as I speak.

In Huna a technique for creating change is Haipule, a Hawaiian word meaning prayer, blessing or spell. Within the Starlite zone it is referred to as the enchanted wish.

In reality, it's a process for organizing and strengthening one's thoughts, feelings, and behaviors based on the simple theory that by changing yourself you can change your experience.

The secret of Haipule is in its four basic roots: Ha-i-pule. Translated for the purpose of this technique, they mean energize, verbalize, mentalize, and actualize.

Energize: Increasing your available energy helps to stimulate your organs, strengthen your muscles, nourish your cells, calm your emotions, excite your feelings, and clear your mind.

Verbalize: Directing or redirecting attention can have powerful effects; the third principle of Huna says that energy flows where attention goes, and words can play a useful role in this. They evoke associations that stir up memories, and memories influence behavior.

Mentalize: Some people think that visualizing is the only way to use your imagination. The truth is that imagination can be applied to any of your senses. You can imagine seeing, hearing, smelling, tasting, and touching, and sensations such as pressure, heat, cold, roughness, smoothness, and tingling. Anything that you can experience you can imagine. And if you can do it vividly enough, which means with enough concentrated attention, your subconscious will accept what you imagine as being valid as any external experience.

Actualize: This is where you do something physical that is either directly related to your desired outcome or symbolically related. If you start symbolically, such as designing a picture book of your desire, dream or goal, then at some point it will need to be replaced with real action. –Serge Kahili King

Shoot for the stars and you'll become a star…

1:26 Desiderata

Go placidly amid the noise and haste, and remember what peace there may be in silence.
As far as possible without surrender be on good terms with all persons.
Speak your truth quietly and clearly; and listen to others, even the dull and ignorant; they too have their story.
Avoid loud and aggressive persons; they are vexations to the spirit.
If you compare yourself with others, you may become vain and bitter;
for always there will be greater and lesser persons than yourself.

*Enjoy your achievements as well as your plans.
Keep interested in your career, however humble; it is
a real possession in the changing fortunes of time.
Exercise caution in your business affairs; for the
world is full of trickery.
But let this not blind you to what virtue there is;
many persons strive for high ideals; and everywhere
life is full of heroism.*

*Be yourself.
Especially, do not feign affection.
Neither be critical about love; for in the face of all
aridity and disenchantment it is as perennial as
the grass.*

*Take kindly the counsel of the years, gracefully
surrendering the things of youth.
Nurture strength of spirit to shield you in sudden
misfortune. But do not distress yourself with
imaginings.
Many fears are born of fatigue and loneliness.
Beyond a wholesome discipline, be gentle
with yourself.*

*You are a child of the universe, no less than the trees
and the stars;
you have a right to be here.
And whether or not it is clear to you, no doubt the
universe is unfolding as it should.*

*Therefore be at peace with God, whatever you
conceive Him to be,
and whatever your labors and aspirations, in the
noisy confusion of life keep peace with your soul.
With all its sham, drudgery and broken dreams, it is
still a beautiful world. Be careful. Strive to be happy.*

– Max Ehrmann 1927

> *Continue to do good and heaven will
> come down to you.*
>
> –Hawaiian proverb

1:27 Tallulah

There was a gentle sway of the carriage as it rocked in rhythm with the train trundling along on this bright October day. Streams of sunlight hit my face as I looked out the window marveling in the golden glow of autumnal colors; the leaves were floating down from their elevated positions to take up residence at ground level and cover the earth with a warm bed of winter protection. Taking in a deep breath of the beauty surrounding me I turned over the page of the *Metro* newspaper and read:

> *Fat, ugly and worthless*
>
> *A "beautiful" teenage ballerina repeatedly scrawled "fat", "ugly" and "worthless" in her diary before throwing herself in front of a train, an inquest heard yesterday.*
>
> *Tallulah Wilson's obsession with her appearance – and her mistaken belief that she was overweight – was fueled by people she met on social networking websites, a jury was told.*
>
> *The coroner described two sides to the 15-year-old: one a confident, lively, engaged, lovely-looking girl who was a gifted dancer; the other a troubled teenager who suffered from self-loathing and was wrongly convinced she was extremely unattractive.*
>
> *She wrote dozens of messages about her depression and posted images of her self-inflicted injuries on photo-sharing website Tumblr, where internet users encouraged her to harm herself and*

Part One - *Shine like a star*... *the aloha way*

share images of it, the inquest heard. The teenager had gained 18,000 followers on such sites.

Tallulah, who lived with her family in a £1million house in West Hampstead, north London, was found dead at St Pancras station in October 2012, a few hours after her mother saw her off to a dance class.

DS Adrian Naylor of the British Transport Police, who investigated the death, said that diaries found at her home showed disturbing writing relating to self-loathing and self-harm. "It is pretty dark, pretty sad and pretty bleak," he said. "She had written 'I am fat' repeatedly, over and over again."

On one page she wrote in large black-inked letters "ugly."

Another page said, "What am I? You are nothing" and repeated the word "worthless."

The teenager had gained 18,000 followers on sites such as Twitter and Tumblr after posting about drinking and taking cocaine, and uploading pictures of herself with cuts she had made. She regularly posted messages such as "I will never be beautiful and skinny."

Her dance teacher told the inquest that Tallulah was his most confident pupil and a talented ballerina when she began her dance course in January 2012. "She began as very outgoing and well liked, she was the leader of the group," he said.

"Because Tallulah was naturally very gifted at dance she also had a brilliant sense of humor and in many ways she was the most able member of the group.

"Although she was a very beautiful, lovely-looking young woman, she did appear to lose some of her 'spark' later in the year but appeared to have improved again, producing some brilliant work just a week before her death. But it appeared from the diary that Tallulah sadly had very low self-esteem."

– reported by Tom Kelly

I sat there looking at the picture of this pretty young lady and thought how sad, what a waste of life, a waste of an opportunity to experience life in all its wonder. Why would someone so talented, so young, and so beautiful, someone who appeared to have it all, why would someone like that see themselves as fat, ugly and worthless – why?

Perception is not truth; just because you think something or others tell you something, it does not make it true. However, if you believe the lie to be true, and you keep repeating that belief, then it has the ability to become true, at least in your own mind. What Tallulah and many others like her need is a change of perception, a paradigm change of belief. They need to see themselves as they really are, a beautiful entity, an angel of light embodied to have the human experience. You are not your body, you are not your clothes, you are not even your mind; you are an enchanting spirit, a spark of light, part of the divine creation of life, you are beauty personified.

> *Don't worry how your body looks. Know that it is beautiful at all times. Love yourself, bless your body. Speak to your soul, which is the lord of your being and command it to bring forth the enzymes of youth.* –Ramtha

> *Huna represents a unique expression of oceanic indigenous wisdom, and is made up of two short Polynesian words: Hu-Na; Hu refers to all things masculine and Na to all things feminine.* –Kala H. Kos

The principles of Huna are based on an ancient psychology and a way of living called the "way of aloha." Aloha is the Hawaiian word for the divine essence of life force energy, a spirit of unconditional love. It occurred to me that if we can share the fruit of aloha, the food of unconditional love, with people like Tallulah then they can see who they really are and believe in who they really are through experience of the self.

*Part One - **Shine like a star**... the aloha way*

The seven principles of Huna are:

1. **The world is what you think it is.**
2. **Energy flows where attention goes.**
3. **There are no limits.**
4. **Love is to be happy with.**
5. **All power comes from within.**
6. **Now is the moment of power.**
7. **Effectiveness is the measure of truth.**

Unfortunately we are brought up on a diet of self-hate in a world that constantly tells us we are not good enough. Some of our religions state that we are born in sin, and that we must ask for forgiveness simply for being a child here on earth – what a start in life! Then we are picked on and ridiculed for our differences. We are tested at school and told we will amount to nothing if we don't pass the grade. Our TVs show people living the "perfect" life and our own dysfunctional families don't match up. Our magazines portray airbrushed models as the ideal body beautiful image, and when we look in the mirror we see something different; no wonder we struggle to accept another reality. To help me understand Tallulah's reality I used the seven principles of Huna and found the following:

1. *The world is what you think it is* ~ wake up in the morning and decide how you want your day to be, you choose. Tallulah chose to see herself as fat, ugly and worthless.

2. *Energy flows where attention goes* ~ remember like attracts like. You choose what you want and focus on it. Tallulah focused on fat, ugly and worthless and that's where her energy flowed.

3. *There are no limits* ~ you can be as happy or as sad as you want to be, it's your choice. Tallulah chose to be sad and see herself as fat, ugly and worthless.

4   **Love is to be happy with** ~ aloha is love and acceptance, implement the principles above, live the way of aloha, and happiness and contentment is assured. Tallulah could not accept that she was a beautiful, talented young lady. She rejected happiness (not considering herself as worthy) and embraced self-harm.

5   **All power comes from within** ~ it all starts with a thought, you decided which one. Tallulah decided to think of herself as fat, ugly and worthless.

6   **Now is the moment of power** ~ you can stop this at any given moment, no matter what has gone on before, you can change your life or end it… right now!

7   **Effectiveness is the measure of truth** ~ you can use the mind to bring pain or pleasure to the body, and you can use the body to bring pain or pleasure to the mind.

There must be something I can do, some way I can help the Tallulahs of this world, I thought as I closed my eyes and drifted gently to the edge of the twilight zone (Starlite zone), the place between awake and asleep; with each rhythmical movement of the train I moved one step nearer a new knowing.

My mind started to flow.

I teach a form of bodywork that is infused with Starlite energy (entanglement of physical and metaphysical energy).

Starlite was designed as a method of connecting to the divine essence of life force energy and transmuting it into the healing arts. To do this we introduce the therapist to the principles of Huna and employ them to adopt the way of aloha as a method of self-empowerment bringing balance, synergy and harmony to their very core. When they reach a point of universal equilibrium it becomes a simple step – and conversely also a quantum leap – to embrace the joy of their own beauty, greatness and wonderment. Acknowledging and accepting their authenticity as great, powerful, and mighty spiritual beings of light, living in a physical world with dignity, direction, and purpose. Only then can they radiate the true essence of this love energy to others in need of compassion and healing.

If only I could somehow share the way of aloha, the food of life, with a skeptical world, a world of troubled teens and unsatisfied adults. But how, how can I get urban teenagers, and city professionals, and frustrated parents interested in a 35,000-year-old Hawaiian way of life? Please help me…

Then the thoughts started to pop into my head…

Make it cool *(awesome and great)*

Make it relevant *(applicable and significant)*

Fat, ugly and worthless *(address these issues)*

Very low self-esteem *(common denominator)*

Show them the light *(self-empowerment)*

Redress aloha, it needs a makeover; just like the character Sandy did in the movie *Grease,* get rid of the frills, the lovey-dovey elements and the "niceness." Give it a pair of jeans, a black leather jacket, turn aloha into a rock chick, give it **attitude!**

45 million Americans diet each year as they battle with low self-esteem, and many consider themselves as fat, ugly and worthless. Many teenagers self-harm and/or develop eating disorders for the same reasons. Eating disorders are often blamed on the social pressure to be thin, as young people in particular feel they should look a certain way. However, in reality the causes are usually more complex.

78% of teenage girls don't like their bodies. –Cameron Russell, US model

What they need is a diet of aloha, a program where the "fruit of life" can be enjoyed one baby bite at a time. It needs to be fun and relevant, like an online computer game, backed and supported by the stars – people whom teenagers relate to and get their inspiration from. A program that they can participate in without stress or pressure from outside forces.

Jennifer Lopez was ordered to diet when her career started and was told that she was too curvy for show business. "There's nothing wrong with me or my shape or who I am, you're the one with the problem," she told them, standing up for herself. Her family are also credited with boosting her confidence. "They made me love who I was and what I looked like," said J-Lo.

What you put into your body (food and thoughts) not only affects your physical well-being, but it can also impact your overall psychological well-being. Food and thoughts influence mood and contribute to the experience of both positive and negative feelings. Therefore, making healthy choices can contribute to a variety of improvements to your overall mental and psychological state. Choosing options that are healthy and nutritious for both mind and body can give you a sense of control and allow you to feel proud of yourself. These increases in positive feelings for yourself and improvements in your appearance can result in improvements to your overall self-esteem.

> *The only way we can be great to ourselves is not what we do with our bodies, but what we do with our minds.* –Ramtha

Then, as they work through the program and grow in confidence, their natural beauty will start to glow and they will see that they are loved more than they could imagine, and they will express splendor beyond comprehension.

In the last part of this book I share with you the two incarnations of "Sandy" in the form of a 30-day diet of aloha that may just help to change lives. One is presented in a traditional Hawaiian setting embracing the love of aloha. The second is presented through the eyes of an urbanized, fashion-conscious teenager with issues and attitude.

*Part One - **Shine like a star**... the aloha way*

This version is to be made available as a separate entity provided at a budget rate and with all profits supporting the Starlight children's foundation that brightens up the lives of seriously and terminally ill children. This is done in the spirit of aloha and as a way of honoring Tallulah for her inspiration leading to this action.

> *With beauty before me; May I walk*
> *With beauty behind me; May I walk*
> *With beauty above me; May I walk*
> *With beauty all around me; May I walk*
>
> Navajo

1:28 Beautiful You

You never knew how beautiful you were, for you never really looked at yourself. You never looked at who you are and what you are.

You cannot truly see or be aware of the beauty of all life or express the depths of love and compassion for others until you have first seen your own sublime beauty and expressed love and compassion for yourself. Once love of self has become real in an understanding, then you have a basis from which to expand your understanding to embrace life outside of you.

The greatest part of your love for your wife was giving her the things that she adored so much. And in that regard you have done quite well, save for this: you never loved yourself enough to allow her to love you in spite of all the things you gave her. You never really appreciated how grand you truly are, the giver of all these things.

You think your body is you? It is not. Your body is only a cloak that represents the unseen essence that is your true identity: the collection of feeling attitudes, called your personality self, which lies within your embodiment.

Ponder this for a moment: What do you love about another entity? Is it the body? No, it is the essence of another that you love, the unseen personality self that lies behind the eyes. What you love about another is the unseen essence that makes the body work, that makes the eyes flicker, the voice melodious, the hair have sheen, the hands have touch.

You are loved greater than you ever imagined.

You are not a flesh entity. You are a rounded, fiery, pure-energy, light principle living within a body to obtain the prize of creative life called emotion. What you truly are is not what you inhabit; it is what you feel. You are known by your emotions, not your body.

What you truly are is spirit and soul, a light entity and an emotional entity combined. Your spirit – this little point of light – surrounds all molecular structures of your body; thus it houses and supports the mass of your embodiment. Your soul lies within the mass, near your heart, in a cavity under a shield of bone wherein nothing exists except electrical energy. Your soul records and stores, in the form of emotion, every thought you have ever entertained. –Ramtha

The word serene might be used to describe internal beauty in a person. Serene means calm, peaceful, unruffled or unagitated, especially when faced with disturbing activity.

But what goes around comes around.

Not only does making yourself feel beautiful on the inside boost your self-esteem and self-confidence, it also helps to improve the lives of those around you, and that in turn makes you happy.

> *If we lose this thing called aloha*
> *Then we are just another sand and surf destination*
> -Rex Johnson

Part One - **Shine like a star**... *the aloha way*

1:29 The Aloha Spirit

The Aloha Spirit is a well-known reference to the attitude of friendly acceptance for which the Hawaiian Islands are so famous. However, it also refers to a powerful way to resolve any problem, accomplish any goal, and also to achieve any state of mind or body that you desire.

In the Hawaiian language, aloha stands for much more than hello or goodbye or love. Its deeper meaning is the joyful (oha) sharing (alo) of life energy (ha) in the present (alo).

As you share this energy you become attuned to the divine power that the Hawaiians call mana. And the loving use of this incredible power is the secret for attaining true health, happiness, prosperity and success.

The way to tune into this power and have it work for you is so simple that you might be tempted to pass it off as being too easy to be true. Please don't let yourself be fooled by appearances.

This is the most powerful technique in the world, and although it is extremely simple it may not prove easy, because you must remember to do it and you have to do it a lot. It is a secret which has been given to humanity over and over again, and here it is once more in another form. The secret is this:

> **Bless everyone and everything
> that represents what you want!**

That's all there is to it. Anything that simple, however, does need some explanation.

To bless something means to give recognition or emphasis to a positive quality, characteristic or condition, with the intent that what is recognized or emphasized will increase, endure or come into being.

Blessing is effective in changing your life or getting what you want for three reasons: First of all, the positive focus of your mind stirs up the positive, creative force of the Power of the Universe. Secondly, it moves your own energy outward, allowing more of the power to come through you. Thirdly, when you bless for the benefit of others instead of directly for yourself, you tend to bypass any subconscious fears about what you want for yourself, and also the very focus on the blessing acts to increase the same good in your life. What is so beautiful about this process is that the blessing you do for others helps them as well as you.

Blessing may be done with imagery or touch but the most usual and easy way to do it is with words. The main kinds of verbal blessing are:

Admiration: This is the giving of compliments or praise to something good that you notice, for example: What a nice sunset; I like that dress; you're so much fun.

Affirmation: This is a specific statement of blessing for increase or endurance, for example: I bless the beauty of this tree; blessed be the health of your body.

Appreciation: This is an expression of gratitude that something good exists or has happened, for example: Thank you, God, for helping me; I give thanks to the rain for nourishing the land.

Anticipation: This is blessing for the future, for example: We're going to have a great picnic; I bless your increased income; thank you for my perfect mate; I wish you a happy journey; may the wind be always at your back.

In order to gain the most benefit from blessing, you will have to give up on the one thing that negates it: cursing. This doesn't mean swearing or saying bad words. It refers to the opposite of blessing, namely criticizing instead of admiring; doubting instead of affirming; blaming instead of appreciating; and worrying instead of anticipating with trust. Whenever any of these are done they tend to cancel out some of the effects of blessing. So the more you curse the harder it will be and the longer it will take to get the good from a blessing. On the other hand, the more you bless the less harm any cursing will do.

Here, then, are some ideas for blessing various needs and desires:

Health: Bless healthy people, animals, and even plants; everything which is well made or well-constructed; and everything that expresses abundant energy.

Happiness: Bless all that is good, or the good that is in all people and all things; all the signs of happiness that you see, hear or feel in people or animals; and all potentials for happiness that you notice around you.

Prosperity: Bless all the signs of prosperity in your environment, including everything that money helped to make or do; all the money that you have in any form; and all the money that circulates in the world.

Success: Bless all signs of achievement and completion (such as buildings, bridges, and sports events); all arrivals at destinations (of ships, planes, trains, cars and people); all signs of forward movement or persistence; and all signs of enjoyment or fun.

Confidence: Bless all signs of confidence in people and animals; all signs of strength in people, animals and objects (including steel and concrete); all signs of stability (like mountains and tall trees); and all signs of purposeful power (including big machines, power lines).

Love and Friendship: Bless all signs of caring and nurturing, compassion and support; all harmonious relationships in nature and architecture; everything that is connected to or gently touching something else; all signs of cooperation, as in games or work; and all signs of laughter and fun.

Inner Peace: Bless all signs of quietness, calmness, tranquility, and serenity (such as quiet water or still air); all distant views (horizons, stars, the moon); all signs of beauty of sight, sound or touch; clear colors and shapes; the details of natural or made objects.

Spiritual Growth: Bless all signs of growth, development and change in nature; the transitions of dawn and twilight; the movement of sun, moon, planets and stars; the flight of birds in the sky; and the movement of wind and sea.

The ideas above are for guidance if you are not used to blessing, but don't be limited by them. Remember that any quality, characteristic or condition can be blessed (e.g., you can bless slender poles and slim animals to encourage weight loss), whether it has existed, presently exists, or exists so far in your imagination alone.

Personally I have used the power of blessing to heal my body, increase my income, develop many skills, create a deeply loving relationship with my wife and children, and establish a worldwide network of peacemakers working with the aloha spirit. It's because it has worked so well for me that I want to share it with you.

How to enhance your power to bless

There is a technique practiced by Hawaiian shamans which enhances your power to bless by increasing your personal energy. It is a simple way of breathing that is also used for grounding, centering, meditation and healing. It requires no special place or posture, and may be done while moving or still, busy or resting, with eyes open or closed. In Hawaiian the technique is called piko-piko because piko means both the crown of the head and the navel.

The Technique

1. Become aware of your natural breathing (it might change on its own just because of your awareness, but that's okay).
2. Locate the crown of your head and your navel by awareness and/or touch.
3. Now, as you inhale put your attention on the crown of your head and as you exhale put your attention on your navel. Keep breathing this way for as long as you like.
4. When you feel relaxed, centered, and/or energized, begin imagining that you are surrounded with an invisible cloud of light or an electromagnetic field, and that your breathing increases the energy of this cloud or field.
5. As you bless, imagine that the object of your blessing is surrounded with some of the same energy that surrounds you.

Variations

a. Instead of crown and navel, shift attention from shoulder to shoulder or sky to earth.
b. To help focus the energy field, imagine it in color, as a tone or chord, or as a tingle.

Serge Kahili King © 1990

Feel free to distribute this page in any manner, under the condition that it is not to be sold.

This page has been produced and shared as a gift of aloha~ please pass it on.

Thousands of candles can be lit from a single candle, and the life of the candle will not be shortened. Happiness never decreases by being shared.

Buddha

1:30 Act of kindness

We can never know how far an act of kindness can travel. It might alter someone's behavior, causing them to be softer or gentler through the rest of the day. Without it, who knows? Maybe they would cause someone pain.

No action ever stops with itself. One kind action leads to another.

–Amelia Earhart

Kindness is good for us and others. A simple act of kindness can bring a smile to a person's face for a whole day. It can be just the tonic for them.

Self-compassion is defined as "being open to and moved by one's suffering, experiencing feelings of caring and kindness toward oneself, taking an understanding, non-judgmental attitude toward one's inadequacies and failures, and recognizing that one's experience is part of the common human experience." We can be our worst enemies, beating ourselves up not only for things that have happened in the past but also for how we've dealt with situations. We often treat ourselves worse than we treat others.

Self-compassion is not to be confused with self-esteem. Self-esteem is having positive thoughts about ourselves and feeling valued by other people. Self-compassion, on the other hand, is caring for ourselves. When we move toward self-compassion this will eventually breed greater compassion for all and allow kindness to flower in our heart.

*Kindness is not just something that you do.
It's something that you are.*

Dr. Wayne W. Dyer

All acts of kindness are good for those who receive them, but they are good for the giver as well. Acts of kindness make us happier and healthier, they relieve the symptoms of depression and they even help us to live longer, healthier lives.

Compassion is also good for us as it strengthens the immune system. Empathy is often the starting point for kindness. We sense and share another's pain, compassion arises and we begin to wish them free of pain, and then we are motivated to do something to help.

When we show kindness, opiates such as serotonin and dopamine are released which lifts our mood and makes us feel more positive and optimistic. In addition, when kindness involves an interaction between people, a hormone called oxytocin is produced and it makes us feel more connected with others as it flows in our brains and bodies. In the brain, it reduces anxiety about being betrayed or taken advantage of, encouraging us to be more trusting. In the body, oxytocin is cardioprotective: it protects us from hardening of the arteries; it dilates our blood vessels, reduces blood pressure; it encourages wound healing; it helps in the construction of fetal heart, and may even help in the regeneration of the heart following damage.

Gratitude is another practice that can make a difference in our lives. It is an expression of kindness because in counting our blessings we are saying thank you to someone or to the world or to a greater spirit. Gratitude can make us happier, alleviate symptoms of depression and even help us get a good night's sleep. It also helps build and strengthen relationships.

Kindness and compassion, and even meditation, produces oxytocin that stimulates the vagus nerve in the brain and reduces inflammation throughout the body. Evidence that has emerged recently shows that we are at our healthiest when kindness, compassion, gratitude, and a positive attitude are a part of our lives. At the deepest biological level in the body we live longer and benefit as well as everyone around us when we express our goodness. –David R. Hamilton

- *Doing the same act several times does not generate as many good feelings as doing a wide range of different things.*
- *Making an effort is important; don't just put money in a tin.*
- *Helpers have highly improved feelings of self-worth.*
- *Seeing someone happy our brain produces a happy state in us, and vice versa.*

When we feel love and kindness toward others, it not only makes others feel loved and cared for, but also helps us develop inner happiness and peace. –Dalai Lama

To the gorgeous lady who got off my bus on Monday night. Your smile made my year. –Ginger, bus driver (Metro)

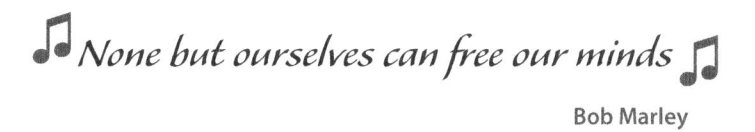

♪ *None but ourselves can free our minds* ♪

Bob Marley

1:31 Happy and sad

Can people feel happy and sad at the same time?

Did you know that it's impossible to be stressed out and relaxed at the same time? Neither can you be happy and sad at the same time.

Of course, you can go back and forth, like an oscillating fan. But let's consider what happens when we focus our energy on one predominant emotion.

Have you ever watched an oscillating fan in action? It blows cool air to one side of the room, and then slowly rotates to the other side.

Our emotions can be like that, oscillating back and forth. Sometimes we have a love-hate relationship: we love someone, but we also hate certain things about them. However, the brain always suspends one emotion while expressing the other.

The reason this happens is due to a protective mechanism in the brain. Isn't that amazing? Our brain attempts to protect us from getting confused, disoriented or shutting down due to "analysis paralysis."

The good news is that we can use our brain's protection mechanism to our advantage. Instead of feeling angry, sad or afraid, we can feel happy, smile and hold our head high.

Perhaps we take a moment to distract ourselves. We think about something that made us laugh or warmed our heart. Or maybe we whisper a quick prayer, thanking God for being in control of our lives, and working in the midst of a difficult situation.

Of course, there are times when we need to express negative emotions, such as sadness, grief, frustration or anger. It's normal and healthy to express these feelings. However, it can become disempowering if our feelings make us miserable, sap our energy and strength, or spiral into despair.

Consider for a moment what happens when you're struggling with negative emotions, but you stop to let go of them… and smile. At first, you feel some tension from the competing emotions. Your brain is wrestling with your feelings. Which feelings will you give in to?

Suppose you keeping on smiling. What happens then? Your negative emotions are pushed aside and scattered to the wind. They may not be completely gone, but they are temporarily suspended.

Whenever we let go of negative emotions, we're able to think more clearly. We have the energy that we need to recover, let go, heal and get on with our lives. Now we can think clearly and decide what to do next. There is tremendous power in letting go and releasing tension from the mind and body.

Sometimes it is hard to smile in the midst of a stressful situation. However, the simple act of lifting up the corners of your mouth will help you to reverse the direction of the fan. Instead of fanning the flames of anger, sadness and fear, and making those coals even hotter, you turn to the other side. By letting go, you activate feelings of calm, energy and emotional release.

> *Consider the power of your smile. When we let go of tension and anxiety, we stay on the road to less stress.*
> –Nicky Van Valkenburgh

> *Groundbreaking research has proved that emotions can follow facial expressions as well as preceding them. Biochemical changes take place and hormones make you feel better and more positive, so a person's facial expression actually does control emotions.*
> –James Borg

We don't just smile because we are happy. We also feel happy because we smile. One of the most important things you can do to bring more pleasure into your life is to act joyful. Years before Darwin, Guillaume-Benjamin Duchenne studied the musculature involved in smiling. He determined that a legitimate smile required the combined movement of two muscle groups: the zygomatic majors (around the mouth) and the orbicularis oculi (around the outside of the eyes). While these muscles work involuntarily when we feel happy, they can also be consciously controlled to let the brain know that you need a little happiness.

Look in the mirror, and smile by lifting your lips from your teeth, raising the corners of your mouth, and squinting. The muscles around your eyes are important pleasure senders, so pay particular attention to them. Now notice how you feel. Chances are, unless your brain is distracting you with such thoughts as don't do that, you look silly, you will feel a little better than you did before smiling. If your muscles are sore from this exercise, that signals another symptom of delight deficiency syndrome, but you can build them up by "smile-icizing." –Paul Pearsall

> *Watch your thoughts, they become words.*
> *Watch your words, they become actions.*
> *Watch your actions, they become habits.*
> *Watch your habits, they become your character.*
> *Watch your character, it becomes your destiny.*
>
> Unknown

1:32 Stop negative thoughts

See the positive side, the potential, and make an effort.

–Dalai Lama

You can't get rid of the butterflies, but you can teach them to fly in formation.

–Paul McGee

Our minds cannot process a negative; to the mind a thought is just energy, therefore it is extremely important to focus on what we want, not what we don't want.

We see tens of thousands of images, sounds and other external stimulating sensations each moment of every day. It is only those to which we pay attention that have the ability to become a thought within our being.

That thought is neither good nor bad until we choose it to be, we decide the feeling and eventual emotion that we want to attach to it. Through our choice we become what we think about: worried, sad, in pain, or happy, glad and healthy. The way we feel is solely determined by how we think.

The question is why would we choose to attach negative elements to our thoughts? This happens because most people don't realize that they have the power of choice. Instead they let a thought develop and affect the way they feel without control, often feeling quite powerless over their emotions and feelings.

The negative feelings that many of us apply to thoughts are not even our own. They come from our beliefs, our values, our religions, our prejudices, which in most cases have been given to us by other people.

You must take responsibility for your emotional and physical state and you do this by taking responsibility for your thoughts.

Acknowledge a thought, reframe it, choose to see it differently and move on. Just a little change can make a big difference.

You control your mind – your mind does not control you.

> *When it gets dark enough,*
> *you can see the stars.*
>
> –Koko

How to…

Purchase a rubber wrist band from a charity or association that is meaningful for you and place it on the wrist of your prominent hand.

Now I am going to give you a list of negative words; choose one or more that you wish to work with on any particular day, write them down or put them in your cell phone/PC, in any place that will help you remember. Now if you use any of them acknowledge the fact with a deep breath, take off the wrist band and breathe out through the hole in the band, clearing the negative thought with it. Now place the band on the other wrist, reframe the thought with a positive one (examples are below) and smile in the knowledge of your positive action. Do the exercise throughout the day, changing wrists as many times as needed.

Slowly, word for word, day by day, you will remove negative language from your thought processing as you reclaim power over your thoughts.

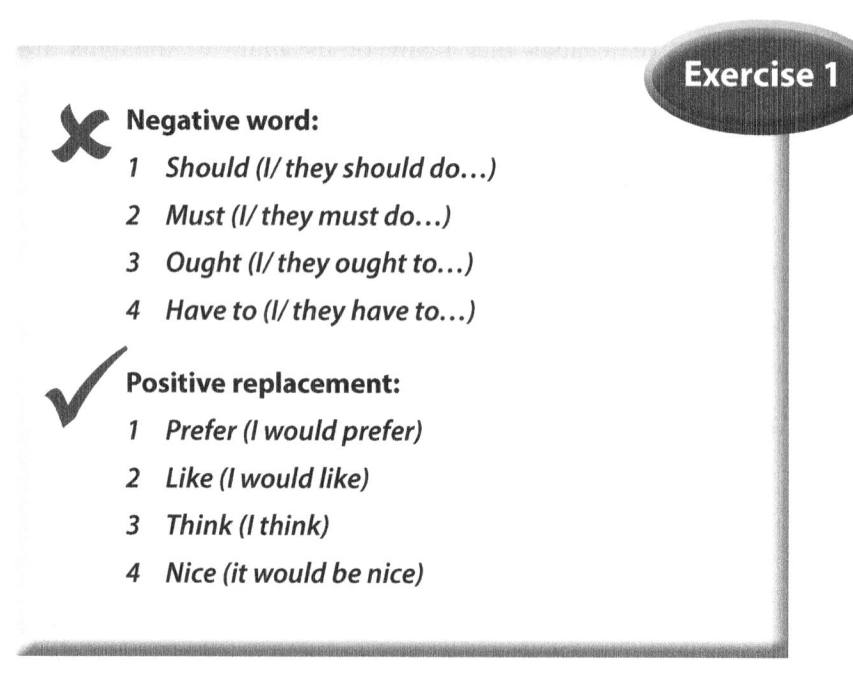

Exercise 1

Negative word:
1. Should (I/ they should do…)
2. Must (I/ they must do…)
3. Ought (I/ they ought to…)
4. Have to (I/ they have to…)

Positive replacement:
1. Prefer (I would prefer)
2. Like (I would like)
3. Think (I think)
4. Nice (it would be nice)

Here we have changed demanding words that have no flexibility that can lead to bad feelings with more flexible words of desire which creates less bad feeling.

Exercise 2

❌ **Negative word:**
1. But
2. Why (why did you do that?)
3. You (you must have the last word, mustn't you?)

✓ **Positive replacement:**
1. And
2. Please try
3. I think/seem/need

Here we deflect from a word associated with a lack of empathy to one of union.

Why and you are often used in a negative judgmental way, and this puts people into a defensive mode.

Exercise 3

❌ **Negative word:**
1. Unlucky
2. Loser
3. Idiot
4. Unhappy

✓ **Positive replacement:**
1. Lucky
2. Winner
3. Smart
4. Happy

In this exercise the object is to stop feeling sorry for yourself. You can add or replace any of these words with others that might reflect your personal position.

*Part One - **Shine like a star**... the aloha way*

The right way is the left way

Always work to the **left** side of your "but."

Notice how often your inner voice speaks to you, only to be followed by "but"s and excuses for not following through. By staying on the left side of your "but" you can choose what you want rather than what you *should* want in life.

- *I'd love to go to the party, but I need to get up early in the morning.*
- *I want to leave this meeting, but I will get criticized.*
- *I'm really hungry, but I shouldn't eat yet.*

When making statements such as these, stay to the left of the "but." In other words, do what you initially say, and forget what follows the "but." –George McClendon

Always work to the **left** side of the "not."

Instead of saying I cannot do this or that, instead of saying I do not know this or that, by working to the left of the "not" you change a negative into a positive: cannot becomes can, and do not becomes do.

Believing you can is self-direction, not self-deception.

One small negative thought can turn into a huge, speeding ball of ugliness. On the contrary, a small positive thought can have the same effect, blossoming into a beautiful outcome.

*Human beings, by changing the inner beliefs of their minds, can change the outer aspects of their lives.
What you believe you can achieve.* –R.L. Wing

Finding a balance

Being told to "grin and bear it" or "put a brave face on it" or "turn that frown upside down" can be infuriating when you're feeling low, but new research seems to back up the clichés, suggesting that, to some extent, you really can fake it 'til you make it when it comes to happiness.

The study, carried out by a team of researchers at Washington State University, revealed that people who act like extroverts – even when this goes against how they're actually feeling – are more likely to be happy. Respondents from all over the world reported more positive emotions when they acted more confidently.

This is the latest in a long line of work that has come to a similar conclusion: that acting a certain way can affect your mood. As far back as 1872, Charles Darwin suggested that emotional responses influence our feelings, writing: *The free expression by outward signs of an emotion intensifies it.*

More recently, the University of Cardiff suggested that people whose ability to frown is impaired by botox injections are happier than people who can frown.

The relationship between outward behavior and inward mood is cyclical, and forcing yourself to act more confidently can be beneficial. Pretend to feel confident and assertive, try and get a real sense of how it actually feels; it's a bit like trying on a new outfit, only you are trying on a new personality.

Behavior affects mood, and mood affects behavior. Just try acting out being very calm and relaxed and notice how those around you then become calmer and more relaxed too. At the same time as learning to act more confidently, try to appreciate the things that are going right.

> **It's important to live your life with your glass always half full, knowing you can fill it right to the top if you so choose. All of us are capable of far more than we believe, so throw off the fear. If you must tempt fate, then tempt fate to provide you with good things in life.** –Diana Parkinson, counselor

You don't have to be positive all the time

There's something tyrannical, however, about being told to think positively *all* of the time; after all, life can be sad and difficult. Don't constantly try to eliminate the negative. Negative thoughts are part of life and by putting too much focus on eliminating them, you only encourage more.

By pretending to be confident and happy when you're actually miserable, you may be ignoring a problem that you would be better off acknowledging then moving on from. Many people with depression cope by acting in ways far removed from how they feel – a form of escapism – but while this may be a good way of remaining functional, it doesn't mean inner feelings should be ignored.

Change "fake it till you make it" to "act as if."

The word fake implies deceit, and most of us are uncomfortable with being untruthful; those wanting to improve self-confidence should act being super confident. Acting, as opposed to faking, makes for a positive attitude, bringing about feelings of self-confidence and self-worth.

Walking tall and acting more confidently may make you temporarily happier and can be a good coping mechanism to get through the day. However, if you're feeling miserable, it's vital to talk to your friends, family or GP about what's going on and to acknowledge it yourself. Adding guilt about your negative feelings to the other unpleasant emotions will only make you feel worse.

Learning to be in touch and honest about your emotions, rather than denying them, is the first step, and letting go can follow. Recognize negative feelings and deal with them. Do not let them fester; it may sound corny, but love is everything, live your life in a loving way and you will be happy.

Cheerfulness is something we can control much more than happiness. We can choose to behave cheerfully in dismal or dispiriting circumstances, in part to sustain our own strength, in part as an act of courtesy to the people we love. When we are miserable around them, we rob them of energy. Rather than pulling them down, we try to be cheerful in order to pull them up. Then an interesting thing begins to happen: we find ourselves feeling happier. The outward behavior influences the inward feelings. –Beverly Sills, opera singer

The important thing is to know that you have the choice and ability to change from a negative state to a positive state, at will.

> *Don't go through life, grow through life.*
>
> Eric Butterworth

1:33 Cock-a-doodle-do!

A wisdom keeper once said:

If you have lost the business, your house and your wife, after you have been pronounced terminally ill and life has dealt you the worst blows, there is only one duty left. That duty is to crawl, if you have to, over to the nearest mirror, hoist yourself up, look deeply into it and with your last breath, say aloud seven times…

"COCK-A-DOODLE-DO!"

When you hear someone say cock-a-doodle-do, you know that another friend along the way has seen through the illusion. Another shaman is receiving his enlightenment. It was years before I realized the simple Hawaiian wisdom of this humor. Cock-a-doodle-do is the rooster acknowledging the light of a new day… a new beginning. –Pali Chiles

Part One - *Shine like a star*… *the aloha way*

> *Stop chasing what your mind wants*
> *And get what your soul needs.*
>
> Kushandwizoom

1:34 The bowl of light

> *Every child born has at birth a bowl of perfect light which represented their true identity's "spirit greatness." If he tends his light during his life it will grow in strength and he can do many things: swim with the shark, fly with the hawk, know and understand all things. If, however, he becomes resentful or envious, he drops a stone into his bowl of light. Since light and stone cannot hold the same space, a little of the light goes out. If he continues to put stones in his bowl of light, the light will eventually go out and he too will become a stone. A stone does not grow and a stone does not move. But at any time he tires of being a stone, all he needs to do is huli (turn) the bowl upside down. The stones will all fall away and the light will come back. His light will shine once more upon the world around him and he will begin to grow and shine with the spirit of light, the way he was meant to be. This story reflects the pure nature of the individual soul, and the power of forgiveness.* –Hank Wesselman

> *Remove suffocating negative thoughts,*
> *allow new positive thoughts to bloom…*

1:35 Flick the switch

> *How do you change from the state of negative thinking to that of positive thinking? You do so by flicking the switch in your mind from pessimism to optimism – this will introduce you to a whole new way of thinking and your life will change immeasurably.* –James Borg

STARDANCE - Flow with Energy

Remember emotion follows thought and action follows emotion, or to put it another way, you think-feel-behave. If you have negative thoughts, you will feel negative (pessimistic-worried) and you will then behave in a negative manner; no wonder you get negative results.

Change your thinking, change your life…

A small change in thinking can lead to a completely different destination.

There is a big difference between knowing something and living it. Stop thinking negative thoughts and it will not get any worse; start thinking positive thoughts and it will start to get better, it's that simple!

But it's not easy to stop thinking negative thoughts when you have built a whole world of negativity around you. Here is the good news: we can trick the body/mind into action because the think-feel-behave sequence also works in reverse. Start to behave in a positive manner, hold your body up in a positive way, and behave as though you already have the result of your desire. The more you act as if you are already in a positive place, the stronger the positive feelings that follow will be. This in turn will create even more positive thoughts, increasing positive feelings and encouraging positive actions.

> *You can make a wish or you can make it happen.*
> -Hawaiian proverb

1:36 Act as if

> *Heisenberg's principle states that 100% certainty doesn't exist. Successful people take risks because they accept that they will never know everything they need to know. But they act as if they do know and take the plunge.* –Lindsay Agness

Part One - **Shine like a star**… *the aloha way*

I once watched a TV series called *Fake it till you make it;* the idea was to take a complete novice and teach them the skills of a different job (famer to dancer) and then let them try to fool the experts. To do this they were mentored in everything from the basic skill requirement to body language, terminology and knowledge of the industry all in a few weeks. The subject would then act as if they had been practicing all their life.

The secret here is to gain confidence from knowledge (not false confidence), understand totally what you want, and how you want to feel, then with confidence act as if you already have it. It's a great way to "flick the switch"; as your portrayal of confidence produces success, it will generate real confidence. Act and behave in a happy confident manner and you will become happy and confident. When we choose to live with a strong faith in things not seen, not proven, and not guaranteed, we tap into the power of the possible and we supersede the literal and predicable.

> *Knowing how to appear confident is a valuable asset in any job. It's a skill to be able to walk in and act like you know what you're doing even if you don't. Allowing yourself to build and applaud that skill – without practicing any intentional harm or deceit – will help you feel credible even when you're out of your comfort zone.* –Nadia Goodman

> *Confidence can be crucial to success, but it's not the only key to achieving it. You also need to develop competence. Self-confidence might spur you on to seek help and support from others, but ultimately it's developing your skills and learning from experience that will cement your success.* –Paul McGee

> *Give us the grace to accept with serenity*
> *the things that cannot be changed*
> *Courage to change the things*
> *which should be changed*
> *And wisdom to distinguish*
> *one from the other.*

1:37 Learn to accept and love yourself

An old Hawaiian saying is that when you see yourself for the first time for the "aloha sparkler" that you are, you will never have a problem with self-esteem again.

The desire to belong is basic human nature. But in order to feel like you truly belong, you must accept yourself for who you are. Acceptance of yourself and others is crucial if fear is going to loosen its grip on you.

Look in the mirror first thing in the morning; concentrate on the eye that attracts you. Look deep into the eye, through the membranes into the soul, say hello to your spirit within. Say good morning and thank you to your body of light for supporting you and for giving you this opportunity to learn and grow on the physical plane. Say I love you and really mean it.

> *Everything you want to be, do, or have comes from love. The positive force of love can create anything good, increase the good things, and change anything negative in your life.*
> –Rhonda Byrne

Acceptance of reality – no matter how unpleasant it seems:

1 *We practice unconditional self-acceptance*
   - *Accept the fact that you are a fallible person who has both good and bad points like everyone else.*
   - *There's no reason why you should not have flaws of some sort.*
   - *You are no less worthy than anybody else, despite your good and bad points.*

2 *We practice unconditional other-acceptance*
   - *Accept that other people will inevitably treat you unfairly on occasions.*
   - *There is no reason why they must treat you with fairness.*
   - *The people that do treat you unfairly are no more worthy and no less worthy than other people.*

2 We practice unconditional life-acceptance

- Accept that life doesn't unfold the way you'd always like it to.
- There's no reason why life should turn out the way you want it to.
- Life may not be what you regard as pleasant but it is not awful and in most instances it is certainly bearable.
- Nothing has any power over you other than that which you give it through your daily thoughts.

> Mistakes are lessons~ not comments
> on your self-worth

How do we fall in love? Falling in love is first to have worked upon ourselves, honed ourselves. We cannot fall in love if we are begging illness, if we are begging poverty, if we are begging victimization. We don't fall in love; we only get relief, but that is not love.

We have to work on ourselves and we have to love what we are, like we would love us as children. We cannot look at our face in the mirror and say it is too fat or it is too old or it is too ugly, my nose is too big or my eyes are too far apart or my eyes are black and blue is pretty, or blue is ugly and black is beautiful. We can't take ourselves apart like that. We have to love us like we would love a child of ours that suckles at our breast or is protected in our arms.

Love is its own beauty. Body parts don't make beauty. Soul and spirit make beauty.

What do we do when we fall in love? When we have worked on ourselves, when we have rooted out our secrets, found the source of our anger, rooted out our self-guilt, told the truth, because you can't love someone when you are battling your own guilt. Turn your attention to you, take your life apart, clean your vessel, and put it back together again.

Then we start being active in our life. We start forgiving ourselves by telling the truth, that we can forgive. Then we know love. –Ramtha

May we hold our hearts as gently as we would the feather of an angel. –Ku'uleialoha

What makes someone beautiful is that they appreciate the beauty in other people without any jealousy or mimicry.
A beautiful person can look at you and they actually see you, accept you and recognize the beauty and the divine in you, which is what makes them beautiful.
Their presence and ability to be with you, and alive in that moment, and appreciate what they're seeing and sensing makes you think Wow! what a beautiful person.
–Brendon Burchard

I can live for two months on a good compliment

-Mark Twain

1:38 Compliments are little gifts of love

Let the sun shine in…

The sun is always shining in people; you just have to move to a place to see it.

Giving compliments

Take a look at the person and see what you like about them. Pay attention to the details and make a mental note of how it makes you feel.

Now let the magic begin…

And yes this is the hard part.

Go up to the person and give them the compliment, be sincere, be specific, be genuine and be warm.

"I like (or I love) the way you have…" is a good introduction.

They are powerful gifts. But compliments only work if they are sincere reflections of what we think and if they are given freely and not coerced.

Be Genuine

A genuine compliment is not given with the expectation of getting anything in return. You are simply saying what needs to be said at that moment.

Be Specific

Giving a general compliment is good, but being specific is always better, it turns good to great.

Be Unique

This requires an extreme amount of attention to detail and a genuine interest in the other person. Being unique is a challenge, but it will set your compliment apart and give it far more impact.

Acknowledge their effort

People will like the compliment even more if you acknowledge that effort. It shows that you appreciate what was going on behind the scenes to make it happen.

State how it makes you feel

People like hearing about how they affect others. If you let them know that they have positively impacted you in some way, it will make them feel better.

> *The time of separation is over and the time of connection is beginning.* –Hank Wesselman

Compliments backfire if they are not genuine, and false flattery is usually highly transparent. A false compliment makes the speaker untrustworthy.

Always put yourself in the other's shoes. If you feel that it hurts you, it probably hurts the other person too.

Compliments are one of the most extraordinary components of social life. If given right they create so much positive energy that they make things happen almost as if by magic. They ease the atmosphere around two people and kindly dispose people to each other.

> *A careless word may kindle strife. A cruel word may wreck a life. A timely word may level stress. But a loving word may heal and bless.* –Anonymous

Accepting compliments

See accepting a compliment as a compliment in itself.

In accepting a compliment, you are telling the other person that you trust their judgment, their wisdom and their sense of self. Accepting compliments also tells the other person that you appreciate what they have to say about you.

More than anything, focus on *receiving* the compliment rather than on its content. This helps you to acknowledge the compliment and express appreciation for it being given to you.

Most importantly, since giving a compliment is a form of uttering an opinion, stop yourself from disagreeing with it or you risk downplaying someone else's opinion.

Smile – when taking a compliment, smiling says a lot without requiring you to say anything.

It is good to say thank you very much or just thank you. You can expand on this with something like thanks, that means a lot to me.

Part One - Shine like a star… the aloha way

Remember when a person has complimented you and note that it's nice and courteous to return it in a short space of time. Simply say something nice about the person who gave you a compliment. A great way to return the favor is to compliment on something of theirs and smile.

> *Be the aloha that you wish to see in the world.*
> —Hawaiian proverb

Natural forces within us are the true healers of disease.

–Hippocrates

1:39 Saturation praise

Hawaiian mind-body medicine teaches that any criticism, whether of your boss, yourself or the weather, leads to tension in your body, raising blood pressure, blood sugar and stress hormones. For instant relief from this mental stress, spend just one minute doing "saturation praise," complimenting everything you like about yourself, your boss (if only his tie), your family, your chakras, your world, and watch relaxation set in. –Becca Chopra

Since the Ku (the body-mind) considers itself connected to everything, criticism of oneself or others is felt as an attack. Even mentally criticizing something stresses the body, which in turn inhibits energy flow, awareness, and memory. Of course, all of this can weaken you and make you more susceptible to illness. –Kala H. Kos

In a recent discussion with Serge Kahili King, PhD, teacher of the Hawaiian Huna philosophy, he explained how everyone's body can achieve instant healing if there is no stress or tension. So that's where healers come in; they teach you to do yoga, meditate or chant, balance your chakras, do Qigong, exercise, breathe deeply, eat healthier food, perhaps take a pill to remove pain so that you can relax and heal. "All power comes from within," as King teaches in the Huna principles and that includes our power to heal. But we are all here on earth to help each other, and healers can help others to release the blocks in the flow of their healing energy, King suggests, in practicing "saturation praise" consciously, repetitively, and persistently. Here's how: spend at least a minute at a time telling yourself everything you like about yourself, everyone around you and your environment.

When you find yourself in a critical state, throw a mental switch and immediately notice any good in your life, in your body, in the world. Notice beauty and appreciate it.

Acknowledge the blessings you do have in your life.

In no time you'll be feeling a deep sense of relaxation spreading over you and your energy will be renewed.

There was a gentle hum, the energy of the woods embraced our small group as we sat joined hand to hand and heart to heart, breathing as one...

Eeeeeee Aloha Mai... the chant started.

Eeeeeee Mana Mai... it continued, raising the vibration all around, the sound of the living wood got louder.

Eeeeeee Pono Mai...

The young lady in the center of the circle smiled, a smile that would light up a thousand eyes.

Eeeeeee Ola Mai...

Part One - **Shine like a star**... *the aloha way*

We all basked in the glow, the beauty radiating from her.

Amama ua noa...

So be it, it is done...

The weekend retreat was coming to an end and Amanda had been transformed right before our very eyes. I could not help thinking back, reflecting on what had happened.

We had arrived late Friday evening, the last few miles were through the dark Welsh woodland and it had been hard going, it rained heavily and our car slid constantly on the wet track up the lower side of the mountain. On arrival we received a warm welcome, a hot drink and an invitation to sit near the open fire, an embrace of warm energy from the discarded limbs of the earth.

Everyone was excited at the thought of what waited ahead, what journeys we would go on at this shamanic retreat. The room was buzzing, alive with conversation, but my attention was drawn to a plain-looking young lady sitting on her own, clearly wrapped up in her own internal world, no one seemed to notice her as she slowly withdrew into her shell. I wandered over to where she was sitting and introduced myself, asking for her name in the process. "Amanda," she replied, as she tried to force an acknowledging smile.

We engaged in polite conversation and it slowly emerged that her boyfriend of two years did not want her to come on the retreat, they had had an argument before she left home on the three-hour journey to Wales, she didn't want to be here, and if it wasn't for the bad weather outside, she would be on her way back home right now. To make matters worse, there was no phone line, this was before cell phones existed – yes there really was such a time! I could sense that there was something much deeper that was bothering her, something that affected her whole personality, her whole way of being. But we had only just met and it was not my place to probe into her personal affairs, and besides I was here to expand my shamanic knowledge, this weekend was for me... or so I thought!

I woke, with the morning light shining through the gap in the drapes, and turned over to see the bed next to mine was empty. David had mentioned the night before that he was looking forward to an early morning run in the woods. I got up, opened the window, took a deep breath of fresh Welsh air, air that had been kissed with the elixir of morning dew, and then I sat down on the bed gathering my thoughts before taking a shower.

There was a knock on the door, and to my surprise Amanda was standing there in her pajamas; she asked to come in and was obviously in distress. I invited her in, left the door slightly ajar for David and sat on the bed. Without another word she burst into tears, sobbing her heart out; I put my arms around her and just gave her the reassurance and security that they offered. Eventually the crying slowed down, she wiped her eyes and apologized. I reassured her that there was nothing to apologize for and as today's weather was dry she could just leave and go home.

This started her crying again as she said, "But I don't want to." I asked her what the problem was, what was really bothering her. I reminded her that there were only the two of us here in the room and a group promise of what was said on the retreat stayed on the retreat.

She spent the next half-hour sharing a most desperate story, a story of a bullying boyfriend who verbally abused her on a daily basis. He would tell her that she was ugly, fat (she was thin) and unattractive. He told her that she was lucky to have him as no one else would look at her. For two years he was constantly undermining her confidence and eroding her sense of self-worth as he took control of her life, bit by bit. Yesterday she had stood up to him such was her determination to attend the retreat, and that had ended in a heated row which in turn resulted in the abuse turning physical; she showed me the bruising on her arm, and asked me what to do.

I simply reminded her that for the next two days she was in a safe environment, and surrounded by kind-hearted souls. I encouraged her to share her story with the group. Later that morning she did so, and this is what happened...

Let there be light, let there be love
Koko

After sharing her story with the group, she asked for help, help to heal herself so that she had the strength to change her life.

As a group we engaged on a shamanic journey; carrying the question of "how can we help Amanda?" we traveled with intention, willful and conscious. After almost one hour we had all arrived back and shared our experiences. Laulima was the unanimous feedback followed by a weekend of saturation praise.

Laulima means many hands coming together and that weekend was to be the longest and most amazing Laulima experience of my life.

Laulima is the practice of the aloha spirit where we all have a spiritual connection with each other and with our land through loving touch. It is the activity of divine light prevailing through each person present. It is the ultimate in grace receiving gratitude.

"Come and experience the giving and receiving of healing and the ultimate gift of love," said the retreat leader. One by one we connected to the divine energy and slowly placed our hands on Amanda. As each member of the group added to the joyous flow of light and love energy, all feelings of anger, frustration, and unhappiness left the supine body lying on the floor, and this negative energy was transmuted into healing energy and passed into the earth for use somewhere on the planet. Amanda said that she could feel the weight of the world leave her body as her energy expanded to "into infinity and beyond" – she really did say that!

After lunch we had a group saturation praise session where we blessed everyone and everything that represented beauty. We blessed and recognized the beauty in the surroundings, the trees, the air; we acknowledged the beauty of each other, our differences, and our uniqueness. We blessed Amanda for giving us the opportunity to work with her.

Throughout the rest of the weekend everyone and anyone who had contact with Amanda, no matter how small that contact was, would comment about her beauty, her inspiring story, we told her that she looked lighter, that she was glowing with health and vitality. People said how they loved her hair, her eyes, and her personality; how she made us feel, her energy, her achievements, the love she shared, every aspect of her was blessed with focused acts of good intents, energy and power.

She was encouraged to affirm her beauty, by saying to herself "I am beautiful" over and over again throughout the weekend. The intention here was just to make her more comfortable with the idea, no more than that.

What is important to remember here is that we are not just blessing physical beauty, whatever that is; as a group we are *behaving with beauty* so that Amanda's own innate natural beauty can shine through, through all the negative abuse that she has received.

And what is so beautiful about this process is that the blessing you do for others helps them as well as you. By the time we had our final sharing circle, Amanda was glowing, transformed by the attention of love, the energy of aloha in action. This was not the same girl: her hair shone, there was a twinkle in her eyes, her voice was vibrant with enthusiasm, and she was born anew.

That is the power of saturation praise!

Action

Take a piece of paper and make a list of all the things you like about yourself, anything good you have done or do. Go through each aspect of your life: family, friends, work, hobbies etc.

Include any good comments or praise you have received, any memories where you have been proud of yourself.

Now go down the list one item at a time, think about it, allow yourself to remember the feelings. Give yourself praise and a compliment for each item before moving on to the next

Thinking about yourself in this way could be one of the healthiest things you do. Your subconscious will acknowledge it, it will do more of it and improve on it.

> *Inner beauty gives you a richness which outer beauty alone can't accomplish.*
>
> Rajin Niku

1:40 Inner beauty

Food for thought

In the United Kingdom a woman government minister recently stated: "Parents should stop telling their children they look beautiful because it places too much emphasis on appearance and can lead to body confidence issues later in life."

Ms Swinson (who does not have any children of her own) suggested that "praising them for their skill in doing a jigsaw and all these other things that they are doing, their curiosity in asking questions and a whole range of things" was more appropriate than commenting on looks.

She told parents to watch what they say about their bodies in front of children.

"Maybe parents themselves have significant issues with body image; when saying 'does my bum look too big? I need to get rid of this tummy,' they should remember that children copy, and they learn.

"Research shows that when children have no body confidence at school they're less likely to put their hand up in class and ask a question. In extreme cases, you'll have people suffering from body dysmorphia, a psychiatric disorder, where people might not feel happy to go to school and you get truancy as a result of this. So it can have an impact on education, either in an extreme way or even in feeling less able to participate."

This view was then questioned by others.

"What's wrong with telling children they're beautiful?" asked Natalie Cox from *The Guardian newspaper*. "Jo Swinson worries about image being overemphasized, but faced with today's media, children's self-esteem needs bolstering."

What this approach to boosting your child's self-esteem fails to address, however, is that children will take an interest in both how they look and what other people say about them in terms of their appearance, good or bad. We live in a society where those in the public eye are constantly criticized in the media for their appearance. Rather than ignoring the fact that we all get judged on how we look, we should be encouraging our children to have a positive opinion of themselves and their appearance. Beauty is, after all, subjective.

I'm advocating balance and encouraging children in all the aspects of life that matter to them, from their education, to social skills, and how they feel about themselves. "Beautiful" is not inherently sexual; it is not intrinsically tied up with misogynistic viewpoints, and it is not about trying to achieve impossible ideals pushed on us by the beauty and fashion industries. Feeling beautiful goes hand in hand with self-acceptance, which is something that any parent would want for their child.

*Part One - **Shine like a star**… the aloha way*

She also makes the very valid point that adults need to watch what they say in front of children when criticizing their own bodies, to prevent their children copying the negative rhetoric.

We need to be doing everything possible to counteract the damage done to our children's self-esteem by the barrage of appearance-based criticism that celebrities endure in the media, and which men and women are encouraged to emulate with reference to their bodies. Our children are growing up in a culture where zooming in on a pop star's cellulite is a news story, or where an actor's weight gain makes the front page. Pretending that appearances aren't judged is impossible, so let's do our best to make sure our children have the thickest armor possible by killing body image woes with kindness.

For every beauty there is an eye somewhere to see it.
For every truth there is an ear somewhere to hear it.
For every love there is a heart somewhere to receive it.

Ivan Panin

Appearances are generally deceptive. Beauty is the essence of life but inner beauty is the essence of the soul. Who knows that a person with a beautiful face may have an ugly heart? You don't need trendy clothes, designer handbags and stylish accessories to be beautiful, all you need is to give your body and your mind a little tender love and care.

Inner beauty gives you a richness which outer beauty alone can't accomplish.

The person who is beautiful from within is blessed with an aura and fullness that external beautification will never find. Your thoughts, your values, make up your inner beauty and if they are pure they give life a better meaning. External beauty fades with time, but internal beauty is with you forever. Real beauty is not the physical beauty all the time. It lies in human character and human heart. Handsome is he who handsome does. Physical beauty is short lived. It fades away too soon. But the beauty of heart is eternal joy giving, and ever-growing gentility of heart and nobility of character are the hallmarks of one's personality.

> *The real test of a person lies in their deeds and not in their words, in their character and not in their appearance.*
> –Rajin Niku

> *Girls of all kinds can be beautiful – from the thin, plus-sized, short, very tall, ebony to porcelain-skinned; the quirky, clumsy, shy, outgoing and all in between. It's not easy though because many people still put beauty into a confining, narrow box… Think outside of the box… pledge that you will look in the mirror and find the unique beauty in you.* –Tyra Banks

> *There are no cosmetics for beauty like happiness.*
> Maria Mitchell

1:41 Charisma

Are you simply born with charisma, or can anyone be taught the art of "lighting up a room?"

The English term *charisma* is from Greek which means favor freely given or gift of grace. The term and its plural *charismata* derive from *charis,* which means grace. It also has two senses: 1. compelling attractiveness or charm that can inspire devotion in others; 2. a divinely conferred power or talent.

Charisma was the difference between Norma Jean Baker and her alter-ego Marilyn Monroe. In 1955, the movie star rode the

New York subway unnoticed by her fellow passengers because, she explained, she had chosen to adopt "Baker" mode. But when she emerged onto the city sidewalks, she asked an accompanying journalist, "Do you want to see *her?*" She fluffed her hair, struck a pose. Suddenly, onlookers reported, magic seemed to flow from her

A charismatic person has three attributes, says Professor Wiseman, a psychologist:

- *They feel emotions themselves quite strongly.*
- *They induce them in others.*
- *They are impervious to the influences of other charismatic people.*

"When you see someone else who has charisma, without realizing it, you're mimicking their posture and their facial expressions," says the professor. "An obvious example is when someone smiles at you and you smile back. And how you hold yourself influences your emotions. You're unaware you're mimicking this person, although you know they make you feel happy."

But don't despair if you haven't got these qualities because you can learn them. Professor Wiseman estimates charisma is 50% innate and 50% trained. His tips include keeping an open body posture and communicating your ideas clearly. Broadcaster and confidence tutor Jeremy Milnes agrees that techniques can make a huge transformation, and says nearly all the people he's worked with have improved. Key areas are listening, asking questions and not trying too hard to be the center of attention.

"Charisma isn't innate, it can be controlled at will," says Fox Cabane, who is transforming what was considered an art into a science, one that is frankly scary at times. "It's all about learning to play chemist with your brain," she explains. "If you're able to flood your body with oxytocin [the love hormone] whenever you want, your body language will be transformed. People will want to be near you."

Give your charisma a kick-start:

- *Conquer reserve.*
- *Make yourself vulnerable.*
- *Become comfortable with discomfort.*
- *Assume the alluring alchemy that makes some people so inexplicably attractive.*
- *Boosting one's charisma involves projecting more of three qualities: presence, power, and warmth.*
- *Neuro-shaping: playing chemist with our own brains to achieve remarkable powers of charm and persuasion.*
- *Push the boundaries of your comfort zone. Increase your ability to fully focus and absorb. Reduce the fear of failure or embarrassment.*

Focus your attention on your toes for one minute. This forces your mind to sweep through your body, helping you to get into the physical sensations of the moment.

In conversation, lower the intonation of your voice at the end of sentences, reduce how quickly and how often you nod, and pause for two seconds before you speak.

Stretch your comfort zone by chatting to a stranger. This can be someone in a queue, just share general conversation. For example: while waiting in a coffee queue ask the person behind you, "I am trying to decide which is the more sinful: the muffin or the brownie. What do you think?"

Become the "big gorilla" when you want to feel and broadcast confidence before a key meeting or an encounter with someone a bit intimidating. Take a wide stance, plant your feet firmly on the ground, stretch your arms to the ceiling then out to the walls on either side of you. Try to take up as much space as possible, roll your shoulders up and then back, puff up your chest, broaden your shoulders and put your arms behind your back.

Think of a small vulnerability you could share, and ease it into a conversation, saying, "You know, I have to tell you..." Or prepare the terrain by saying, "I am feeling a bit nervous about saying this, but...." Ask for confidentiality – people love secrets.

Total focus is "presence" which is charisma's vital component. It's often said of Obama that he makes people feel like the only one in the room – he isn't distracted, he's truly present. It's easier said than done. Our brains are wired to be distracted. Our ancestors survived by registering every new stimulus, before it killed them or they killed it, and today we're bombarded by electronic diversions. A recent Harvard study revealed that 50% of the average person's time is spent mind-wandering. People who can control this are rare – and can make others feel extraordinarily special. We all think we can fake paying attention, but when we do it, our reactions are delayed. The human mind can read facial expressions in about 17 milliseconds, so subconsciously the person you're talking to will feel the lag and feel brushed off. Presence should be underscored by two further qualities: warmth and power.

Charismatic people always combine the two. "They give the impression that they have a lot of power and also that they like you, or could like you, a lot," says Fox Cabane

People seek out a good and charismatic chiropractor/therapist because they know they'll be treated well and the encounter will leave them feeling better about themselves for having the interaction.

The rules of charisma

- ◆ *Be present. Give people your full attention. If your mind wanders, refocus by concentrating on physical sensations, like your breathing.*
- ◆ *Exude power and warmth. Adopt a powerful posture (wide stance, straight back, broad shoulders) and cultivate warmth by focusing on three things you like about the other person.*

- *Accept introversion. If you're naturally shy, "warm up" before important interactions – visualize moments when you felt confident, or listen to mood-boosting music.*
- *Be vulnerable. There's a fine line between charismatic and intimidating. Encourage a human connection with someone by revealing a weakness or sharing an embarrassing secret.*
- *It's all in the voice. Create an air of confidence by speaking in a measured tempo and lowering your intonation at the end of sentences. Increasing the warmth in your voice is even easier: just smile.*

Live and breathe aloha, it's the gift of grace and with grace comes charisma.

♪ *Good morning starshine; the earth says hello*
You twinkle above us; we twinkle below ♪

Hair

1:42 All day energy

Plug into the flow of energy and beat fatigue, morning, noon and night.

Sunrise:
Create a morning burst of energy:

- *Open the drapes and let the daylight in.*
- *If it's dark outside use a time-glow alarm.*
- *Greet the day with a few stretches, to get the body moving and the blood pumping.*
- *Take a few deep breaths, bringing much-needed oxygen to the awakening brain.*
- *Do a few yoga sun salutations.*
- *Use good morning affirmations.*

Part One - **Shine like a star**... the aloha way

- *Refill your fuel tank, it's nearly empty.*
- *Have a good healthy breakfast – protein and fat are essential for energy.*
- *Your brain needs a continuous supply of glucose to function optimally.*
- *Try oatmeal with skimmed milk. A morning smoothie. Bran and fruit.*
- *"Don't just rely on coffee; it will mask your low blood sugar level by temporarily stimulating your brain but won't do any thing to satisfy your need for energy."–Professor Dan Benardot*

Sunshine:
Sustaining midday energy:

- *Don't eat like a bird or skip lunch.*
- *Your digestive system peaks at lunchtime.*
- *Have a healthy combo lunch with nourishing wholesome, unprocessed ingredients, comprising protein, good fats and vegetables or salad.*
- *Add extra fiber to slow down the passage of food through the intestines to ensure a long continual release into the bloodstream.*
- *Snack on grapes or an apple to stabilize your blood sugar.*
- *Take a few deep breaths and open your chest.*
- *Do a midday focus exercise.*
- *Go for a walk, and share an aloha moment with someone.*

Sunlight:
More useful energy-boosting tips:

- *Have a playlist of different kinds of music. It has the ability to change your mood.*
- *Surround yourself with energetic people as their vitality will rub off on you.*

- Do a hobby that you love.
- Spend time with people and/or pets that you love.
- Laugh a lot, watch something funny, see a comedy, and spend time with funny people. Don't take life seriously.
- Create a balance in your life: if you have a brain-based office job, go outside and exercise; if you have a physical job, relax, do a pub quiz, read a book, paint, listen to music, write.
- Go out for a meal with good company.
- Tired or not, these energy-boosting ideas are fuel for the body and soul.

Sunset:
Easing into the evening:

- Play sport or do some exercise.
- If too tired try a restorative yoga exercise.
- Have family time.
- Have fun, laugh be happy.
- Watch TV, play music.
- Unwind while preparing your evening meal, get the family involved.
- Plan a variety if possible using lean meats, skinless chicken or turkey breast; oily fish, such as tuna, mackerel, salmon; and vegetarian substitutes. Try some different side dishes such as rice, pasta, couscous, jacket potato, bread or salad. Aim to eat different vegetables with each dinner.

Sundown:
Creating a restful night:

- Power down your body.
- Remove any stimulating negative energy, TV news or bad vibes.

Part One - **Shine like a star**... the aloha way

- *Take a "chill pill" and relax; have a bath and re-energize, play music.*
- *Have a hot drink; milk contains amino acid tryptophan which helps in the production of serotonin and aids sleep.*
- *Herbal tea contains calming infusions such as chamomile, ginger, orange, peppermint and honey.*
- *Don't touch alcohol, cocoa or coffee as they raise the heart rate, the last two contain sugar and caffeine which will take several hours to process.*
- *Power down your home.*
- *Turn off all electrical gadgets.*
- *Reduce any light in the room.*
- *Light stops your melatonin levels from rising, which you need for a good night's sleep.*
- *Do your evening reflection of gratitude.*

> *Habit is habit, and not to be flung out the window by any man, but coaxed downstairs one step at a time.*
>
> Mark Twain

1:43 Breaking bad habits

Habits are a part of life, good or bad we all have them. One of the ways you can start to take control of your life is by changing your habits – reducing the bad ones and increasing the good ones.

Nearly all of us have made positive changes only to revert to old habits, with each forward leap followed by a backslide. This is due to a natural, subconscious attachment to familiar patterns.

Your body and subconscious mind get accustomed to a familiar weight, activity level, and other patterns of behavior. This applies to good habits, neutral habits, or negative habits. Once a pattern is in place, we all tend to resist change.

Breaking a negative habit or starting a positive one happens in two stages: first, making the desired change; second, maintaining the change. Patterns tend to reassert themselves unless you can maintain the new pattern long enough for it to become familiar.

Habits are relatively simple to develop. Look at all the habits you *don't* like. If you examine your undesirable habits closely, you will find that they all have something in common. They all give you some type of feeling that is rewarding to you. Why do people spend hours watching mindless TV? Why do people smoke? They do it because it gives them a certain feeling – in this case, relaxation, stress reduction, or even excitement.

You see, we're not addicted to the actual activity. What we're addicted to is the *feeling* that activity gives us. Just think of any habit you have that you find undesirable. What positive feelings does it give you? Know that you're getting a "reward" for those bad habits, that's why you continue doing it. We don't do things habitually that make us feel bad, at least not at the moment that we're engaged in doing it.

To start, make a list of all the bad habits you would like to stop. Then reduce that list down to the top five, and then reduce it further down to three. Once you have three put them in order of preference. If you find yourself struggling to decide the order, do it in reverse: ask yourself if you had to drop one which one would it be then place that habit at number three on the list. Now you have two, either repeat the question above or ask yourself if you only had a chance of losing one habit which one would you choose. You now have your priority habit, the one you have the most desire to break.

Part One - *Shine like a star*… *the aloha way*

Step 1 - Conscious attention: using bullet points list the times, places and circumstances that you engage in the bad habit.

- *Are any feelings attached to it?*
- *Why is this habit bad?*
- *What's holding me back from getting rid of it?*
- *What things or people stop me from breaking the habit?*

Step 2 - Conscious action: can be divided into three parts: (a) create barriers (b) change the environment (c) flick the switch.

- *Have a habit jar and put money in every time you do the habit.*
- *Find someone who doesn't like your habit and spend time with them, ask them to point out to you every time you engage (subconsciously) in the bad habit.*
- *Limit your interactions with people who encourage your habit (they may also have the same bad habit).*
- *If your habit takes place in a particular environment, change the environment or don't go.*
- *I have known many moms who have broken the habit of their children's pacifier sucking by going away for a few days and "forgetting" to take it.*
- *Flick the switch is about replacing one bad habit with a better one, e.g. smoking an electronic cigarette. This should be seen as a temporary step.*
- *Or maybe instead of smoking you take a ten-minute walk around the block.*

Step 3 - Conscious consideration:

- *Behavioral conditioning is a long process, and breaking a habit takes time; as much as you'd like to, you probably won't stop doing it overnight. Set realistic goals and plan to have the behavior wiped out in 30 days. If you get to the end of a month and find you need more time, take another 30 days. As long as you're still improving, don't pay too much attention to how long the process is taking. You'll get there eventually.*

Reward: *Reward yourself for breaking the habit; if you don't repeat the habit for 30 days then use the money from the habit jar to do or have something nice.*

> *Words that enlighten the soul are more precious than jewels.*
>
> Hazrat Inayat Khan

1:44 Way of learning

We sit here supreme in our scientific knowledge of our subject matter, but still the skill of hand-eye coordination eludes us, as we expect to develop motor memory with less effort than that given to our conceptual thinking. But that is the western way: learn the science and develop the application after a limited amount of time.

In the islands the traditional way was to start young, sit, watch, listen, don't talk, practice skill development, help others, sit, watch, listen, question, explore and find the hidden meaning, practice skill development. This would go on for years so by the time the student "graduated" he had been in practice for more years than his western counterpart may have in his professional career.

The island way is not compatible with the fast pace of modern society and the western way is not compatible with the development of spiritual touch. There has to be a compromise somewhere.

The where is at the azurii massage school. Here the kumus give westerners the "little what" (what about the science); they receive just enough science of what, why, when, where, and how to light a flame of encouragement, then it is skill development, practice, practice, and practice. Only when the student has demonstrated the required level of commitment and improvement are they given the "bigger what," the expanded picture. Here they understand the process and time required for a new skill to move from the conscious mind and into the subconscious mind, and then only on arrival into the subconscious can the newly learned skill be developed into an art form, then with layer upon layer of daily practice can the form develop the artist.

There are no mistakes only lessons,

> *In the martial art aikido, the fighter blends with the direction of an opposing force, moves with it, and uses its power to defuse the attack. If you view a setback as an opposing force, you can still accept and blend with it and internalize its lessons to your advantage. By doing this, the power of the opposing force no longer exists. You direct the force and forge ahead.* –Chungliang Ali Huang

> *We are what we repeatedly do. Excellence then, is not an act, but a habit.*
> Aristotle

1:45 Developing new habits

How do you make doing something continually look easy? The answer is by developing habits that make your actions automatic. The goal is to get yourself to do something long enough until it becomes a habit. Once it becomes a habit, you don't have to put much effort into it anymore. It'll almost be automatic, and that's the beauty of creating habits that align with your goals and dreams.

How long does it take to create new empowering habits? It is largely determined by the intensity of the emotion that accompanies the decision to begin acting in a particular way. Habits of medium complexity can be developed quite easily in 21 days through practice and repetition (medium – like getting up earlier). How long it takes really depends on how fast you can get to the point where it becomes effortless, but for practicality's sake, set a goal to do it for at least 30 days.

The main reason why people fail to develop a good habit (New Year resolution) is that they focus on the negative (bad feeling) that is associated with it (I must lose weight, I don't like the way I look).

Change this to a positive (good feeling) such as I will look great in that lovely bikini this summer and you will change the outcome; focus on the positive reward of your actions. Reward yourself at various stages as you progress. If your target is to lose 20lbs, then reward yourself with something you really want (a new pair of shoes) at 10lbs. This way you are creating good feelings and focusing on the positive.

Step 1 - Conscious statement of intent: decide clearly that you are going to begin acting in a specific way 100% of the time, whenever that behavior is required.
- *What is the end goal?*
- *Know the end result required.*
- *Write down how you are going to get there.*

Step 2 - Conscious clarity: it is very important that you have strong reasons for obtaining the end results because it will be the fuel that will drive your actions in forming the desired habits.
- *What are your reasons for developing this habit?*
- *List all the good points and reasons for achieving this goal.*
- *Write down how you will feel once you have reached your goal.*

Step 3 - Conscious commitment: never allow an exception to your new habit pattern during the formative stages.
- *Don't make excuses or rationalizations.*
- *Don't let yourself off the hook.*

Part One - **Shine like a star**... *the aloha way*

- *Discipline yourself to repeat the developing habit until this becomes automatic.*

- *Kick out the gremlins – you know, the charming little voice in your head that comes up with about a dozen excuses to not take action.*

Step 4 - Conscious recruitment: tell others that you are going to begin practicing a particular behavior. It is amazing how much more disciplined and determined you will become when you know that others are watching you to see if you have the willpower to follow through on your resolution.

- *Find a friend who wants the same goal.*
- *Talk about your progress with others.*
- *Surround yourself with people who will encourage you.*
- *Remove yourself from people and situations that will discourage you.*

Step 5 - Conscious creation: visualize yourself performing or behaving in a particular way in a particular situation. The more often you visualize and imagine yourself acting as if you already had the new habit, the more rapidly this new behavior will be accepted by your subconscious mind and become automatic. Create an affirmation that you repeat over and over to yourself. This repetition dramatically increases the speed at which you develop the new habit.

- *See yourself as already doing the new skill/habit.*
- *See yourself as already having the result of your desire.*
- *Put a photo or inspirational quote on the refrigerator.*
- *Create an affirmation and put it in your computer and cell phone.*

Step 6 - Conscious carry-on: resolve to persist in the new behavior until it is so automatic and easy that you actually feel uncomfortable when you do not do what you have decided to do.

- *Keep going for 30 days.*
- *Resolve never to give up.*
- *If you forget or miss a day, don't worry, keep going.*

Reward: *Give yourself a reward of some kind for practicing the new behavior. Each time you reward yourself you reaffirm and reinforce the behavior. Soon you begin to associate, at an unconscious level, the pleasure of the reward with the behavior. You set up your own force field of positive consequences that you unconsciously look forward to as the result of engaging in the behavior or habit that you have decided upon.*

> *Nothing we ever imagined is beyond our powers,
> only beyond our present self-knowledge.*
>
> Theodore Roszak

1:46 Developing a skill

How long does it take to develop a new skill? It depends on the complexity of the skill. However, developing a new skill (bodywork or otherwise) will go through the same stages of progress before it becomes a habitual skill that can be performed subconsciously.

Skills of medium complexity can be developed quite easily in 21 days through practice and repetition. How long it takes really depends on how fast you can get to the point where it becomes effortless, but for practicality's sake, set a goal to do it for at least 30 days.

*Part One - **Shine like a star**... the aloha way*

To learn a new bodywork skill to the level of subconscious competence requires on average 30 days of continuous habit building, with the last five days being regarded as the golden period of reinforcement. But studies show that this practice of a skill does not have to be of a physical nature only. Visualization works as well; if you visualize doing the skill you will trigger the same muscle memory and subconscious response.

The five stages of progress are:

1. *Unconscious incompetence*
2. *Conscious incompetence*
3. *Conscious competence*
4. *Unconscious competence*
5. *Integration*

Stage 1 - Unconscious incompetence:
(You Don't Know that You Don't Know)

- *Also known as the "pool of bliss."*
- *So you don't care.*
- *You have no idea about your incompetence in the subject matter.*
- *At this level you are blissfully ignorant: you have a complete lack of knowledge and skills in the subject in question.*
- *We are not aware of the existence or relevance of a skill, or that we're deficient in the skill area. We may also not see the relevance or usefulness of a skill, and dismiss it. "Oblivious" could describe us in stage one.*
- *On top of this, you are unaware of this lack of skill, and your confidence may therefore far exceed your abilities.*

Symptoms: Inexperience, naiveté, immaturity or (technically speaking) cluelessness.

Remedy: There isn't one. Understandably, at this stage we don't have a clue.

Stage 2 - Conscious incompetence:
(You Know that You Don't Know)

- *A period of frustration as you become aware of the skill you don't have.*
- *At this level you find that there are skills you need to learn, and you may be shocked to discover that there are other people who are much more competent than you. As you realize that your ability is limited, your confidence drops. You go through an uncomfortable period as you learn these new skills when others are much more competent and successful than you are.*
- *We move into this state when we realize that if we improve the area of deficiency in a new skill we will become more effective.*

Symptoms: *Awareness, knowledge, interest or (technically speaking) the "a-ha! moment."*

Remedy: Accepting the fact that a deficiency exists and welcoming the opportunity to learn.

Stage 3 - Conscious competence: (You Know that You Know)

- *You can now do the activity, but you still have to think about it as you go.*
- *We begin to achieve conscious competence when we can perform or demonstrate a skill reasonably well. We still have to think about it, but we don't need a lot of assistance to execute it.*
- *At this level you acquire the new skills and knowledge. You put your learning into practice and you gain confidence in carrying out the tasks or jobs involved. You are aware of your new skills and work on refining them.*
- *You are still concentrating on the performance of these activities, but as you get more practice and experience, these become increasingly automatic.*

Symptoms: *Strong skill development, continuous improvement, ability to demonstrate skill or (technically speaking) "I might actually be good at this."*

Remedy: Practice is the most effective way to move from stage three to stage four.

Stage 4 - Unconscious competence:
(You Don't Know that You Know – It Just Seems Easy!)
- *You can do the skill without thinking about it; it has become a subconscious act, an imbedded habit.*
- *At this level executing your skills becomes second nature, and you perform the task without conscious effort and with automatic ease. The subconscious almost takes over and the skill execution is automatic. At this stage, you can not only perform the skill, but also do other things at the same time.*
- *This is the peak of your confidence and ability.*

Symptoms: *Ability to multi-task, ability to teach the skill or (technically speaking) "I could do this with my eyes closed."*
Remedy: The only concern at this stage is to check whether we've missed an opportunity to learn still more. Often we master a skill, but with new technology or innovation, we can develop it even further.

Stage 5 - Integration: you have integrated your new skill with all your other skills; it is now a part of you.

Each stage can be broken down further into four phases:
1. **Engage:** in which a student's interest is captured and the topic is established.
2. **Explore:** in which the student is allowed to construct knowledge in the topic through facilitated questioning and observation.
3. **Explain:** in which students are asked to explain what they have discovered, and the instructor leads a discussion of the topic to refine the students' understanding.
4. **Extend:** in which students are asked to apply what they have learned in different but similar situations, and the instructor guides the students toward the next discussion topic.

I hope this is a prescription that will help you understand yourself and others better. It will certainly provide you with some great one-liners the next time someone asks you, "Do you know what you're doing?"

1:47 The man who thinks he can

If you think you are beaten you are.
If you think you dare not, you don't.
If you'd like to win but think you can't,
It's almost certain you won't.

If you think you will lose, you've lost.
For out of the world you'll find,
Success begins with a fellow's will,
It's all in the state of the mind.

If you think you're outclassed you are.
You've got to think high to rise.
You've got to be sure of yourself,
Before you can ever win a prize.

Life's battles don't always go
To the stronger or faster man.
But soon or late, the man who wins
Is the man who thinks he can.

Walter D. Wintle

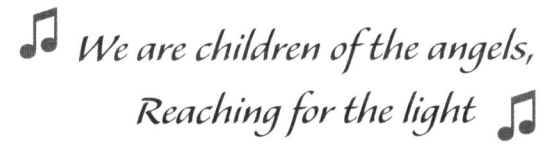

♪ *We are children of the angels,*
   Reaching for the light ♪

Walela

Truly, it is in the darkness that one finds the light, so when we are in sorrow, then this light is nearest of all to us.

–Meister Eckhart

Part One - **Shine like a star**... *the aloha way*

1:48 Web of light

Imagine… imagine. Before you were born you were just a little spark of light connected to the creative force of the universe. You looked down on this great earth. What a beautiful planet filled with wondrous life forms. You started to ponder the possibilities of life on earth. Do you remember the preciousness of life and that all life was created to experience love, light, joy, harmony, peace, equality, and abundance for all? If you can feel this in your bones, then you know it is true.

–Sandra Ingerman

The underlying principle of esoteric beliefs is that all life is made of light. As human beings with egos we often forget our true nature and we over identify with our personalities and bodies. We are light in bodies.

We are light and we came here to shine. But most of us have forgotten our true nature as well as why we came here. We were created from love and light and we are love and light. It is our birthright to shine as fully as we can in the world.

Many of us have been taught at an early age not to shine too brightly. If we shine too brightly no one will love us. There can only be a few "stars" and it is not you. Does this sound familiar?

Why can there only be a few stars here on earth? I have never heard anyone say when looking up at the stars in the sky: I wish that star wouldn't shine so brightly, it is outshining other stars. Why do we have that belief here?

It is time for all of us to shine our light, which will reflect back the beauty of the night sky above us. We need to find our shine again so we can light up the dark places of the world.

We need to create a human web of light. This will not only bring light to places that need it right now, but it will heal us and help us remember our true nature, which is light.

This formula will help us in remembering our light and letting it shine forth: intention + harmony + love + concentration + focus + union + imagination = transmutation.

Begin to practice with letting your light shine through you. And next practice breathing in light and breathing out light throughout the day.

As you get in touch with your own light and shine it in your life you will change your vibration. As we gather our lights together and share it in the world we change the vibration of the planet. It's crucial to stay focused on your intention.

I suggest that you add no prayers or words as you do this. Just simply shine and allow yourself to join with a planetary web of light that will reach out to touch all the dark places in the world.

It will also be quite healing to know that you are connecting with thousands of others who are remembering that we are light. As we share this concept with others our web of light will grow, which I know will have an impact on the earth and all life on it.

> *Remember all life is of the light. You are light, we all are light, we can join together in a great web of light.*
>
> –Sandra Ingerman

Everywhere is the center of the world.
Everything is sacred…
                                                -Black Elk

1:49 The zone

What a useless map! I thought.

Now let me explain, I love maps and as a youngster I was interested in cartography; give me an old map or a globe and I would be lost for hours. Today we have GPS systems to show us "the way" to

*Part One - **Shine like a star**… the aloha way*

anywhere and Google Earth is a fantastic form of entertainment that completely locks my interest. But every map becomes useless without the little arrow that indicates "you are here."

On a hot Sunday afternoon I was in a maize maze; that's right, a giant maze made out of maize, and in a clearing was a group of people agitated and in a state of confusion, while looking at the map on the board. Which way out? What path do we take? Where do we go? Question after question came from the group followed by theories but no real sense of direction. Why? Because someone had removed the sticky arrow that said "you are here."

It's the same in life: in order to move forward we need to step back and reflect on where we are, and where we want to go. The process of creating a path between both points then becomes a lot clearer and easier.

Ancestral masters say that peace and love come from within and to experience peace and love we must look within; at any given time we live in one of three zones:

- *The zone of darkness*
- *The zone of smog*
- *The zone of light*

The zone of light is where your dreams manifest into reality; it's where you live a full and fulfilling life. It's a zone where you can bask in the glow of great relationships. It's a zone of brilliant achievement. This zone is accessible to anyone who lives with direction and purpose in their love of life.

The zone of smog is where the majority of people spend their lives. Smog is a gray thick fog where you struggle to see beyond that which is in front of your eyes. They get comfortable in their jobs, relationships and day-to-day activities. It's not good but it's not bad – it is safe and it is familiar, the sound echoing in the mist. In the illusion of the "mist of acceptance" they fear change, they can't see anything better, and therefore they settle for a dull gray life – after all it's not the zone of darkness so it must be okay!

The zone of darkness is where we slip when we let the light in our lives fade. We can enter the dark zone through a traumatic life-changing event or simply by a build-up of frustration of unfulfilled potential or from the unhappiness of year after year living in the smog of a wasted life.

The good news is it's never too late to change, you always have a choice. Don't be one of those poor spirits who live in the mist that knows neither victory nor defeat. Let the light back in, sprinkle your life with the magic of stardust, re-energize and soar into the heavens; shine like the star you were born to be.

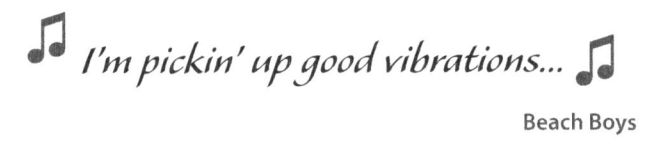

♪ *I'm pickin' up good vibrations...* ♪

Beach Boys

1:49 The flow

> *Oceanic philosophy teaches that each of us resonates with the other and that there is a rhythm that throbs through every person, rock, bird, and fish. Some people refer to this as "sending out vibes" but Polynesians speak of "becoming in harmony" with the natural rhythm of the world.*
>
> *Whether we call it sending out vibes or getting a good feeling, most of us know that beyond the brain, the heart, endorphins, and the neurohormones there is an energy that we feel and send all the time. Something seems to tell us when something is good or bad for us. We often can't find words for it, but there is an internal wisdom that draws us to or diverts us away from certain people or things. We must remember that we too are sending out approach or avoidance signals.*
>
> –Paul Pearsall.

Go with the flow and life becomes easy and you become happy. Fighting the current makes life hard and you get nowhere.

Have a relationship not with a person but with an art – something you love to do – and you create a field of energy that is in harmony with the energy of your thoughts, resulting in good vibrations.

Also known as the flow – when your sense of time is forgotten during an activity, you get so absorbed that when you do look at the clock, you can't believe where the time has gone. You feel safe and secure in where you are and what you are doing, the good vibrations of the energy flow produce happiness.

However, stepping out of your comfort zone every now and then evokes feelings of greater happiness (even though at the time it felt uncomfortable). This is because after the event you recall the courage it took, how you have grown because of it, and how satisfying that feels.

The happiest people balance risky endeavors with safer experiences so they can benefit from both. Savor the moments, enjoy the good vibrations of being in the flow, reflect and remember the happy moment and you will get even more satisfaction as the good vibrations grow. Project those feelings into the future, look forward to doing it again, it makes you feel more positive about the future.

Don't worry about feeling sad or upset, maintain a perspective, process the feelings and bounce back. Happy people tend not to worry about whether they are happy enough. They live their lives to the full and enjoy daily positive experiences, no matter how small. –Dr. Alison Boyes

The spirit of these islands comes from the people. People who are unselfish and radiate joy, they are full of the spirit of Hawaii.

Monsignor Charles Kekumano

1:51 What is the secret?

"What is the secret?" asks yet another student.

"It's a magical ingredient," I reply.

"Could you let me have a bottle, please?" said another.

I'll do better than that, I thought to myself. If I give them a "bottle" (a bottle of this magical elixir), they can enjoy themselves for a night; but if I show them how to access this pool of enchanting energy, then they can drink from it for life.

> *This was another beautiful treatment from Kevin. The feeling of peace and love that this treatment gives leaves you feeling the love for days afterwards.*
>
> –Karen Wade, massage therapist

That was three years ago; now, when asked, I can say, "Let me point you in the right direction, I will even walk with you, if you wish." These seekers come from all countries, all faiths, and all types of complementary therapy. If they are committed and ready for what is the greatest adventure known to man, or woman, then they receive a map, a treasure map unlike any other, for the "pot of gold" at the end of this rainbow holds the most precious and valuable jewel in the universe.

The map is titled "The Starlite zone, a place of self-discovery." Within its pages is a pathway that reveals clues and unveils many secrets along the route. One step at a time, one baby step at a time, you are encouraged to explore beyond your perceived limitations, search for new possibilities, uncover one golden nugget at a time and investigate the energy of each new dawn as it rises from within. At your own gentle pace you will discover the energy frequency of each level and connect to its vibration. You will ride wave upon wave, from trough to crest you will ride, increasing the energy pulsation of your very being as you build the rainbow bridge between the human body/mind and the cosmic spirit/soul found within.

> *When you align with this divine energy, you hold the key to joy, success, and fulfillment in whatever you do. Surfing the wave requires no special knowledge or learning; you simply need to follow the laws of nature.*
> –Chungliang Al Huang

As you grow in ecstasy so will your (complementary) practice grow, expanding in all directions dreamed and undreamed.

> *This was an absolutely amazing treatment, transformational. Kevin is an expert in his field. I felt totally safe in his hands. I could feel the changes in my body's energy. Subtle at first, by the end of the session I felt like a new person, revitalized!*
> –Lindsay Gill, Reiki Master

Starlite is a method of self-discovery, growth and connection to the divine essence of universal energy. Stardance is all about the application of the Starlite method, enhancing your life and practice by infusing this magical energy into both on a daily basis. Become one with life force energy, light up your life and shine on the lives of those around you by radiating the pure essence of love energy; develop and deploy the sacred touch of aloha.

Starlite energy can be applied by any therapist and to any therapy, it can only lift and enhance your being and your treatment. Everything else is just technique – but do not dismiss technique; expand your mind, seek out and discover new techniques, new ways of healing; never stop, never listen to those who would restrict you, who would limit you to "their way" only. Techniques are your tools of the trade: the more choice you have and the more proficient you are in using them, the more diversity and options you can offer your clients.

> *If your only tool is a hammer, then every problem will tend to look like a nail.* –Abraham Maslow

After a lifetime working in and attending hundreds of workshops in the healing arts, I can say that many therapies claim to be holistic, but unless they include all techniques and/or all options of using all techniques, they are holistic but not whole. You, however, must endeavor to become both wholistic and holistic, become a therapist supreme, add the "magical elixir" and let your light shine on the world.

All you need is an open mind and a loving heart.

> *Thank you so much for a wonderful treatment. Kevin's manner was very warming and I felt instantly at ease with him. The treatment was very thorough and it felt as if he was treating every part of the body. I fell asleep in the afternoon and woke the next day refreshed and energized. Thanks for this amazing experience.*
> –Sophie Caws, complementary therapy spa owner

> *Love cures people - both the ones who give it and the ones who receive it.*
> –Karl Menninger MD

When you wish upon a Wish upon a star...

> *You are not in the universe, you are the universe, an intrinsic part of it. Ultimately you are not a person but a focal point where the universe is becoming conscious of itself. What an amazing miracle!* –Eckhart Tolle

Starlite

Starlite is an inspirational and transformational wave of cosmic energy that transcends the spiritual and the physical, creating a cosmic interface ~ in and around the body. An entanglement of cosmic energy, swaying to the vibration of creation, transmuting metaphysical energy into a physical existence, and turning dreams into reality.

Part One - **Shine like a star**... *the aloha way*

Riding the waves between science and spirit, between the light forces of the cosmos and the dense frequencies of matter, vibrating, circulating and resonating to the movement of beauty, love and aloha. A galaxy of wonder, gracefully gliding effortlessly to the tune of the universe, and creating a dance... a stardance!

Starlite is also a method of connecting to the divine essence of life force energy and transfusing it into the healing arts. To do this we introduce the therapist to the principles of Huna and employ them to adopt the "way of aloha" as a method of self-empowerment bringing balance, synergy and harmony to their very core. When they reach a point of universal equilibrium it becomes a simple step – and conversely also a quantum leap – to embrace the joy of their own beauty, greatness and wonderment. When something or someone has been "Star-Lite" they have experienced life within the zone of transformation, the Starlite zone. Not only have they experienced magic, they have also experienced life as magic.

The following secret of "the light" has been kept hidden in the culture, psychology and esoteric knowledge of ancestral wisdom keepers of the earth. Our true might lies in the fact that we are unique "sparks of divinity." Acknowledge and accept our authenticity as great, powerful, and mighty spiritual beings of light, living in a physical world with dignity, direction, and purpose.

That's right; inside each of us is a tiny spark of light – the true essence of our being – and it is part of the very creation of life: divine consciousness. We have simply forgotten who we really are and using the Starlite method we can rediscover, reconnect, and through that connection give and receive abundance. We can shine like a star when connected to the light of the divine.

After creating the ideal conditions for this ancient wisdom to enhance modern complementary therapy we can then radiate the true essence of this love energy to others in need of compassion and healing: aloha in action.

This is the plane of three-dimensional form called matter. This plane is the density of matter because thought has been expanded into a vibratory frequency to become electrum, and from electrum to become gross matter, and from gross matter to become the solidity of this plane. The matter of this plane is thus light that has been slowed in its vibratory frequency and taken to its densest form. Every thought you contemplate and embrace for an understanding has a vibratory frequency, which is experienced as a feeling. Thus if you are mastering the understanding of pain, you are contemplating the more limited thoughts associated with pain, which gives rise to the lower vibratory frequencies that are emotionally experienced as pain. If you are contemplating and mastering the understanding of love and the expression of it, you will be experiencing the elation of the higher vibratory frequencies of the thoughts of love shared and expressed. –Ramtha

The science

A new scientific explanation of spirituality states that proto-consciousness, platonic values, goodness, and truth exist at this fundamental level of space-time geometry which can influence your actions if you believe in them.

When using the Starlite method in the healing arts always remember that whatever your consciousness is predominantly focused on will be expressed through the magnetic field of your aura.

- *Raise the vibration to a level of healing.*
- *Focus on love, happiness and joy.*
- *Be young at heart.*
- *Give good vibrations.*
- *Willful – the ability to influence through mental power.*
- *Conscious – a knowledgeable stream of awareness.*
- *Intent – concentrated attention to a specific purpose.*

In the Hawaiian story that reflects the true nature of the soul, *The Bowl of Light,* when things get dark they simply turn the bowl over and light will shine once more upon the world around them and they will begin to grow and shine with the spirit of light, the way it was meant to be. In modern times it might be helpful to identify the light of your soul/spirit as a glowing intense light controlled by a dimmer switch. This dimmer switch is turned up or down by your thoughts, actions and deeds. You have the ability, at any time, to change the direction that you turn the switch no matter how dark your situation may feel. Start by simply *stopping:* turn the switch down toward the off position, no more negative thoughts, stop beating yourself up over things you cannot control. Then *start* moving it toward the open position by accepting that you are good enough as you are, appreciate the good things in life. With the change of direction will come more light, things will start to look brighter, this in turn will increase your confidence, happiness and well-being. You can then let your light shine brightly on the world.

Stardancer

The term stardancer can be applied to a master of the Starlite method, an expert waverider surfing the cosmic ocean of all probabilities and possibilities. They have experienced life in the Starlite zone and have chosen a new way of being and live that difference daily in the spirit of helping and supporting others through the medium of the healing arts.

> **They know that love, appreciation, and gratitude are life-affirming qualities that infuse our bodies with vitality and our world with peace. By accepting their connection to the source of creation and living this wisdom with compassion, trust and love, they send consciousness a blueprint for new possibilities and upgrade our reality.**
>
> –Gregg Braden

When you learn to master judgment against your thoughts and allow yourself to receive all thought, you have the power and the ability to become anything through thought. You can take your thought, concentrate it on the body, and command the body to vibrate faster. The body will then elevate toward the ideal that the thought holds steadfast for it. The whole of the body will begin to vibrate at a greater speed. As it does so, the temperature of the body will rise and the body will begin to glow. As it continues to vibrate faster, the matter of the body will go into pure light and then into pure thought. Then that which is seen is seen no longer. –Ramtha

> *O'hana~ means family, and family means nobody gets left behind… or forgotten.*
>
> Hawaiian proverb

1:52 In this moment

It is Friday, and I am ready for the day to be over. It has been a long week; I have business concerns, bills to pay and phone calls to make. I ache a little, need a hot bath and an appointment with my chiropractor.

My last client is a retired schoolteacher and educational consultant. He served in World War II and is now described as part of the greatest generation. He receives a treatment on his birthday and possibly one other during the year. It has been a year since his last treatment. His wife, also a retired schoolteacher, is a monthly client. She has scoliosis. She says that the treatment keeps her body moving. Sadly, she has also told me she does not expect to have her husband with her for another birthday. She has confided many family secrets in the hours she has spent on my couch, trusting me not only with her body but her heart as well.

Her husband loves the treatment and expresses his appreciation with groans, moans and an occasional resounding "yes!" Today I notice that he has lost weight since I last touched his transparent skin. He tells me he has a new nose since the skin cancer was found on his face last year. His legs are scarred with long blue streaks where doctors have gleaned the materials necessary to perform his by-pass surgeries.

Although it speaks volumes, I know more about this man than his robe of flesh can tell. He has spent his life giving of himself to his family, his country and the school of children he has taught. In confidence I know he cannot afford the treatment he loves so much. This is not because he did not plan carefully for his retirement, or make sacrifices in order to live a quality life in his old age. Rather it is because his son is disabled and totally dependent on him for support. His devoted wife buys him a treatment on special occasions such as this, his 75th birthday.

As we start, my client's eyes close, he wears a grand smile, moans, and again says "yes" out loud. For one hour he is in heaven and I am no longer working; the labor of my hands has become an act of service. With every stroke, I give as much love, compassion and appreciation as my heart can express. Being exceedingly aware that this may be this precious man's last treatment, I am honored and humbled.

I am reminded that no matter what is going on in my life, a completely different reality is occurring for my client. The hour he has chosen to spend with me is for the purpose of meeting specific needs and expectations, and I am the privileged facilitator. For this moment in time the music, lighting, oils, linens, and my touch and expertise will resonate with conscious intent for both the mortal and the eternal. None of my worries will be allowed to sway my attention.

The only thing of importance is to be present, in this moment, for the benefactor of human touch. For this hour it is no longer Friday. It is forever!

– Donna Anderson

I Keia Manawa... 'uhane nui au.
In this moment... I am spirit greatness.

This simple mantra brings you into balance (pono) with the universe and acknowledges the greatness of your spirit being.

1:53 Love is the secret of healing

Papa Henry was a Hawaiian healer and a keynote speaker at the Alternative Therapies Conference held in Hawaii in 2000, the same year that he passed over on New Year's Eve eight months later at the age of 94. At the conference held at the Mauna Lani Orchid Hotel, Papa stood at the podium in the hotel ballroom and looked out at the sea of faces of those who had come to hear what he had to say, medical practitioners all.

At that time, it was said that Papa had cured more than 12,000 people with terminal cancer. Papa's admonition to the medical community was this in a nutshell:

"Healing is 80% spiritual and 20% medical...." Long pause and then, "True healing can only come from a place of love. If you are not in a state of love when you are trying to help your patients, don't be a doctor!"

> *In addition there was her spiritual practice. Jill's choice was to go through her arduous treatment for cancer in a strongly positive state, echoing the thoughts of our great Hawaiian friend, the kahuna nui Hale Makua: "Either you're in love or you're in fear," he often said, "and when love moves out, fear moves in." And with his insight held in mind and heart, Jill drew closer and closer to her Oversoul, her immortal spiritual Self from which she was sourced into this life, and the one who loves her unconditionally.* –Hank Wesselman

> *Some medical sources report that 70-90% of illnesses are psychosomatic, leaving people helplessly ill because they don't know how to change their minds.* –Serge Kahili King

*Part One - **Shine like a star**... the aloha way*

Never tell your problems to anyone; 20% don't care, and the other 80% are glad you have them". –Lou Holtz

> *Your true strength lies within you.*

1:54 Cosmo-human body

For a scientific explanation we turn to Deepak Chopra's book *Quantum Healing*.

> *If you see your body as it really is, you would never see it the same way twice. 98% of the atoms in your body were not there a year ago. The skeleton that seems so solid was not there three months ago. The configuration of bone cells remains somewhat constant, but atoms of all kinds pass freely back and forth through the cell walls, and by that means you acquire a new skeleton every three months.*
>
> *The skin is new every month. You have a new stomach lining every four days, with the actual surface cells that contact food being renewed every five minutes. The cells in the liver turn over very slowly, but new atoms still flow through them, like water in a river course, making a new liver every six weeks. Even in the brain, whose cells are not replaced once they die, the content of carbon, nitrogen, oxygen and so on is totally different today from a year ago.*
>
> *To get an idea of how limited our current knowledge is, consider the structure of a neuron. The neurons that compose the brain and central nervous system "talk" to one another across gaps called synapses. These gaps separate the tiny branchlike filaments, the dendrites that grow at the ends of each nerve cell. Everyone possesses billions of these cells, divided between the brain and the central nervous system, and as we saw, each one is capable of growing*

dozens or even hundreds of dendrites (the total estimated at 100 million million), meaning that at any one time the possible combinations of signals jumping across synapses of the brain exceed the number of atoms in the known universe. The signals also communicate with one another at lightning speed. To read this sentence, your brain takes a few milliseconds to arrange a precise pattern of millions of signals, only to dissolve them instantly, never to be repeated again in exactly the same way.

The discovery of neuropeptides was so significant because it showed that the body is fluid enough to match the mind. Thanks to messenger molecules, events that seem totally unconnected – such as thought and a bodily reaction – are now seen to be consistent. The neuropeptide isn't a thought, but it moves with thought, serving as a point of transformation. The quantum does exactly the same thing, except that the body in question is the universe, or nature as a whole.

A neuropeptide springs into existence at the touch of a thought, but where does it spring from? A thought of fear and the neurochemical that it turns into are somehow connected in a hidden process, a transformation of non-matter into matter.

The same thing happens everywhere in nature, except that we do not call it thinking. When you get to the level of atoms, the landscape is not one of solid objects moving around each other like partners in a dance, following predictable steps. Subatomic particles are separated by huge gaps, making every atom more than 99.999% empty space. This holds true for hydrogen atoms in the air and carbon atoms in the wood that tables are made of, as well as all the "solid" atoms in our cells. Therefore, everything solid, including our bodies, is proportionately as void as inter-galactic space.

–Deepak Chopra

Part One - **Shine like a star** … *the aloha way*

> *Being made of Stardust you are much like a star. You shine with light, give warmth, and burn with inner fire. You don't need outside energy...*
> *You are Energy.*
>
> —Emily

Stellar sound-bites allude to universal phenomena and are not empty, airy-fairy metaphors. Although in olden times we had no way to explain that we share common origins with stardust, we do now.

1:55 To be a star

The metaphoric reference "to shine like a star" is a factually accurate reference to its highly combustible source of fusion power.

The sun is a star. This is a statement of fact, not a poetic metaphor. As a fairly average, medium-sized, type G (G2V) classification of yellow stars, the sun gives off heat in the form of electromagnetic radiation.

All solar energy comes from nuclear fusion in the sun's core. The energy of fusion gradually migrates to the sun's surface. By convection, conduction and radiation, the sun transfers heat as energy waves into space. This is the heat that we experience here on earth as ultraviolet radiation.

Solar radiation is nuclear and radioactive. The sun's rays are so powerful it takes them just eight minutes to travel 93 million miles from the solar surface to the surface of the earth.

A star is formed when a large amount of gas (mostly hydrogen) starts to collapse in on itself due to its gravitational attraction. As it contracts, the atoms of the gas collide with each other more and more frequently and at greater and greater speeds – the gas heats up. Eventually, the gas will be so hot that when the hydrogen atoms collide they no longer bounce off each other, but instead coalesce to form helium. The heat released in this reaction, which is like a controlled hydrogen bomb explosion, is what makes the star shine.

Not only does the sun's nuclear energy sustain life on earth, but beneath our very feet, at all times, lies a massive molten iron core that provides the structural foundation upon which we build our cities, homes, and infrastructures.

Below the surface of the earth are the strata of subterranean plates of hardened volcanic lava. This is known as the earth's crust. Nearly 1800 miles below earth's various mantle-crust masses we come to the inner and outer core of our planet, which is composed of molten iron. It is a convection of extremely hot liquid iron that annually generates 10.3 ergs of energy – the equivalent of 1,000,000 Hiroshima-sized nuclear bombs (that is just the amount of energy reaching the surface from the core that can be measured). The core temperature may be as high as 13,040 degrees F (7227 degrees C) – hotter than the surface of the sun.

Do you realize that in energy healing practices, when you are told to "ground your center" you are literally grounding the oxygenated portions of your blood via bio electromagnetic hemoglobin (iron) to the massive molten magnet deep in the planet's core?

In this post-quantum-physics, modern-cosmology, information-age era, to be a star, to use Starlite energy implies that power-for-power you have the awareness, capacity, and information database to match the power of nuclear radiation.

To reiterate: the universe's light comes mainly from stars – hot balls of gas that generate energy through nuclear fusion in their core. In physics and cosmology, radiation is energy that is emitted from a source and travels through space and some types of matter. Today, the latest and catchiest stellar sound bites allude to universal phenomena and are not empty, airy-fairy metaphors. Because

Part One - *Shine like a star*... *the aloha way*

whichever way we go, up or down, into solar systems or away from them, we seem to be running into nuclear energy.

Be careful what you ask for! Can you really handle the power that comes from shining like a star?

Ancient stardust

We are all made of stardust. It sounds like a line from a poem, but there is some solid science behind this statement too: almost every element on earth was formed at the heart of a star.

The expression "with every fiber of my being" may profoundly implicate our existential derivations from stardust.

Just as stars shine, some of them also burn out. Stardust is created from the ashes of burned-out stars.

The gas within and around galaxies is made mainly of hydrogen and helium atoms. Some clouds inside galaxies also contain atoms of heavier chemical elements and simple molecules. Mixed in with the galactic gas clouds are dust – tiny solid particles of carbon or substances such as silicates (compounds of silicon and oxygen). Fusion powers stars and has created the atoms of all chemical elements heavier than beryllium8 (Be4).

Every element in the periodic table has come to exist in its current form from this basic primordial process. For example, it is how earth's atmosphere came to be composed of mostly nitrogen (78%) and oxygen (21%) with traces of argon, carbon dioxide, and water. By mass, earth is composed mostly of iron (35%), oxygen (30%), silicon (15%), and magnesium (13%).

Hold on to your seat. I'm taking you for a ride on quantum waves again.

In our bodies, the atoms of hydrogen (H1), carbon (C6), nitrogen (N7), oxygen (O8), sodium (Na11), phosphorus (P15), sulfur (S16) chlorine (Cl17), potassium (K19), calcium (Ca20) – and the list of bio-available elements goes on and on – share common ancestry with stardust.

The biological fibers of a human being are composed of cells, which are formed out of molecules, which are formed out of atoms; the protons and neutrons of these are held together by the strong nuclear force which radioactively decays – in our case exceedingly gradually – via the weak nuclear force; this pulses very tiny electromagnetic waves which interact with the gravitational force.

The plants that feed us utilize photosynthesis to break down the metabolic process. Each time you ingest food, whether it be vegetarian or carnivorous, you are consuming various combinations of our planet's elemental compositions. These elements facilitate our multitude of physiological functions. Without them, we would be unable to sustain life.

Deep in the recesses of our collective consciousness exists the mysterious knowledge that elementally we share the same basic building blocks as stardust. We are, in a sense, made of the same pool of source material as stardust. The basic elemental components of our bodies share the same origins as the basic compositions of stars, supernovas and galaxies, all of which are different forms of manifested energies, cosmic waves of universal energy.

Every one of us is already riding (cosmic) quantum waves.

We are connected to our elemental origin, the stars. You only have to look within yourself to know you are a distant relative of the stars. An elemental memory of our stellar relationship pulses in every molecule, element, atom, and subatomic particle that makes up the physical body. This memory compels us to aspire for a reunion with our stardust origins. Out of this compulsion our desires are born. In stardust terms this means your desires are pulsing into the furthest reaches of galaxies so far away that the sheer magnitude in distance is beyond our wildest imagination. Conversely, a reciprocal *creative spark is coming back to you from a very distant place.*

Regardless of our religious, spiritual, philosophical, and/or intellectual inclinations, we are innately plugged into the nebulous realm of our will's inexplicable driven impulse to continually "wish upon a star." To ride this wave of truth is, in my humble opinion, to be connected – intimately, existentially and profoundly in a deep way as a celestial child of the universe.

Although in former times we had no way to explain that we share common origins with stardust, we do now. This existential knowledge should not be relegated to science fiction. A paramount truth in the universe is that energy (or its equivalent in mass) can neither be created nor destroyed.

There isn't even anything mystical about it. It is simply the way of the universe. She recycles everything. A particle of dust – whether it haphazardly blew into your eye or floats in a galactic gas cloud – is not judged by the universe to be better or worse. Nor does she label it profound or ordinary.

–Barbara Chang

Live your life while the sun's still shining.

-Hawaiian proverb

1:56 Solar and lunar

The two great lights that shine on the earth – the sun and the moon – affect all that happens on the land and in the waters of our world.

The energy from the sun provides life on earth by way of heat and light. The light from the sun not only provides day and night, but also seasonal influences on our systems, which bring about physiological and emotional changes.

The moon creates the great movement of the tides, and as our bodies are largely made up of water, we too respond to this tidal effect.

Although it generates no light of its own, the moon is nevertheless the night's major source of natural light, a borrowed light far removed from the sun in color and intensity.

The sun is our nearest star and its life-giving starlight energy is referred to as sunlight or daylight by day and moonlight by night; although they are from the same source they manifest differently and resonate at a different energetic vibration.

> ***The light of day*** *is the combination of all direct and indirect sunlight outdoors during the daytime.* ***Sunlight*** *is a portion of the electromagnetic radiation given off by the sun, in particular infrared, visible, and ultraviolet light. On earth, sunlight is filtered through the earth's atmosphere, and is obvious as daylight when the sun is above the horizon. When the direct solar radiation is not blocked by clouds, it is experienced as* ***sunshine,*** *a combination of bright light and radiant heat.* ***Moonlight*** *is the light that reaches earth from the moon, consisting mostly of sunlight, with some starlight and earthlight reflected from those portions of its surface which the sun's light strikes.* –Wikipedia

The light from our nearest star shines onto the surface of the moon and the surface becomes starlit with light; a transmuting process occurs before the moon's surface projects its lunar version of light onto the earth. This process of transmutation that happens betwixt and between the solar and the lunar is known as "star-lit-e", the "e" representing the change in energy vibration.

In the healing arts the inspirational and transformational energy referred to as Starlite consists of both physical and metaphysical energy. Its power lies in the duality with both elements retaining their identity but combining to become something else, something more powerful than the sum of the two parts, a quantum entanglement infused with aloha.

Physical energy is masculine and metaphysical energy is feminine; the bonding is completed through an entanglement of aloha unconditional love. Scientists have recently found that the coupling of male/female energy increases positive results to nearly six times that of single operators, and by adding aloha energy the positive results increase to startling proportions.

> *"The blood of man is increased or diminished in proportion to the quality of moonlight," wrote Pliny the Elder, Roman naturalist. Two thousand years later, modern medical research has reported that postoperative bleeding peaks around the time of the full moon.*
>
> *When we honor the natural rhythms of energy we start to synchronize with them, all aspects of our being take part in this dance of light and energy – this stardance.*
>
> –Jan Morgan Wood

1:57 Betwixt and between

> *Magic occurs "betwixt and between" and under conditions that are "neither this nor that." What is meant by magic is transformation, change, an alteration in the flow of our own consciousness. With proper method and intention, we can send our altered consciousness or spirit to places betwixt and between the elements, places where the elemental spirits are engaged with each other, working their own magic, weaving their own spells. We can alter our consciousness so that it mingles with the consciousness of the elements, leaps the gulf between spaces, and bridges the space that separates us as physical beings.*
>
> *We are in places where things begin and end, where objects touch each other, where auras blend, where energy is transferred. Here we can hop back and forth across the boundary line of the mind.*

We are on the edge of things, in the world of betwixt and between, in realms that are neither this nor that. The stroke of midnight is in neither the old day nor the new. Midnight, the "witching hour" is betwixt and between the days, a time of magic, mystery, and power. Dawn and dusk are periods between day and night; they come from nowhere and at no measurable point in time.

Twilight (twin light) is a mysterious light, which has a dual quality of both solar and lunar brightness; the air feels different when the blue hour arrives, twilight is a time of magic.

The magical quality of moonlight comes from the moon's betwixt and between status as a source of light. Moonlight is neither bright nor dark, and even thought it allows us to see, it casts an obscure pallor on objects, making them easy to mistake for something else.

Shapeless and shape shifting, fog, smoke, mist and cloud are ethereal composites of more than one element – air, water, heat, particles and light – that pass through them, they are elusive wanderers and seem to belong to a world of their own, merely passing through ours. They are always verging on their own extinction, hanging onto a momentary existence in our visible world by the frailest of means.
They disappear and leave no trace. –Tom Cowan

1:58 The science of spirituality

Go outside on a clear evening and look at the night sky, and you will see a panoramic view of a starlit universe laid out on a cosmic canvas, physical energy dancing in the light of the stars.

Not so long ago, scientists became involved with quantum mechanics, noetic science, and astrophysics. This explosive mixture has given birth to a new understanding that life and consciousness are fundamental to the universe. *It is consciousness that creates the material universe, not the other way around.*

A 1996 Time Magazine poll relating to a story on Faith & Healing found that 82% believed that prayers could heal.

Placebo at best is regarded as a supernatural phenomenon that requires an expanded view of human consciousness to understand.

But for years our experiences have been systematically dismissed as impossible, or ridiculed as delusionary, by influential academics who have assumed that existing scientific theories are inviolate and complete.

Classic science is commonly regarded as a method of studying the natural world, a supernatural phenomenon is by this definition unexplainable by, and therefore totally incompatible with, science.

It's become very clear that they cannot be fully understood without significant, possibly revolutionary, expansions of the current state of scientific knowledge.

Ancient philosophies embrace the concept that mind is primary over matter and yet western science has for hundreds of years firmly rejected the idea as mere superstition, mumbo-jumbo, pseudo-spiritual claptrap.

For years we knew that it worked but had no way of explaining it – we do now! The evidence is right here and it's all about noetic science.

Noetic science uses rigorous scientific methods to investigate the role of consciousness in the physical world and the ultimate nature of reality.

Noetic, from the Greek word *noesis*, meaning intuition or direct inner knowing, is defined as: states of insight into depths of truth unplumbed by the discursive mind.

I have been working in the healing arts since 1970 and have had many great results using energy, placebo and mind over matter as a healing tool. In the early days it was considered as dangerously heretical nonsense, but gradually opinions started to change largely because of hundreds of studies of the placebo effect and the spontaneous remission of serious disease. Now it has become widely accepted that the body's hard physical reality can be significantly modified by the more evanescent reality of the mind. After many years of ridicule, I can go out and shout it loud and proud, that the placebo effect (the power of consciousness) is real and highly effective. To those skeptics who have only just come to terms with this fact, I wish to propose another very simple idea: **as the mind moves, so moves matter.**

> *There are no unnatural or supernatural phenomena, only very large gaps in our knowledge of what is natural.*
> –Edgar Mitchell, astronaut

In science, the acceptance of new ideas follows a predictable, four-stage sequence.

Stage 1: *skeptics confidently proclaim that the idea is impossible because it violates the laws of science. This stage can last for years or centuries, depending on how much the idea challenges conventional wisdom (the flat world theory).*

Stage 2: *skeptics reluctantly concede that the idea is possible but claim that the effects would be very weak.*

Stage 3: *begins when the mainstream realizes not only that the idea is important but its effects are much stronger than previously imagined.*

Stage 4: *is achieved when the same critics who previously disavowed any interest in the idea begin to proclaim that they thought of it first.*

–Dean Radin

> *When you have eliminated the impossible, whatever remains, however improbably, must be the truth.*
> –Sir Arthur Conan Doyle

> *We delude ourselves with the thought that we know much more about matter than about a "metaphysical" mind or spirit and so we overestimate material causation and believe that it alone affords us a true explanation of life. But matter is just as inscrutable as mind. As to the ultimate things we can know nothing, and only when we admit this do we return to a state of equilibrium.*
>
> –Carl Jung

> *The same scientific mindset that thrives on high precision and critical thinking is also extremely adept at forming clever rationalizations that get in the way of progress.*
>
> –Dean Radin

> *It's one thing not to see the forest for the trees, but then to go on to deny the reality of the forest is a more serious matter.*
>
> –Paul Weiss

Huna is the ancient philosophy of the Pacific islanders; it describes in detail not only the concepts of the mind/body link but also the way of using the mind to lead a healthy, invigorated, and spiritually balanced life. Contrast this to the following statement from physicist Nick Herbert: "Science's biggest mystery is the nature of consciousness. It is not that we possess bad or imperfect theories of human awareness; we simply have no theories at all. About all we know about consciousness is that it has something to do with the head, rather than the foot."

The underlying principle of esoteric beliefs is that all life is made of light. That we are spirit beings of light, an expression of universal consciousness in creation that derives from the web of light, entwined in perfect harmony with both physical and metaphysical energy, weaving light and love from a divine center. I refer to this enchanting web of light as a Star-lite Universe-ity, a place of universal knowledge.

This view is not too distant from Buddha's expression of the universe as a vast net woven of a countless variety of brilliant jewels, each with a countless number of facts. Each jewel reflects in itself every other jewel in the net and is, in fact, one with every jewel... everything is inextricably interrelated.

> *It may exist. It may be important to human and physical behavior. Yet it may not be explainable until long after its discovery.* –Nobel Laureate Richard P. Feynman

In other words, if something is real, it can be put to use even if we don't understand it very well.

> *The day science begins to study non-physical phenomena it will make more progress in one decade than in all the previous centuries of its existence. To understand the true nature of the universe, one must think in terms of energy, frequency and vibration.* –Nikola Tesla

Scientists have begun to recognize that everything in the universe is made up of energy. Quantum physicists discovered that physical atoms are made up of vortices of energy that are constantly spinning and vibrating. Matter, at its tiniest observable level, is energy, and human consciousness is connected to it, human consciousness can influence its behavior and even restructure it.

I offer these points not to convince or convert, but simply to inspire those who are now at the edge of a new beginning and are wondering whether they can in fact fly.

starlite
spirit of aloha ~ in action

*Part One - **Shine like a star**... the aloha way*

1:59 Stargate

The world in which we live is composed entirely of energy. We are forever immersed in and surrounded by energy. It is a powerful elemental force, in effect whether we acknowledge it or not.

So how do we access this energy and use it?

There are many ways, a lot of mystery and also a lot of misunderstanding about how to access and use the energy that surrounds us.

The secret of channeling healing energy is allowing yourself to feel connected to a source of positive energy and then allowing that energy to flow through you so it can be shared with someone else. It's that simple.

Remember you are not doing the channeling, you are allowing it to happen, and the energy is actually channeling itself.

There are many therapy systems and methods that teach you how to connect and use universal energy for healing. The one you choose to learn will be dependent on your background, your beliefs, and your intentions. There is no one supreme system, method or therapy.

All of us have the power to access this energy, you just need to be shown how. No one has the power to "tune you in," it is your right; when you are ready, you claim it by your authenticity. Never give away your direct power to the divine source, to a so-called "master." Learn many methods and use the one you feel most comfortable with; it may even be a mixture of many systems.

Here are the secrets of using energy, no matter what system you decide to learn.

A good therapy will teach you the physical element of channeling, laying on of hands, and creating the proper mindset before engaging in a healing activity.

Portal

In order to channel metaphysical energy for healing in our physical existence, we need to find a key to the access point, also called a portal, a doorway, a stargate, the Starlite zone.

These keys are our minds, our imagination, our memories, our fantasies, and our bodies.

The secret is in finding ways to use these keys to trigger the opening of the portal, and this is found in our feelings and our emotions. There's no point having a memory, imagination or even an active mind if it doesn't trigger feeling and emotion.

Most of us have had at some point in our lives an experience in which we were flooded with so much happiness that we were almost overcome by it. That memory is a key to the doorway; the emotion resulting from the memory is the trigger that can open the door and give you access to the very vibration of creation.

Concentration condenses energy, your concentration and focus increases its power and actually creates a movement in the universe's energy that brings about the object of your sustained attention. This is an esoteric entanglement of metaphysical and physical energy.

Having gained access we can then use our keys (minds, imagination, memories, fantasies, and bodies) to tune into our desired wave of energy. And we have a great number of choices ranging from colors to sounds, from white light to bright light, and from the caring vibrations of love right through all its frequencies to the divine source itself. There is an art in choosing the right energy for the right situation.

The guideline to remember is that you can always add more, but too much, too soon, can become overpowering for the receiver. A good analogy here is that it's like adding sugar to a drink: you can't remove it once it's been put in. Don't be the over-fussing aunt from your childhood.

At this point most healing systems will tell you that the energy will flow through you unrestricted as though you were a straw. This is not true.

We act more like a straw with many paper filters running through it, each defusing the quality of the healing energy as it passes through us. Individual therapists have a role to play in determining the purity of the energy passing through to the receiver.

These filters are called our beliefs, our egos, our thoughts, our prejudices, our desires, our frustrations, and our needs, to name a few. Each of us working as a therapist has an individual responsibility to address these issues. The more filters you reduce or remove, the greater the energy field surrounding you will become, and as your light shines brighter you will attract people and clients like a moth to a flame.

Understand this: we can't see it but we all know that the earth has an atmosphere, which is an electromagnetic field. Our bodies also have a kind of electromagnetic atmosphere around them. It's harder to detect than the earth's but it's just as real and is called our "aura."

The aura is made up of etheric energy and an electromagnetic field, which becomes denser nearer the body. A good therapist will become sensitive enough to feel and interact with someone's aura as they channel energy.

> *Inside the aura we have seven energy centers called chakras which vibrate at different color frequencies and are associated with different parts of the body. Chakras are not physical, they are aspects of consciousness and function as pumps and valves, regulating the flow of energy through our energy system.*
>
> *Energy is the fuel of excellence. The higher your energy level the better you feel, and the better you feel the more astounding your results will be.*
>
> –Lindsay Agness

Chakra Seven	Crown	Violet
Chakra Six	Brow	Indigo
Chakra Five	Throat	Blue
Chakra Four	Heart	Green
Chakra Three	Solar Plexus	Yellow
Chakra Two	Sexual	Orange
Chakra One	Root	Red

> *Lots of people talk to animals, not many listen though… that's the problem.*
>
> -Benjamin Hoff

1:60 Laulima Hae 'aoe

A dog is the only thing on earth that loves you more than he loves himself. –Josh

Laulima * Reiki * Trust Technique * Starlite * Healing beyond words

Each lifelong relationship between an animal and his person is a unique heart-to-heart dance: elegant, graceful and flowing. To be able to be present with an open heart is a beautiful gift. To be able to support animals and their people, to hold a meditative space of compassion, peace and love in that moment whatever it looks like – happy, sad, hopeful or uncertain – this is the true highest calling of the animal practitioner.

Animals that live closely with human companions are very much in tune with the emotional states of their people. In their efforts to protect and take care of them, animals often take on their worries, anxieties and sometimes even their physical problems.

Part One - **Shine like a star**… *the aloha way*

Laulima can help animals live closely with their people while protecting their own health so that the animal can be there at their best for their people.

Laulima can help people as well as animals to resolve and release past memories, patterns, behaviors and other influences that hold them back from the best and highest expression of their true selves.

This work complements both conventional and alternative therapies and can enhance their actions and lessen any side-effects.

It helps heal on a mental, physical and emotional level, hence maintaining your animal's health and allowing them to be happy, peaceful, relaxed, healthy, calm and stress-free.

It also provides compassionate support to help an animal make the transition, when the time has come to pass away, more peaceful for all concerned.

One of the aspects of this gentle, non-invasive therapy is that it releases endorphins into the body. Endorphins are our (and our animal's) natural opiates which act as pain relief and give us a "feel good" factor.

Releasing endorphins into our system can:

- *Strengthen our immune system.*
- *Decrease the intensity and awareness of physical pain.*
- *Activate the emotions that are vital to maintenance of good health.*
- *Reduce the incidences of attitudes such as chronic hostility that negatively arouse and damage our bodies.*
- *Multiply the benefits to our body's systems provided by stress relief.*

Breathing in, I calm body and mind. Breathing out, I smile. Dwelling in the present moment I know this is the only moment. –Thich Nhat Hanh

Using different techniques

If you feel comfortable or get an intuitive message to get closer to an animal, you can then try performing with your hands hovering above it. You can eventually move into an actual hands-on session.

Because animals can't give their express permission for you to perform healing, make sure you approach any animal in a slow and respectful manner when starting to give energy. Doing so gives the animal the opportunity to understand what you are doing and lets the animal make its feelings known.

You may want to start by beaming energy to the animal from across the room. This technique may be sufficient for treating an animal.

Intention is the single most important factor in the success of a treatment. Intend for the highest level of healing for the animal and that you can be a pure channel of energy. Healing is not from you, but through you. Be clear about your role as a therapist and why you are treating the animal.

azura supporting the Blue Cross animal hospital and Paws rescue service

Not every person knows how to love a dog. But every dog knows how to love a person. – Koko

In every culture and in every medical tradition before ours, healing was accomplished by moving energy.
– Albert Szent-Gyorgyi, Nobel Laureate in Medicine

Here are the general techniques to use on animals:

- **Distant Laulima or Reiki:** *This type of Reiki can be performed from anywhere, so you don't need to be near the animal to do this. You can use this technique to treat any trauma an animal might have suffered in the past or to help the animal with any event in the future.*

- **Beaming Laulima or Reiki from across the room:** *When you are with the animal, start with beaming to connect with the animal from a safe distance. You and the animal then get a chance to connect with each other before moving closer.*

- **Laulima or Reiki with hands hovering over the body:** *Some animals tolerate this type of Reiki for a longer period of time than hands-on Reiki.*

- **Hands-on Laulima or Reiki:** *Adapt the standard hand positions for humans to the animal. Even with smaller animals the basic idea of anatomy is the same.*

- **Group Laulima or Reiki:** *For larger animals, especially horses or large dogs, a few people can perform Reiki simultaneously, sending much love and healing at once.*

The Trust Technique is a synergy of both healing and communication principles, delivered in a simple-to-use format for anyone to use effectively with any type of animal. It helps animals and people resolve problems by finding confidence and trust, while tapping into a delightful world where true animal intelligence can be seen, felt and interacted with. – James French

Energy healing is not a substitute for professional veterinary treatment.

The Veterinary Surgeons Act of 1966 prohibits anyone other than a qualified veterinary surgeon from treating animals, including diagnosis of ailments and giving advice on such diagnosis.

However, the healing of animals by contact, by the laying on of hands or distant healing is legal. The Protection of Animals Act 1911 requires that if an animal clearly needs treatment from a veterinary surgeon the owner must obtain this. To give emergency First Aid to animals for the purpose of saving life or relieving pain is permissible under the Veterinary Surgeons Act 1966 Schedule 3 (taken from the UK Reiki Federation Code of Ethics and Standards of Practice, March 2002).

This is a non-medical therapy that complements and supports all other healing therapies, including veterinary medicine, and is a valuable part of a combined approach to healing and health maintenance.

Make some aloha today...

In the calm beauty of Hawaii a traditional lomilomi massage gets under way.

1:61 Lomilomi

Imagine yourself being gently rocked into a state of deep bliss, your body being massaged from head to toe, with a harmonious blending of movement, breath and open heart. Using long continuous strokes, the massage becomes a beautiful dance on your body. And with the hands touching you imbued with love, you are able to do more than simply relax, but also free your mind and actuate healing, as your soul is caressed by the waves of the ocean. Such is the experience of receiving a lomilomi massage.

Lomilomi differs from other forms of massage in many ways; it is an experience that overwhelms the mind with sensations and at the same time communicates an acceptance and a nurturing of inner self. Lomilomi is a deeply nurturing, incredibly relaxing, transformative massage that is truly unique and not like any other form of bodywork. To truly understand what makes lomilomi different we have to travel back in time to a land called Lemuria (the land of light), the original home to the ancestors of the Hawaiian people.

Here lomilomi was a way of life, and a complete healing system, nurturing and supporting life of both human and spirit bodies. *We are spirit beings, beings of light, here to have the human experience.* And it's this connection to the ancestors, to our inner spirit and to the divine energy of creation that is still present in all true lomilomi work. For to lomi is to weave, weave light, weave love, weave spirit through the energy waves of the body, creating a web of healing light. It was known as Ke Ala Hoku or pathway to the stars, referring to the cosmic energy connection.

This old traditional lomi bodywork would combine whole body rhythmic movement with chanting, drumming, and deep breathing, along with the application of coconut and other nature-infused healing oils. The session the participant would undergo aimed to reach down into the center of our being and bring up our life force energy, letting it flow through our entire bodies which in turn would flow into our lives. It would start with pule/prayer requesting the presence of healing mana/energy. This was followed by a deep cleansing process which included fasting, herbal preparations, sweats in the steam vents of the volcano and bathing in the mineral enriched ponds. The receiver would empty from the heart all anger, jealously, envy, forgiveness, and any other emotions that cause stress, before the sun sets. In ancient times the massage session could last for hours or even days.

> *Traditionally, everyone in the o'hana knew lomilomi and massaged each other every day.* –James Jackson Jarves, 1843

Modern lomilomi massage

Over the centuries lomi massage has divided into two distinct groups. The people's lomi for relaxation and rejuvenation was shared by members of the extended family or O'hana; today this branch (which was first shared with non-Hawaiians by Auntie Margaret) is referred to as Big Island Style. The second branch was practiced by priests or kahunas as a sacred rite of passage; this transformational lomi (which was first shared with non-Hawaiians by Kahu Abraham Kawai'i) is referred to as Temple Lomi. Both use pule/prayer, and loving touch. Today there are many varieties of lomilomi but all modern versions originate from these two branches.

Lomilomi today

Today lomilomi massage can be divided into two categories: Hawaiian and Oceanic, each unique to their geographical location. As mentioned, there are many versions of Hawaiian lomilomi practiced. Oceanic lomilomi (Honu) massage is a melting pot of Hawaiian styles, and in addition includes techniques from many Pacific islands that pre-date the settlement of Hawaii. All styles are deeply rooted in aloha and contain prayer, presence, breath and touch to offer a space of unconditional love and healing.

Lomilomi bodywork (Hoku) is a modern adaptation and presentation of the old art of lomilomi, a complete and sacred bodycare system that blends together a synthesis of techniques: old with new, ancient with modern, shamanism with quantum physics – a truly magical loving touch therapy. This healing system is derived from the ancient Polynesian methods of realigning and balance to the body, mind and soul. Lomilomi practitioners are trained to see life as a flow of energy. They follow the notion that the flow can be congested or even blocked by muscle tension, joint immobilization and mental stress. Oceanic lomilomi bodywork (Hoku) is a technically advanced Pacific island healing art and only practiced by masters of the art.

Using a beautifully choreographed dance, the practitioner gracefully and systematically weaves their way through the soft tissue of the body, creating harmony, balance and alignment of the musculoskeletal system. In an ebb and flow of cosmic waves, blocked energy is released, and fresh new light energy introduced. The practitioner constantly alternates between soft tissue release techniques and energy enhancement techniques; the result is a "magical dance of the tissues." The combination of the practitioner's focus on love/aloha energy and specialized bodywork techniques helps to release tension and restore energy flow in new directions and patterns. The outcome is greater levels of clarity, joy and health.

> *During a genuine lomilomi session, the therapist is aligned with divine energy, and keeps his or her heart and mind clear for spirit to move through them as a conduit for healing energy.* –Tamara Mondragon

Space - receiving a lomi session is like being loved and nurtured in a way that for some people hasn't been present since childhood, if at all. The sacred space created for the session is like a womb securely embracing a new being, and readying it for birth. In this place of gestation, old physical and emotional patterns are released, opening up a space for new, healthier patterns to take root and grow. In this safe environment participants can have a unique experience to discover, acknowledge and embrace all aspects of who they are.

The space we work in is "alive" and we treat the space as being sacred in the sense that we infuse it, to the best of our ability, with a positive, balanced energy.

> *Early Hawaiians knew what modern medicine has now proved.* – Mary Kawena Pukui, 1972

Philosophy – In Oceanic philosophy everything is energy, universal energy from one vibrating, living entity, a source presenting itself in various forms, a universe within universes.

> *An example of this idea in the context of massage and the human body is found in any major anatomical, physiological, energetic system. Let us consider the circulatory system. This is an overall system with many individual parts, each performing its own function in relation to the others. These parts cannot be separated to function independently and all together they function as one larger, more complex organism. On the largest scale there is the phenomenon of the collective circulatory systems and hearts of mankind, all contained in the one universal heart of creation. No matter how far this system is projected downward into the microcosm (the cellular level) or upward into the macrocosm (the cosmic level), there is relationship, connection, and ultimately sameness. Client and practitioner become one being and together enter into a synergetic and dynamic exchange of energy and information with the multidimensional forces and levels of existence.*
>
> –Rosalie Samet

Dance – Lomilomi has been called a dance. The movement starts from the feet up to the hips and through the arms; the giver is completely relaxed, using their forearms for most of the session. This movement, or dance, is more Tai Chi in nature and very graceful, the beautiful long strokes re-weave areas of the body that were once disconnected. These continual and rhythmical massage strokes create an immense outpouring of energy, and help to lull the receiver into a deep state of bliss, thus creating a loving, sensual massage. At the finish of each section of the body, a feather-light touch is used in gentle loving strokes.

Hawaiians look at things in terms of energy flow, following the idea that a thought or belief can block energy flow as much as muscle tension can. Lomilomi helps release the blockages, while at the same time giving the energy new direction. Thus lomilomi is not just a physical experience; it also facilitates healing on the mental, emotional and spiritual levels as well.

Lomilomi usually commences with a stillness between the practitioner and client, with the giver's hands resting on the back of the receiver. In the stillness the practitioner will quietly say a blessing or prayer asking for whatever healing is needed to take place during the massage. The massage is given in fluid, rhythmic motion using forearms as well as hands, using upper and under body strokes to free energy. The giver works all areas – different parts of the body are massaged at the same time, not working an area in isolation creates a deep sense of balance and harmony.

Lomilomi can be done by one person or by two or more people working together. Having two people massaging tends to send the recipient into an even deeper level of relaxation as you can't focus on four hands doing different things – it really is a blissful and fairly mind-blowing experience.

–Tracy Courtney

I felt as if I was floating on a wave of light and energy. Even though I was in a room full of people and I was wearing very little, I was made to feel totally safe and secure. They were so in tune with each other that although it was tandem it felt like one person, flowing, and no difference in pressure between the two. The wave moved up and down my body in rhythm soothing every inch of my being. I've never experienced anything remotely like this and would highly recommend it. If everyone had this opportunity we'd live in a very peaceful, giving, sharing world.

–Sally Gurnham

The secret

The secret of lomilomi massage technique lies within the practitioner, for they are the creators and weavers of the magic. Receivers of lomilomi are treated as spirits in a body, sacred at their core.

While the technique is an important part of the massage and associated healing, it is the little bit extra that the practitioner brings that turns the massage from ordinary to extraordinary. It is a culmination of life process, experience, understanding, and the ability to let the energy of unconditional love flow freely that makes a lomilomi massage master, someone who freely gives the gift of aloha. Only by looking inward, restoring balance and harmony, practicing self-healing, striving to understand the spiritual element of the esoteric knowledge of Huna can a practitioner achieve a semblance of mastery.

Echoes of joy

The waves faded out to tribal drums overlaid with Hawaiian chants as forearms kneaded and rolled across the landscape of my body. She lifted and cradled me, rocking me in the arms of the mother, sweeping me into her grace. I became wide open and receptive. In the spirit of aloha, unconditional love, I felt like a newborn babe, soft and silky.
~from Sweet Your Prayers by Gabrielle Roth

I am so grateful for Kevin's help, love and support without which I would be living my life from a wheelchair.
~Linda Sharrett, specialist midwife, King's College London

Loving, healing, renewing lomilomi is not just a wonderful massage technique; it's a journey for the soul, a clearing for the mind, an opening of the heart, a dance with life. A very human experience of aloha.
~Anita J. Webb

I was able to achieve a state of rapture that felt like I was dancing in the heavens. Lomilomi creates the vehicle to be transported and nurtured in a way that puts you into a total trust of the moment and allows you to free yourself.

~Peter Roth

Kevin is an expert in his field. I felt totally safe in his hands.

~Lindsey Gill

The feeling of peace and love that this gives leaves you feeling the love for days afterwards.

~Karen Wade

What a beautiful gift. Not only are you transported to "lomilomi land" but you feel like the goddess that you are. This is a spiritually cleansing experience.

~Rev. Debbie Steinke

Reflections

The cells of my body vibrated higher and freer as the kahunas danced through the layers of my being with incredible mana and grace. Connecting with all that I am. Reaching out in fluid ripples to my gene pool. A call to higher consciousness.

Raindrops from heaven blessed me as they poured from the soft dark skin of the kahunas. Imbued with great mana, each drop fragrant as pikake merged with the ocean of movement that freed me in my body. I swam in the spaces where past and future cease to exist. Surrendering to the power of moment,

Manawa.

May this peace, expansion and knowingness run through the blood and bones of all my relations. May we be pono in truth and may we reclaim our inherent aloha. Love beyond description, and mana, divine power, my prayer continued to call out. The lights of heaven reflected me like an intricate map in the starry night.

Remembering, remembering. Deeper, further. The vials between the worlds dissolved as I found the bridge within my own being. The heart of the mother entering mine with a love and compassion so great as to open my floodgates with ocean sobs, the longing now fulfilled. Breaking down any residue, my true heart, one in hers.

A golden pink sunburst of light was freed from within in an instant. Connected to the heart of infinity, I was absorbed into her radiance beyond words. The never ending harmonic sound of my vibration caressed and guided me. In trusted abandon, I was no more. At last, one with all creation. There are no more words.

–Iolani Negrin

As the lomilomi comes to an end the receiver slowly opens her eyes and sees the world in a sacred light.

1:62 Hoku

Hoku lomilomi is a full body musculoskeletal alignment treatment that uses a top-to-toe regime in which the therapist uses his/her hands and arms, making use of their finely tuned sense of touch (palpation). Superficially it may seem as though the treatment is methodically the same each time. This is far from the truth. The treatment flow (order in which treatment takes place) is there to make sure everything is checked in order and nothing gets forgotten, but each treatment is individual. The therapist only stretches, mobilizes and aligns what is required on the day.

The aim is to check the alignment, range of motion and mobilization of the joints, and to stretch and ease any tight (hypertonic) muscles that may affect the skeletal alignment and smooth operation of the body. The aim is: (a) to ensure that there is no hindrance to correct nerve and blood flow to every part of the body; (b) that the body is free to move in any direction from a center of correct alignment and balance. Chiropractors and osteopaths around the world have used traditional island techniques with many being adopted into their treatment regime. By contrast, therapists practicing Hoku will remove muscular inhibition, joint dysponesis and somatic dysfunction using non-invasive, non-cavitational, soft tissue release techniques.

As therapists we seek to restore the structural integrity and balance of our clients. To do this efficiently we must treat the body as a whole. Every bone, joint, ligament and muscle needs to be visited and checked. Fascia is often the missing element in the movement/stability equation. Understanding fascial plasticity and responsiveness is an important key to lasting and substantive therapeutic change. Hoku is a holistic or even wholistic therapy as it systematically weaves its way through 206 bones, 360 joints, and some 640 muscles, hundreds of ligaments, tendons, and mile upon mile of fascia, a continuous connective tissue not unlike saran/cling-film wrapping.

> *This fascia wraps every muscle, bone, organ, and vessel of the body and changes its name according to what it is covering. Right under the skin, there's a second skin, a body stocking called superficial fascia. This radiates into a deeper layer covering each individual muscle, this layer is called deep fascia. The muscle itself has a second skin composed of the same connective tissue but now called the epimysium. Each muscle bundle is surrounded by perimysium and each individual fiber by endomysium. At either end of the muscle belly, these tissues naturally converge, but now they are called tendons. The tendon attaches to the connective tissue covering of the bone called periosteum. As you can see, we are highly layered in structure. It is important to address the adhesion between or within the layers of connective tissue.*
>
> –David Lauterstein

> *An unexamined life is not worth living.*
>
> –Plato

1:63 Ho'oponopono

If we can accept that we are the sum total of all past thoughts, emotions, words, deeds and actions and that our present lives and choices are colored or shaded by this memory bank of the past, then we begin to see how a process of correcting or setting aright can change our lives, our families and our society. –Morrnah Nalamaku Simeona

- Ho'oponopono is a tool for atonement, for correcting errors, erasing the effects of past actions and memories that cause havoc and grief in our lives, the lives of others and on Mother Nature as a whole.

- The Ho'oponopono mantra "I am sorry, please forgive me, I love you and I thank you," combined with other cleaning practices, breathing exercises and meditations, is used to eliminate whatever the adverse condition is. The mantra is spoken from your human mind and directed to your spirit body and soul. We call this the Hawaiian Code of Forgiveness, and it's an important thought, because when we forgive others, who are we forgiving? Ourselves, of course.

- Ho'oponopono is not a religion and never will become one. With Ho'oponopono there are no teachers, gurus, high priests or middle men. Ho'oponopono practitioners know that the divine source is the only teacher there is. Indeed, there are those who are more experienced in the practice of Ho'oponopono, but they are regarded in the same way you would regard an older brother or sister.

- *Anyone can practice Ho'oponopono – essentially you are seeking a dialogue with the Creator. However, before you proceed further you will need to be comfortable with the following fundamental concepts of Ho'oponopono.*

- *When faced with any adverse situation, the Ho'oponopono practitioner will immediately ask, "What is it in me that is causing this event to take place, this person to behave this way, this sickness to manifest?" etc. Ho'oponopono practitioners know that blaming others is a sure way for making certain of the recurrence of a problem.*

- *If you can pass through this major ego-generated hurdle, I promise you that you will absolutely love Ho'oponopono – and not only that, you will witness miracles in your life and the lives of others.*

- *Those who follow and practice religions of love will quickly recognize that the message of Ho'oponopono is not at all new. But they do point to a higher intelligence that has a very clear and well-planned future for the human race – the emergence of a super race being the first step of this plan.*

- *The following description is by no means a complete training in how to do Ho'oponopono.*

The Process of Ho'oponopono

1. Bring to mind anyone with whom you do not feel total alignment or support, etc.

2. In your mind's eye, construct a small stage below you.

3. Imagine an infinite source of love and healing flowing from a source above the top of your head (from your higher self); open up the top of your head, and let the source of love and healing flow down inside your body, fill up the body, and overflow out your heart to heal the person on the stage. Be sure it is all right for you to heal the person and that they accept the healing.

4   When the healing is complete, have a discussion with the person and forgive them, and have them forgive you.

5   Next, let go of the person, and see them floating away. As they do, cut the aka cord that connects the two of you (if appropriate). If you are healing in a current primary relationship, then assimilate the person inside you.

6   Do this with every person in your life with whom you are incomplete, or not aligned.

    The final test is, can you see the person or think of them without feeling any negative emotions? If you still feel negative emotions when you do this, then do the process again.

You are today where your thoughts have brought you; you will be tomorrow where your thoughts take you.

–James Allen

The winds of grace blow all the time.

-Ramakrishna

1:64 Piko-piko

Piko-piko is a special Hawaiian breathing technique that simultaneously relaxes and energizes the body.

– Serge Kahili King

Piko-piko means center to center. In Huna healing there are many energy centers (piko points), the two most powerful are the navel and the crown of the head. The navel represents your physical source and lifeline while the crown symbolizes your connection with the aumakua, or spiritual realm.

> *The diaphragm, at the solar plexus, the space between the lung and the stomach, is the place where the power to heal comes through. The diaphragm is like a drum, it is a vacuum. Breathing inward activates the light energy; the breath begins and gathers power in the diaphragm, echoes as it moves through the heart, then into the throat where it becomes a healing chant HAAA! The outgoing breath beats the diaphragm like a drum. This in turn raises the vibration.*
>
> – Harry Uhane Jim

Piko-piko (Key points)

Piko-piko breathing is used in the Hawaiian healing tradition. It is not only a stress reliever and body energizer, but also a great aid in relieving pain.

- *You will learn how to breathe mindfully.*
- *You will learn how to relax your whole body.*
- *You will learn to enhance your overall sense of well-being.*
- *You will learn about a very powerful Hawaiian breathing technique.*
- *There are many, many variations of Piko-piko, this is the basic form.*

Piko-piko (Summary)

This is a perfect breathing exercise that takes less than a minute, it can be done anytime and anywhere when you need to relax.

Piko-piko is part of the Hawaiian healing tradition.

You have experienced a deep abdominal breathing technique that not only relaxes the body but is also a great aid in relieving stress and pain and ultimately giving an overall sense of well-being.

The act of centering the attention and moving the attention automatically results in a deeper than normal pattern of breathing, increasing circulation and relieving tension.

You can do this breathing technique wherever you are and no matter what you are doing. The more you use the technique, you will become centered quicker and deeper.

Piko-piko is very good for getting to sleep if your head is full of thoughts or anxiety.

> *"A way to relieve mental stress is to place your attention on what you like, rather than what you don't. Criticism, whether of yourself, another person or even the weather, creates mental stress and thus tension in your body," explained King. He recommended a quick mental stress reliever, "saturation praise," spending one minute focusing on everything you like about yourself or the world.* –Diane Koemar

Piko-piko (Basic)

Exercise Level 1

1. Get in a relaxed position and put one hand on the crown of your head, and the other on your navel. You can use either hand for the positions.
2. Breathe in deeply through your nose and place your attention on your navel and hold for a moment (your hands will help you focus).
3. Exhale out through your mouth with a **Ha** sound, your attention should be on your crown.
4. Breathe in deeply through your nose and place your attention on your navel.
5. Exhale out through your mouth with a **Ha** sound, your attention should be on your crown.
6. Breathe in deeply through your nose and place your attention on your navel and hold for a moment (your hands will help you focus).
7. Exhale out through your mouth with a **Ha** sound, your attention should be on your crown.
8. Your imagination will help move healing energy along with your breath.

*Part One - **Shine like a star**… the aloha way*

9 Continue until you feel energized, grounded and/or de-stressed.

10 This is the basic Piko-piko breathing technique and is used to center the body, re-grounding the body, reducing stress and re-energizing through oxygenation.

Exercise Level 2

Piko-piko (Relax and Energize)

1 Get in a relaxed position and take three cleansing breaths.
2 Breathe in deeply through your nose and place your attention on your navel and hold for a moment (your hands will help you focus).
3 Exhale out through your mouth with a **Ha** sound, your attention should be on your crown.
4 Breathe in deeply through your nose and place your attention on your navel.
5 Exhale out through your mouth with a **Ha** sound, your attention should be on your crown.
6 Breathe in deeply through your nose and place your attention on your navel.
7 Exhale out through your mouth with a **Ha** sound, your attention should be on your crown.
8 Now imagine a ball of living healing light pulsating with energy above your head, and this time as you breathe in, take in the healing energy from that ball of light and at the same time place your attention on your navel.
9 (If you don't connect with using energy this way, feel free to replace it with your God if religious, or whatever healing power you believe in).
10 Exhale out through your mouth with a **Ha** sound, your attention should be on your crown.
11 Breathe in deeply the healing energy through your nose and place your attention on your navel.

STARDANCE - Flow with Energy

12 Exhale out through your mouth with a **Ha** sound, your attention should be on your crown.

13 Breathe in deeply the healing energy through your nose and place your attention on your navel.

14 Exhale out through your mouth with a **Ha** sound, your attention should be on your crown.

14 Your imagination will help move healing energy along with your breath.

16 Continue until you feel energized.

17 Close by thanking and blessing your healing source.

Exercise Level 3

Piko-piko (Self-healing)

1 Get in a relaxed position and take three cleansing breaths.

2 Breathe in deeply through your nose and place your attention on your navel and hold for a moment (your hands will help you focus).

3 Exhale out through your mouth with a **Ha** sound, your attention should be on your crown.

4 Breathe in deeply through your nose and place your attention on your navel.

5 Exhale out through your mouth with a **Ha** sound, your attention should be on your crown.

6 Breathe in deeply through your nose and place your attention on your navel.

7 Exhale out through your mouth with a **Ha** sound, your attention should be on your crown.

8 Now imagine a ball of living healing light pulsating with energy above your head, and this time as you breathe in, take in the healing energy from that ball of light and at the same time place your attention on your navel.

9 (If you don't connect with using energy this way, feel free to replace it with your God if religious, or whatever healing power you believe in).

Part One - *Shine like a star*... *the aloha way*

10 Exhale out through your mouth with a **Ha** sound, with your attention on any part of your body that is in pain.

11 Breathe in deeply the healing energy through your nose and place your attention on your navel.

12 Exhale out through your mouth with a **Ha** sound, with your attention on any part of your body that is in pain.

13 Breathe in deeply the healing energy through your nose and place your attention on your navel.

14 Exhale out through your mouth with a **Ha** sound, with your attention on any part of your body that is in pain.

15 Your imagination will help move healing energy along with your breath.

16 Continue until you feel energized.

17 Close by thanking and blessing your healing source.

18 Another variation of this exercise is to breathe in healing energy from the ball of light and *send any heavy energy with your breath out of your* **feet** *to the center of the earth.* You'll be moving healing energy through the body energizing your chakras and unblocking tension so your body can move into balance.

Piko-piko (Advanced)

Exercise Level 4

1 Get in a relaxed position and take three cleansing breaths.

2 Breathe in deeply through your nose and place your attention on your navel and hold for a moment (your hands will help you focus).

3 Exhale out through your mouth with a **Ha** sound, your attention should be on your crown.

4 Breathe in deeply through your nose and place your attention on your navel.

5 Exhale out through your mouth with a **Ha** sound, your attention should be on your crown.

6   Breathe in deeply through your nose and place your attention on your navel.

7   Exhale out through your mouth with a **Ha** sound, your attention should be on your crown.

8   Now imagine a ball of living healing light pulsating with energy above your head.

9   Now imagine someone, something or some place that you love deeply, really imagine it, and make a picture, feel the feeling of love, hear the sounds. When you are really experiencing the emotion, put the emotion into the ball of light-as-energy.

10 This time as you breathe in, take in the healing energy with the essence from the emotion of love from that ball of light and at the same time place your attention on your navel.

11 Exhale out through your mouth with a **Ha** sound, with your attention on your legs and feet filling them with love and light energy.

12 Breathe in deeply the healing energy through your nose and place your attention on your navel.

13 Exhale out through your mouth with a **Ha** sound, with your attention on your torso and arms filling them with love and light energy.

14 Breathe in deeply the healing energy through your nose and place your attention on your navel.

15 Exhale out through your mouth with a **Ha** sound, with your attention on your head and heart filling them with love and light energy.

16 Breathe in deeply the healing love energy through your nose and place your attention on your navel.

17 Exhale out through your mouth with a **Ha** sound, with your attention on your whole being – let the light and love burst out from your head, hands and feet.

18 Let your eyes sparkle as the light shines from your soul.

19 When you feel completely energized give thanks and blessings to the source, go out and live your life radiating love and light as you go.

20 Mahalo & Blessings.

> *Who looks outside dreams;*
> *who looks inside, wakes.*
>
> –Carl Jung

1:65 Dynamind

Disease occurs when there is a psychic or psychological state of tension that holds the imbalance for an extended period of time with a fair degree of intensity. In energy healing, it is easy for the giver to transfuse light energy into the receiver for healing. The problem is that unless the receiver changes their thinking/attitude, the healing energy can quickly dissipate. Dynamind allows for the required thinking change, or attitude change, in addition to stimulating specific energy points on the body. This combination gives the receiver something to change their healing patterns. Unless the thinking pattern, the attitude, is changed, the condition often returns no matter what technique is used. This is because "energy flows where attention goes" and if the receiver is concentrating on the negative that is what ultimately they will receive.

There are a number of complementary therapy techniques that address this issue: techniques such as EFT (emotional freedom technique) and Dynamind by Hawaiian healer Serge Kahili King.

The Dynamind Technique

1. Choose a physical, emotional, or mental problem to work on. State the issue out loud (headache, anger, sadness).

2. Rate the intensity of the feeling on a scale of 0-10 at the current moment where 10 is the most intense.

3. Bring both hands together with your fingertips touching. Make the following statement, aloud or silently: "I have a problem (state problem as above) and that can change; I want that problem to go away."

4. "Even though my body/mind has this issue/problem, I completely love and accept my spirit-self and my embodiment."

5. With two or three fingers tap these points seven times each: the center of your chest; the outer area between the thumb and index finger of both hands; the bone at the base of your neck.

6. Inhale with your attention focused on the top of your head; exhale with your attention on your toes.

7. Once you have done three rounds of tapping, re-score the intensity of the issue/problem.

8. Symptoms may change in intensity, location, or type.

The Synergy Technique ~ Dynamind with Starlite

1. Focus on a ball of golden light, vibrating just above your head.

2. Breathe in that light concentrating on your heart and head.

3. Breathe out sending the light down and out through your fingers and toes.

4. Make the following statement, aloud or silently: "I am bathed in the light and my (issue/problem) has changed for the better."

*Part One - **Shine like a star**... the aloha way*

5 Breathe in that light concentrating on your heart and head.

6 Breathe out sending the light down and out through your fingers and toes.

7 Make the following statement, aloud or silently: "I am grateful and send my blessings for the benefits I have received."

8 For additional benefit repeat from number one if necessary (redefining the changed issue).

Distant Dynamind

The following is a method for using the Dynamind technique in distant healing applications.

1 Relax by doing some gentle deep breathing or perform a few rounds of Piko-piko. Piko-piko is performed by placing the attention at the top of the head on the inhale breath, and when exhaling, place the attention at the navel.

2 Imagine that you are in your favorite place in nature, or your favorite garden. This is your inner garden, or your "special place" in your mind. Place your attention on any one sound you hear, then place your attention on touching something in the garden, then place your attention upon seeing one thing in your garden. Using the senses like this helps develop and focus your awareness, which helps increase your energy.

3 With your creative imagination, visualize that the individual requiring healing help is mentally there with you in your garden, standing in front of you.

4 Mentally see yourself speaking with them and directing them to place their hands in the Dynamind hand position. Now visualize yourself saying to them (note: in this example, we will assume the person's name is Mary), "Mary has a problem, and that can change, Mary wants the problem to go away." Replace the word problem with a description and location of the health issue/condition Mary has.

5. Now with the Dynamind symbol technique, imagine and make a symbol of the condition and then change that symbol in some positive way to improve it. Now visualize the client, Mary, walking into this symbol, surrounding her body.

6. Then imagine that a healing light is coming down from above, and that you can focus this light just like the iris of a camera can focus light. Imagine that you have focused the light into a small sphere, and that this small sphere of light now has a warm and soothing sensation that relaxes and stimulates.

7. Mentally direct the small sphere of light toward the client, Mary, and see it on her chest. See it blinking on and off seven times. Using the Dynamind tapping process, do the same for the points on the hands and at the base of the skull.

8. See the client again place their hands in the basic Dynamind hand position. Now direct the sphere of light to the top of the client's head, and see the sphere of light illuminate the receiver's body as the sphere slowly descends from the top of the client's head to the bottom of their feet.

9. Now imagine there is a point inside the center of your brain that is radiating out little beams and ripples of light waves or concentric rings. You now mentally think the question, asking the client how the round of Dynamind has changed the issue. See this wave of thought question touch the client, and then, like a radar beam, the client's response bounces or echoes back to you. The answer can be in the form of a feeling, a thought, or a symbol.

Based on the client's return information, it can be decided if further Dynamind treatment is required. –Jim Fallon

You'll see it when you believe it.

– Wayne Dyer

1:66 Hula for health

Dancing the Hula is a healthy activity that makes you feel good; it has a positive effect not only on physical fitness, but also cognitive (mental) function.

Hula is a sacred, spiritual dance that helps dancers connect with nature.

Freeing the mind and connecting with nature eases tension and stress. Hula also increases flexibility while toning the hips, stomach, thighs, calves and arms.

Kahiko hula, being fast-paced, is a cardiovascular exercise, promoting heart health. Hula improves posture and breathing techniques as well.

Auana hula has smoother movements and is ideal for people with restricted physical movement or those with age-related problems.

> *After the age of 35, our brains decrease in mass by up to 3% every decade, so as we get older, we are not as able to store and recall information.* –Professor Terry Eckmann

Hula involves following and participating in sequenced movements, an activity that creates new brain cells. Just as you can develop new muscle at any age, you can develop new neural pathways. It could be used to slow mental decline in dementia patients. Basically, the more brain mass you have, the longer it will take for the disease to eat it away.

> *The evidence of the cognitive effects of exercise is so strong, we now say, "whatever is good for the heart is good for the brain."* –Beth Israel, Harvard Medical School

Dance has a positive effect beyond that of other types of movement. When you dance it makes you happy. When you smile it has a positive effect on the body. Not taking yourself too seriously is incredibly important for your mental well-being. Learning to dance focuses the attention away from any worries, but you also have to forgive yourself for making mistakes, and laugh at yourself.

Using Hula and Huna in a clinical setting is not about pretending everything is all right but learning to take a step back from whatever is bothering you.

Hula is not only a muscle strengthening exercise but it also involves learning new challenging steps, which in turn releases dopamine. People with Parkinson's disease suffer a progressive loss of nerve cells in the brain, leading to a deficit of dopamine. Dopamine plays a key role in regulating movement and a fall in levels is why Parkinson's symptoms include involuntary shaking and muscle stiffness.

Clearly we need more medical research into the "dance of life."

> *Aloha has a healing power all of its own.*
> -Koko

1:67 Emotions and bones

Emotional wellness affects your bone health

When patients come to our healthcare clinic for a bone health evaluation, most are surprised when we ask them about their stress levels and emotional wellness. But stress and emotions have a powerful impact on bone health.

Your body responds to stress by producing a hormone called cortisol. Cortisol has many effects on the body, one of which is mobilizing calcium from bone and increasing its secretion through the urine. In other words, when you're stressed, your bones begin spilling the minerals they need for bone formation into the bloodstream for the good of other tissues. Unfortunately, most of us experience chronic stress, which means your bones are continuously leached of minerals, which often aren't being replaced in the diet.

Depression also negatively impacts bone health. Research shows women with past or present depression have lower bone density than women who have never experienced depression. One explanation for this link is that depression increases cortisol production, much like stress does. Depressed women are also less likely to consume sufficient nutrition for bone health, and are less likely to be active.

Clearly, our emotions play an important role in our bone health. Most women have certain sources of stress that they can't avoid, but we do have the ability to change the way we respond to stress, and lessen its impact on our health.

Exercise can be a wonderful stress reliever, with the added benefit of directly stimulating bone formation. We also recommend meditation, deep breathing, and sleeping at least seven to eight hours per night. Simple dietary changes and medical-grade nutritional supplements can help heal the damaging effects of stress on our adrenals, the glands responsible for producing cortisol.

The Aloha Diet is a great place to start: reduce stress, lift depression and improve health.

Progressive Muscle Relaxation

Progressive Muscle Relaxation was developed by Edmund Jacobsen in the 1930s and is a great way to relax the body in order to help create the beginner's mind state of calm.

Take a reclining position, and breathe in and out three times. Prepare to contract and relax every major muscle group throughout your body. Begin at your feet. Tense your feet and clench your toes. Hold for five seconds, and relax. Tense your calf muscles, raise them a couple of inches off the floor, tense and relax. Lower your legs to the floor. Tense your knees, and proceed to the lower and upper legs, tense for five seconds and relax. Move on to the buttocks and then abdomen, repeating the "tense, hold for five seconds and relax" formula. Next the upper back, chest then shoulders, followed by upper and lower arms then onto the fingers – tense, hold for five seconds and relax. Finally we come to the neck and face.

The idea is to become aware of what tension feels like and to experience the relaxation that follows when you release and let go.

> *The diagnostic curing model is as outdated as the horse and cart.*
>
> -Bowen

1:68 We do not diagnose

Diagnosis can be a hit and miss affair. Many conditions can even be diagnosed differently from doctor to doctor. Many patients also might seem to "fit" the pattern of certain illnesses or conditions. How do we know exactly where a problem comes from? Do we know that one problem is not related to another problem? Even if we diagnose correctly, can we be sure that there are no other factors of the condition that we might have missed? The main point however is that lomilomi is a holistic or even wholistic therapy. It treats the whole body, with the body choosing what it will and will not address.

Professor Malcolm Stemp, a homoeopath for over 40 years and lecturer of osteopathy at Oxford University says, "Any natural therapy must obey the first law of nature cure. This law states that the body be treated as a whole, without reference to named disease."

We do not treat specific conditions

> **We don't diagnose or treat specific conditions. If the body is being treated as a whole, then it follows that any and every condition within any body being treated is being addressed.**

Part One - **Shine like a star**… *the aloha way*

*Presenting conditions are recorded but it is important not to be bogged down by the presenting condition.
We do not chase the pain.*

This "first law of natural cure" also gives us lots of scope. When people ask the question "Can you treat cancer?" the answer is no! If we rephrase the question to "Can you treat people with cancer?" the answer is most definitely yes!

We do not prescribe or alter medication.

While it's important to encourage patients to take a responsible attitude toward their medication, we would be on very dangerous ground giving any sort of specific advice or instruction in this regard. –Bowen

Western medicine takes an aggressive and defensive approach to health. It speaks of winning the war against disease and preventing illness by strengthening the body's defenses, and approaches the body as a machine of muscle and bone, driven by a fluid pump (the heart) and coordinated by an electrical organ (the brain).

The Oceanic view of the body is more musical than mechanical. It sees the body as a rhythmic representation of the spirit of life and a result of all things resonating together to create a harmonious system. In Oceanic culture, the body is referred to with respect, kindness and love, and is not seen as an entity separable from its environment. –Paul Pearsall

> *Weave a rainbow of healing light...*
>
> -Rima A. Morrell

1:69 Rainbow energy

In physics, the law of entropy says that all systems, left unattended, will run down. Unless new energy is pumped in, the organism will disintegrate. Look after your own energy levels.

Rainbow medicine (color energy): pure white light contains the whole spectrum of color and when reflected through water it will display a beautiful rainbow of cascading light energy.

This works by tuning into the vibration of the universe found in the Starlite zone and channeling cosmic energy waves through spacetime continuum into an embodiment here in the physical dimension.

Cosmic energy is simply light energy resonating at various wavelengths. Each wavelength will have a slightly different vibration and be seen in the physical world as a different color.

For the majority of the time a stardancer will find that he or she is channeling pure white light directly from the source. However, there are times when a receiver will require a rebalancing of a specific energy vibration and the color of that wave will become apparent to those with eyes that can see through the vial of the physical realm.

Real vision is seeing the invisible. –Jonathan Swift

Color and bodywork

All life on earth is based in wavelengths of energy called electromagnetic radiation. What we experience as visible light is simply a tiny portion of this continuum. Electromagnetic radiation of this wavelength activates the nerve cells in our eyes.

Within this spectrum of visible light, we perceive different vibrations of light. We call the visible quality of differentiation of vibration color. We perceive different colors according to their vibration and name them accordingly: red, blue, yellow. These colors don't exist in the world on their own, they are simply names for light waves of different energy and frequency.

–Principles of Visual Perception by Carolyn Bloomer

Breathe in the rainbow

This is a lovely and very helpful exercise to encourage a balance of all the seven main chakra colors for our well-being.

Stand with feet slightly apart and arms by your side, relaxed, with palms turned to the front. Relax the shoulders, and concentrate on your breathing, consciously relaxing all of your body from the top of your head to the tips of your toes. Breathe in deeply through the nose, holding for a few moments and then breathing out through the mouth. As you breathe out, imagine expelling all the stress, negativity and toxins from your body. If you can do this exercise outside, all the better, and weather permitting, stand on grass with bare feet.

Affirmations, either spoken out loud or as a concentrated thought, can be helpful as well, to help us focus and stop our minds from wandering. For example, red is the color of courage and strength, we could say to ourselves: the energy of red fills my body and I have the strength and courage to move forward along my life's path. It doesn't matter how we word our affirmations, they will be unique to each individual, but remember the positive aspects of the colors and make sure your statements are positive.

Choose the color that has the positive aspect that you require on this occasion and use this still-point meditation technique to rebalance your being. Remember that white contains all the colors of the rainbow and is considered a sacred color.

Rainbow meditation

Now, close your eyes. Relax and take several deep breaths.

Now let your body tension go.

We are going to take a color trip. Climb a mountain of color. During this trip, I want you to be aware of your breathing. Each time you take in a breath, you will be inhaling a color, which will have a definite effect on your body.

We are at the bottom of a mountain, a mountain of color. Here at the bottom of the mountain, everything is Red: the grass, the flowers, the trees and even the air. Each time you inhale you breathe in Red and as you continue to do this, you feel your energy level pick up. With each Red inhalation, all fears drop away and you have the courage to be yourself. Look around, everything you see is Red.
Feel this Red.

All right now. We have vitalized our bodies and we are proceeding up the mountain. As we arrive at the second level, we see that now everything is colored Orange. Breathe in Orange with each inhalation. As this Orange color enters your body, you feel your inhibitions drop away and you become more aware of both your physical vitality and your mental powers. You feel balanced. Everything you see is Orange.
Feel this Orange.

Now we climb to the next level. As we arrive, we see that here everything is Yellow. Now we are breathing in Yellow with each inhalation. As you breathe in Yellow, you feel your mind expanding. Sense the freedom gained through the use of your mind. You feel Yellow saturating your body with happiness and a joy of living. Look around, everything you see is Yellow.
Feel this yellow.

Now it is time to climb to the next level, and now we feel great peace and tranquility as we enter the Green world. Everything at this level is Green. It is the midpoint in our climb and a time for rest. We are aware that we must alternate activity with rest. Breathe in Green with each inhalation. See the color coming into your lungs. Feel the balance within yourself. The Green is soothing your muscles and relaxing your body and your mind. Everything you see is Green.
Feel this Green.

All right. We have rested. And now we climb further and reach the Blue plateau. Everything is Blue. We begin to sense

Part One - **Shine like a star**... *the aloha way*

eternity, for we have left the valley and our sight has no limitations. We can see both heaven and earth. Breathe in this Blue and feel faith entering your body. The Blue takes away all anxieties as you get a glimpse of true understanding. Everything you see is Blue, feel this Blue.

With this faith within you, we now climb higher and gradually enter the Indigo level. Everything you see has that deep Indigo quality. Breathe in this color and feel your intuitive perception increasing. You are beginning to see the larger picture, beyond the little personal problems, to get a sense of the journey of life. Breathe in the Indigo with each inhalation. Feel this Indigo.

This Indigo breath is filling your body with love – for yourself and for all mankind. For you realize we are all one family.

With this knowledge, we almost float up the mountain reaching the summit. Here we see that everything has turned Violet. As we breathe in this Violet color, we seem to see to eternity. And though it is the unknown, we are not afraid. For we have within us courage, balance, joy, peace, faith, love and understanding. With each Violet breath, feel the understanding of the truth of the universe filling your very being. Your flaws and your faults drop away and you see yourself as shining perfection. Everything you see is Violet. Feel this Violet.

You are truly one with all life. You know it. You sense it. You feel it. You will carry this with you wherever you go.

Everything we learn, we tuck away in our minds. It is all useful at some time and some place. Today we have all come here for a reason. Let's take this knowledge with us and put it to use in our own lives.

This is a good day and we rejoice in the joy of living. All right now, let us slowly come back.

–Louise Hay

1:70 Full Spectrum Energy Technique

1. Visualize a golden/white light.
2. Breathe in to your stomach area through your nose.
3. When breathing out shoot the bright light out through your arms and hands.
4. Breathe in to your stomach area through your nose.
5. When breathing out shoot the bright light out through your arms, hands and head.
6. Breathe in to your stomach area through your nose
7. When breathing out shoot the bright light out through your legs and feet.
8. Breathe in to your stomach area through your nose.
9. When breathing out shoot the bright light out through your head, hands and feet, creating the azurii star of light.
10. Breathe in through your nose directing **red** colored light into your **root chakra.**
11. Breathe in through your nose directing **orange** colored light into your **sexual chakra**.
12. Breathe in through your nose directing **yellow** colored light into your **solar plexus chakra**.
13. Breathe in through your nose directing **green** colored light into your **heart chakra**.
14. Breathe in through your nose directing **blue** colored light into your **throat chakra**.
15. Breathe in through your nose directing **indigo** colored light into your **brow chakra**.
16. Breathe in through your nose directing **violet** colored light into your **crown chakra**.

    Finally:
17. Breathe in the golden/white light into your stomach area through your nose.
18. Fill your whole body with golden/white and rainbow light.
19. When breathing out shoot the bright golden light out through your mouth and fill your aura with its magnificence.
20. You are now fully charged to face anything that comes your way.

azura
spirit of aloha ~ in action

azura~ is a noun and a verb, a seat of energy. It's the essence of aloha, the manifestation of the aloha spirit, living in balance and harmony in an often crazy, fast and furious, world.

azura~ is the spiritual home of the Starlite system and the azurii O'hana.

azura~ is 'the spirit of aloha~ in action'… there is nothing else like it.

Practiced by artisans using skills passed down by generations...
—Koko

We shall extend and display respect to all others which reflects our own appreciation of humanity. We shall carry our pride quietly, neither boasting of ourselves nor speaking badly of others, often a dishonest method of self-praise.
– Hawaiian code of conduct.

STARDANCE - Flow with Energy

1:71 Starlite Energy

Tapping into the Starlite zone is a method of empowerment that can be used to radiate the true essence of aloha love energy to others in need of compassion and healing. Using this ancient wisdom to enhance modern complementary therapy is a great way to show gratitude to the ancestors for the sharing of the secret.

Starlite energy can be used by any therapist and in any therapy to raise the vibration of energy and enhance the quality of healing, making the impossible possible!

The bodywork and massage techniques are practiced by artisans and have been passed down through generations of masters at the azurii beach school of massage on the mystical Isle de la azura who have now been infused with the energy of the Starlite method. As a result two enchanting island therapies – Honu (massage) and Hoku (bodywork) – are now being shared with the world for the first time in over a thousand years.

In my previous book *Starlite ~ The Secret Lomi* I introduced the energy of Starlite into a bodycare system, but Starlite is more than that; it's also a method of self-empowerment that can be used in the healing arts and any other way of life to bring about a paradigm change and a new cycle of human consciousness. It is a bridge between the transpersonal world of spirit and the physical world of form. Western doctors still don't understand the nature of this dynamic, but never in the history of the earth has there been a time like this.

With this expanded understanding I am pleased to present a completely revised, improved and updated healing art, the bodycare course, embracing the principles of the Starlite method and which enables the student to learn Honu (island massage) and/or Hoku (island bodywork) as they proceed through a systematic method of personal growth and empowerment.

When using the Starlite energy in the healing arts, always remember that whatever your consciousness is predominantly focused on will be expressed through the magnetic field of your aura.

- *Raise the vibration to a level of healing.*
- *Focus on love, happiness and joy.*
- *Be young at heart.*
- *Give good vibrations.*
- *Willful - the ability to influence through mental power.*
- *Conscious - a knowledgeable stream of awareness.*
- *Intent - concentrated attention to a specific purpose.*

From the very first module you will be introduced to the mystical techniques that make up the central core of this amazing energy bodycare system and the shamanic principles found within Huna; you will learn how to embrace spiritual energy and apply it to loving touch healing. You will learn the art of Oceanic Laulima, an ancient energy work with special healing powers. Step by step, you will be introduced to aloha touch and active release techniques that make up the central core of this beautiful bodycare system.

You will learn basic to advanced techniques of soft tissue mobilization, how to increase joint range of motion, improve skeletal alignment and anatomical balance of the body. You will learn how to release stress and tension actively, activate the hormonal and chemical interchange in the body and bring about improved health and well-being.

You will learn how to weave loving energy from the cosmos, sparks of light, into these beautifully choreographed techniques, creating a magical shamanic dance, infused with the spirit of aloha.

You will explore the infinite possibilities of this powerful and potentially life-changing esoteric healing therapy, learn to ride cosmic waves and experience a multi-dimensional universe where shamanism and quantum physics merge in an ocean of pure potentiality.

This course is lomilomi in its purest form – spirit touching spirit. It is an adventure in discovering and loving your emotional body, the sharing of aloha, love, caring, and compassion. You will be able to experience the magic of the Oceanic people and have a foundation for the adventure of a lifetime.

Bodywork benefits

Lomilomi (Honu) massage

The benefits of lomilomi (Honu) massage

There are many benefits of receiving a (Honu) massage or a (Hoku) body alignment treatment. This massage can be of benefit for all of the following conditions:

- *Alleviate low-back pain and improve range of motion.*
- *Assist with shorter, easier labor for expectant mothers and shorten maternity hospital stays.*
- *Ease medication dependence.*
- *Enhance immunity by stimulating lymph flow – the body's natural defense system.*
- *Exercise and stretch weak, tight, or atrophied muscles.*
- *Help athletes of any level prepare for, and recover from, strenuous workouts.*
- *Improve the condition of the body's largest organ – the skin.*
- *Increase joint flexibility.*
- *Lessen depression and anxiety.*
- *Promote tissue regeneration, reducing scar tissue and stretch marks.*
- *Pump oxygen and nutrients into tissues and vital organs, improving circulation.*

Part One - Shine like a star… the aloha way

- *Reduce post-surgery adhesions and swelling.*
- *Reduce spasms and cramping.*
- *Relax and soften injured, tired, and overused muscles.*
- *Release endorphins – amino acids that work as the body's natural painkiller.*
- *Relieve migraine pain.*

A powerful ally

There's no denying the power of bodywork. Regardless of the adjectives we assign to it (pampering, rejuvenating, therapeutic) or the reasons we seek it out (a luxurious treat, stress relief, pain management), Honu massage therapy can be a powerful ally in your healthcare regime.

Experts estimate that more than 90% of disease is stress related, and perhaps nothing ages us faster, internally and externally, than high stress. While eliminating anxiety and pressure altogether in this fast-paced world may be idealistic, massage can, without a doubt, help manage stress. This translates into:

- *Decreased anxiety*
- *Enhanced sleep quality*
- *Greater energy*
- *Improved concentration*
- *Increased circulation*
- *Reduced fatigue*

Furthermore, clients often report a sense of perspective and clarity after receiving a massage. The emotional balance bodywork provides can often be just as vital and valuable as the more tangible physical benefits.

Profound effects

In response to massage, specific physiological and chemical changes cascade throughout the body, with profound effects. Research shows that with massage:

- *Arthritis sufferers note fewer aches and less stiffness and pain.*
- *Asthmatic children show better pulmonary function and increased peak air flow.*
- *Burn injury patients report reduced pain, itching and anxiety.*
- *High blood pressure patients demonstrate lower diastolic blood pressure, anxiety and stress hormones.*
- *Premenstrual syndrome sufferers have decreased water retention and cramping.*
- *Preterm infants have improved weight gain.*

Research continues to show the enormous benefits of touch, which range from treating chronic diseases, neurological disorders and injuries to alleviating the tensions of modern lifestyles. Consequently, the medical community is actively embracing bodywork, and massage is becoming an integral part of hospice care and neonatal intensive care units. Many hospitals are also incorporating on-site massage practitioners and even spas to treat post-surgery or pain patients as part of the recovery process.

Increase the benefits with frequent visits

Getting a massage can do you a world of good and getting massage frequently can do even more. This is the beauty of bodywork. Taking part in this form of regularly scheduled self-care can play a huge part in how healthy you'll be and how youthful you'll remain with each passing year. Budgeting time and money for bodywork at consistent intervals is truly an investment in your health. And remember: just because massage feels like a pampering treat doesn't mean it is any less therapeutic. Consider massage appointments a necessary piece of your health and wellness plan, and work with your practitioner to establish a treatment schedule that best meets your needs.

The art of lomilomi (Kalaunu) massage

Kalaunu is a form of relaxing and energizing massage that focuses on the face, head, neck, shoulders, upper back and upper arms which are important energy centers within the body. This form of massage is very relaxing and has a balancing effect on the recipient as it helps them to release stress and tension, creating a sense of peace and well-being. Because this form of massage is done over the clothing in a seated position it can be done anywhere and at any time, making it easily available just about anywhere.

What are some of the benefits of Kalaunu massage?

- *General relaxation.*
- *Improved blood circulation increasing oxygen supply to the brain.*
- *Calms, revitalizes and uplifts the spirit.*
- *Can create a more balanced state of being, and balancing of the chakras.*
- *Relaxes taut and uncomfortable muscles, eases stiffness, breaks down knots and nodules in muscle tissues.*
- *Stimulates blood circulation and drains away accumulated toxins.*
- *Increased joint mobility.*
- *Improved lymphatic drainage which helps in the removal of waste products and toxins helping the immune system.*
- *Stimulation of energy meridians affects the health of the whole body.*
- *Can give your hair a healthy lustrous shine and improve skin condition.*
- *Encourages deeper breathing and deep relaxation; very enjoyable and triggers the release of "feel good" chemicals called endorphins creating an almost euphoric sensation of contentment and happiness.*
- *Promotion of hair growth.*
- *Helps to dissipate mental tiredness, stress and depression resulting in greater mental alertness and concentration and clearer thinking.*

Can also help relieve the following conditions:
- *Eye-strain*
- *Tension headaches*
- *Migraines*
- *Earaches*
- *Tinnitus*
- *Jaw ache*
- *Sinusitis*
- *Insomnia*

Lomilomi (Hoku) body alignment
Benefits of (Hoku) bodywork

Hoku is bodywork which blends the principles of osteopathy, chiropractic and structural integration to relieve chronic pain, and to reduce the potential for the emergence of pain which could become chronic over time. This technique is often integrated into regular massage and bodywork sessions, and it can also be used alone to treat systemic problems.

The basic idea behind Hoku bodywork is that tight, stressed muscles contribute to pain by limiting freedom of movement, while weak muscles provide inadequate support for the body. This in turn leads to posture problems, stiffness, and other symptoms which create an endless cycle of pain. By addressing the fundamental issues in the muscles and fascia, practitioners hope to eliminate the associated symptoms.

Structural integration and alignment both rely heavily on the mobilization of the muscles, fascia and skeletal system with the goal of promoting general musculoskeletal health. The idea behind structural integration is that if someone's body can be aligned properly, their health problems can be dramatically reduced, because the body will work as a whole. Professional practitioners share this idea, arguing that many chronic health conditions are related to musculoskeletal problems. The human brain communicates through the body's nervous system, sending messages through our spinal column, so it's easy to see how taking care of this conduit of messages to every single part of our bodies is so important. Routine chiropractic care is vital to maintaining good overall health and regularly visiting a Hoku practitioner can have a significant positive impact on your overall well-being.

What can Hoku help?

- *Muscle aches and pains*
- *Whiplash injuries*
- *Repetitive strain injuries*
- *Trapped nerves*
- *Frozen shoulder (adhesive capsulitis)*
- *Runners knee (illiotibial band syndrome)*
- *Joint imbalance (one leg shorter than the other)*

Benefits

- *Release of pain and discomfort*
- *Corrects the skeletal frame*
- *Realigns muscles and fascia*
- *Improves posture and deep-seated postural habits*
- *Enhances freedom of movement and vitality*
- *Muscular aches, pains and strains*
- *Repetitive strain injuries (RSI)*
- *Golfer's and tennis elbow*
- *Carpal tunnel syndrome*
- *Nerve pain*
- *Frozen shoulder*
- *Plantar fasciatis and many more*
- *Helps reduce pain and speeds recovery*
- *Relaxes and strengthens weak muscles*
- *Increases circulation and aids in removing waste products from the muscles, such as lactic acid*
- *Aids tissue repair*

Starlite energy (in Honu and Hoku)

Starlite is a method of connecting to the divine essence of life force energy and transfusing it into the healing arts. A therapist would have developed an understanding of a deeper knowledge of spiritual consciousness that comes from the connection to the Divine through the higher self. Life energy, the vital life force or universal life force that is present in all living things and emanates outward from the inner being, is transfused into the treatment.

What are some of the benefits of energy transmission during massage/bodywork?

- *It helps supports the body's ability to heal itself naturally and at an accelerated rate.*
- *There is a re-energizing and integration of the body and soul. This can re-establish a connection to many areas of your life.*
- *It promotes well-being on all levels: mental, emotional, physical and spiritual.*
- *It loosens up any blocked energy.*
- *It cleanses the body of toxins, thereby encouraging healing.*
- *Nervous system is balanced and allows one to deal with life's problems more effectively.*
- *Enhances the body's natural healing process.*
- *Development of healthy positive habits.*
- *Control of one's life.*
- *Freedom.*

> *The role of the mystic is to find love, and reveal the love, that lies latent in every circumstance.*
>
> -Marianne Williamson

Part Two

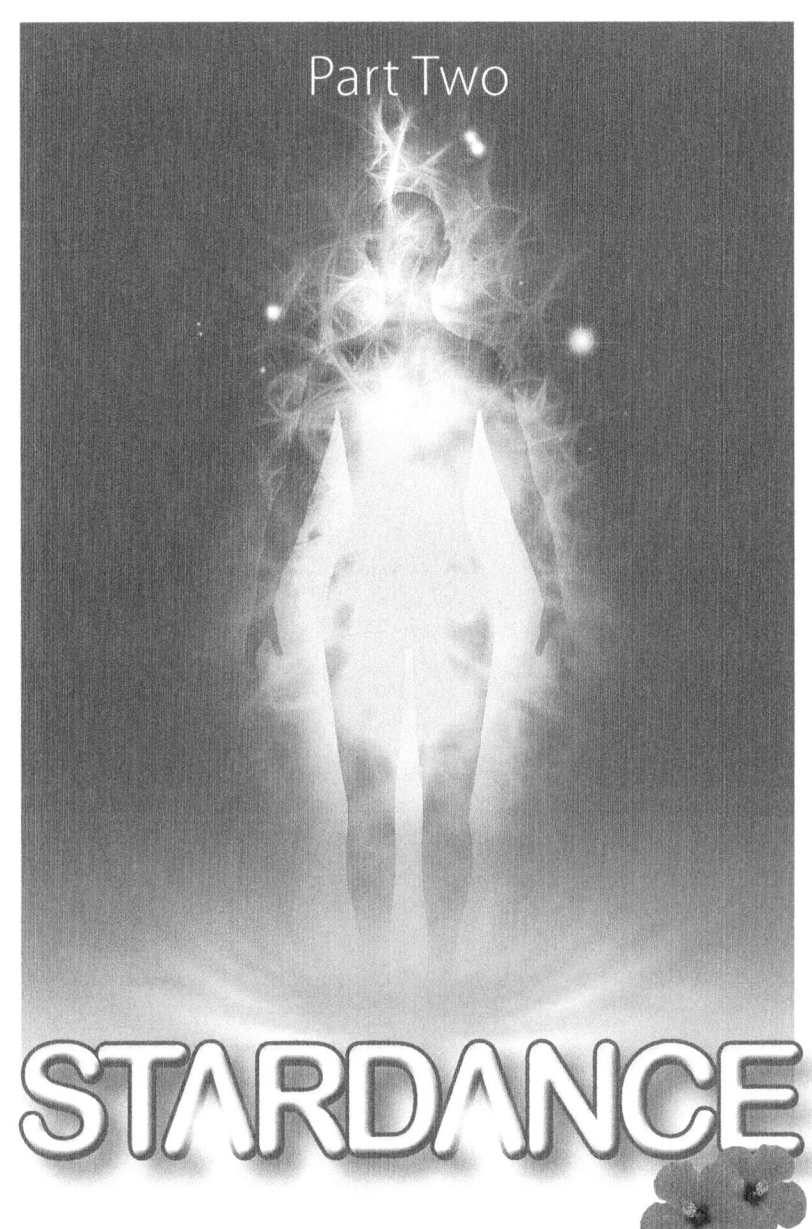

STARDANCE

Flow with Energy
Shine like a star … the aloha way

Part Two

2:72 Aloha philosophy in practice

Managing with Aloha is the name of our philosophy for living a good life with great work. It's something we practice daily, in **living, working, managing *and* leading** with aloha. We welcome you to join us.

> *Every single day, somewhere in the world,*
> *aloha comes to life.*
>
> *As it lives and breathes within us, it defines the epitome of sincere, gracious and intuitively perfect customer service given from one person to another.*
>
> **Managing with Aloha:**
> *Bringing Hawaii's Universal Values to the Art of Business*
>
> -Rosa Say

Aloha is the value of unconditional love, of self and of others. Aloha literally translates to "being in the presence of the life's spirit," and it is a sharing which is therefore thought of as the outpouring and receiving of a person's inner spirit. That inner spirit is more than a simple projection of positive character or personality; it is an incredible source of energy for us as human beings.

2:73 The values of Aloha:

ALOHA:
Aloha is a value, one of unconditional love.
Aloha is the outpouring and receiving of the spirit.

HOʻOHANA:
The value of work: To work with intent and with purpose.

ʻIMI OLA:
To "seek best life." Our purpose in life is to seek its highest form.
The value of mission and vision.

HOʻOMAU:
The value of perseverance. To persist, to continue, to
perpetuate. Never give up.

KULIŪLIA I KA NUʻU:
The value of achievement. "Strive to reach the summit."
Pursue personal excellence in all you do.

HOʻOKIPA:
The value of hospitality, a hospitality of complete giving.
Welcome guests and strangers with your spirit of aloha.

ʻOHANA:
Those who are family, and those you choose to call your family.
As a value, ʻOhana is a human circle of complete aloha.

LŌKAHI:
The value of teamwork: Collaboration and cooperation.
Harmony and unity. People who work together can achieve more.

KĀKOU:
The value of communication, for all of us. We are in this together.
Learn to speak the language of we.

KULEANA:
One's personal sense of responsibility.
I accept my responsibilities, and I will be held accountable.

'IKE LOA:

The value of learning. To know well.
To seek knowledge and wisdom.

HA'AHA'A:

The value of humility. Be humble, be modest, and open your thoughts.

HO'OHANOHANO:

To honor the dignity of others.
Conduct yourself with distinction, and cultivate respectfulness.

ALAKA'I:

The value of leadership. Lead with initiative,
and with your good example.
You shall be the guide for others when you have gained
their trust and respect.

MĀLAMA:

The value of stewardship. To take care of.
To serve and to honor, to protect and care for.

MAHALO:

Thank you as a way of living.
Live in thankfulness for the richness that makes life so precious.

NĀNĀ I KE KUMU:

Look to your sense of place and sources of spirit,
and you find your truth.

PONO:

The value of integrity, of rightness and balance.
The feeling of contentment when all is good and all is right.

KA LĀ HIKI OLA:

The dawning of a new day. Optimism.
The value of hope and promise

-Rosa Say

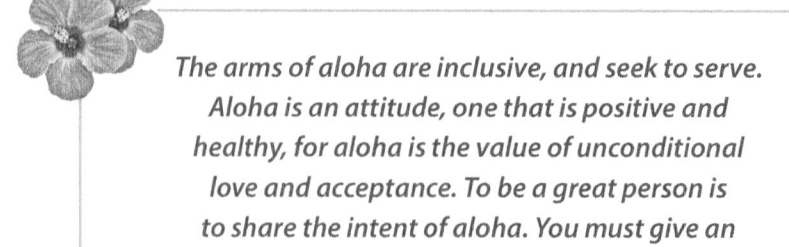

> *The arms of aloha are inclusive, and seek to serve. Aloha is an attitude, one that is positive and healthy, for aloha is the value of unconditional love and acceptance. To be a great person is to share the intent of aloha. You must give an outpouring of your spirit, and you must receive theirs.*
>
> –Rosa Say

2:74 Crossroads

> *For the most part wisdom comes in chips rather than blocks. You have to be willing to gather them constantly, and from sources you never imagined to be probable. No one chip gives you the answer for everything. No one chip stays in the same place throughout your entire life. The secret is to keep adding voices, adding ideas, and moving things around as you put together your life. If you are lucky, putting together your life is a process that will last through every single day you're alive.*
>
> –Ann Patchett

Welcome to the edge of tomorrow, as we say goodbye to today what will the new dawn bring? Will you settle for yesterday's doubts, fears and worries? Or will you embrace a new beginning, a fresh start, with anticipation, courage and a loving heart?

The path ahead is challenging, you will need courage, determination and tenacity to reach the far side. But if you make it, you could find riches beyond all expectation.

Turn the page if you dare…

But once you make your choice and leap into the abyss there is no going back!

Question	A=Yes	B=No
Are you interested in complementary therapy?		
Do you consider yourself as spiritual?		
Are you a parent or carer?		
Do you like soft, gentle, healing music?		
Are you involved with supporting charities?		
Do you like Hula, leis and everything Hawaiian?		
Are you over 25 years old?		
Have your heard of Huna before?		
Do you know who Serge Kahali King is?		

Question	A=No	B=Yes
Are you under 25 years old?		
Do you like indi, garage or Rap music?		
Are you a heavy user of social media?		
Do you get frustrated easily?		
Do you see yourself as a rebel?		
Do you think that nobody understands you?		
Do you go clubbing, dancing or drinking regularly?		
Are you out of work?		
Do you want to scream at the world?		

What is your path going to be? Take the test and see!
Mostly **A**s go to **The Aloha Diet** (page 229)

Mostly **B**s go to **Stardust** (page 269)

Guidelines

a. Choose one or the other.
b. Do not look at the other path (or even peek at it) until you have completed the one you have chosen.
c. Read, do and complete each step in order.
d. Do not look at or read the next step until you have completed the one you are on.
e. You may take an extra day on each step if necessary.

♪ *I Wish you more luck then you need.* ♪

Jimmy Buffet

Welcome
to the beautiful **Aloha Diet**
introducing you to
the food of life

THE ALOHA DIET

... it starts here!

Flow with Energy
Shine like a star ... the aloha way

Aloha Diet

2:75 Aloha diet

I have been fortunate to have worked in the healing arts since 1970, and for the last 15 years or so, I have studied the healing arts of the Pacific islands. This eventually led to a philosophy called Huna – the way of aloha. A way of life that lives and breathes with the essence of love, kindness, compassion and gratitude on a daily basis.

> *We are here and it is now…*
> -H. L. Mencken

I started to apply the principles to my own life and gradually saw many improvements and changes beyond expectation. As I changed so did my practice with astonishing results. I wanted to share this aloha magic with everyone and in particular other healing artists; the Starlite method was designed as a bridge between the spiritual and the physical, a safe passage for new travelers. This method enables those with a practical western mind to explore and discover another reality, one baby step at a time, without abandoning the illusionary safety of their own reality.

> *The rainbow is energy that bridges the earth and the heavens. Starlite is energy that bridges the human spirit with that of the divine.* –Koko

Aloha is the most beautiful word in the world.

Aloha is the divine essence of life force energy – the energy of unconditional love. To live and breathe aloha on a day-to-day basis is the ultimate achievement.

The problem is how we get to that position from where we stand right now with our complicated life issues, problems and concerns. We would all like to have a life full of love and gratitude, where people are helpful and kind. But where do we start, how do we start?

> **One person must choose a new way of being and live that difference to create a paradigm and new possibilities.**
>
> –Gregg Brandon

There are and have been many paths; now, for the first time since the light of the heavens rained down upon the earth, the "spark" of creation has revealed the "pathway of the stars" – an enlightened path, a route that embraces the principles of aloha and encourages you to shine your light on a dark world, become the star of your life.

The Starlite experience has been described as a little diet of aloha; it is a method of self-acceptance, empowerment and love, bringing balance, synergy and harmony to our very core. Our true might lies in the fact that we are unique "sparks of divinity." Acknowledgement and acceptance of our authenticity as great, powerful and mighty spiritual beings of light, living in a physical world with dignity, direction and purpose is the starting point.

When we reach a point of universal equilibrium it becomes a simple step – and conversely also a quantum leap – to embrace the joy of our own beauty, greatness and wonderment. We are then no longer separated from the divine light, we are the light.

> ♪ *Can't stop me now*
> *The world is waiting*
> *It's my turn to stand out from the crowd.* ♪
>
> -Rod Stewart

The science behind the diet

Be all that you can be...

The Aloha Diet has taken the world by storm!

The Aloha Diet is a diet of love, light and aloha (the divine essence of life force energy) – it is the food/fruit of life.

But how does it work? Why does it work? What is the science behind the success of the diet?

This diet is not about giving up eating, it's about abundance. Like all diets it's about reducing the intake of one energy source and increasing the intake of another energy source. But the energy source referred to in the Aloha Diet is not fatty foods, sugar, carbohydrates, fiber or protein. It is about replacing the destructive element of negative energy with the powerful, enhancing, vibrating, loving energy of aloha. It is not too much to state that this is a life-changing diet, for once you have tasted the fruit of aloha you will never want to be the same again.

The science behind the diet can be found within the pages of this book and all the inspirational books listed in the bibliography at the back.

> *The flowers of all our tomorrows*
> *are in the seeds of today.*
>
> – Pacific island proverb

Introduction

How to use this section:

- ✓ *There are a number of steps for you to take over the next 30 days.*
- ✓ *Complete each step before moving on, even if it takes longer than the allotted time.*
- ✓ *The first step is different from the rest and introduces you to three "power foods" which you should use every day at the appropriate time in addition to the requirements of each step.*
- ✓ *From there on each step will give a brief explanation, this is called the "little what" (when, where, why, how).*
- ✓ *Those of you who may want the "bigger what" – the science both physical and metaphysical behind the Aloha Diet –*
- ✓ *should first read Starlite ~ the Secret Lomi.*
- *There is an affirmation related to the step at hand and should be repeated several times every day for the duration of that step.*
- ✓ *Next there is a pre-action which is designed to prepare you for action.*
- ✓ *This is followed by a little action, a comfortable taste of what's to come.*
- ✓ *The main action of each step is designed to push your comfort zone, encouraging personal growth through life experience.*
- ✓ *Before we start, write down five things, pets or people that you love; they must put a smile on your face and evoke feelings of love and joy.*
- ✓ *Finally there is the end of task reflection; you may find it helpful to write down your thoughts when undertaking this exercise.*

STARDANCE - Flow with Energy

Reflection:

*Part Two - **Shine like a star**… the aloha way*

Questionnaire

Answering the questions is a process that can be valuable in itself. It gives you the opportunity to look at many aspects of your values, beliefs and life skills. It gives you the opportunity to think about what is important to you and what aspects of yourself you would like to improve.

Mark yourself between 0-10: zero is low and ten is high; five is average. You are only comparing against yourself, no one else needs to see this questionnaire. Be honest.

Question	Before	After
I get anxious meeting new people		
I find it difficult to take criticism		
I fear being made to look stupid		
I fear making a speech		
I am easily embarrassed		
I feel interior to others		
I get defensive quickly		
I find it difficult to focus on one thing		
I do not set goals for the future		

Question	Before	After
I spend most of my time in a happy mood		
I spend most of my time in an unhappy mood		
I am grateful for the good things in my life		
I focus on the things I don't have in my life		
I find it hard to forgive people		
I often do random acts of kindness		
I often tell those closest to me that I love them		
I am happy about my future		
I find it hard to share my emotions		

Day 1:

Good Morning

What a beautiful day...

Daily power foods~ the fruit of aloha:

Start of day affirmation

- Close your eyes, place your attention on your stomach and breathe in through your nose, keeping your attention on your stomach, switch your attention to your heart, breathe out through your mouth with an audible haaa; repeat three times.
- Say to yourself: what a beautiful (sunny, spring, windy, rainy) day, may my eyes and heart be open to the day's lessons, gifts and blessings.
- And may the spirit of aloha live in and radiate from me.
- Breathe in and out…
- It is done…
- Relax and receive, you have now called upon the spirit of aloha for help and healing.
- Mahalo & Blessings…
- Breathe in and out, this time with a long sigh type of sound.
- In your own good time, when you are ready, open your eyes… welcome to your day, you have connected to the spirit of aloha; the spirit of unconditional love.

Good Night

That was a beautiful day...

Evening reflection

- *The best time is just before going to sleep.*

- *Relax, clear the mind of clutter and take a few deep breaths, just as you would before meditation.*

- *Reflect over the day's events and find something that you are grateful for, and then give thanks. Find a lesson that you have learned, and then give thanks. Find something or someone that you felt blessed about, and then give thanks. You may not find all three in one day, but that's okay, as long as you have one and give thanks with all your heart.*

- *If someone has wronged you or you have wronged someone else, real or perceived, surround the situation with love and light, forgive them and ask for forgiveness in return.*

- *Reflect on the food of love that you consumed during the day's aloha diet activities.*

- *Now think of something good you have done today, maybe something you are proud of, or a simple act of kindness, or a moment of love, of grace. Thank spirit with gratitude from your heart.*

- *Say Mahalo & Blessings then go to sleep.*

Power Break

This is a beautiful day...

Power break

Take a moment's break, inside or outside it does not matter.

Place your attention on your stomach and breathe in through your nose, keeping your attention on your stomach, breathe out through your mouth.

Have a slow look around your surroundings and find something to focus on (it could be a flower, a blade of grass, a dog, or even the clouds) and for two minutes, no more, really focus on the item. If it's a blade of grass, see the colors, the sheen on one side of the leaf and the matt underside. Imagine touching it, really feel it in your fingers, smell it, and really appreciate its beauty.

At the end of the two minutes, give thanks for the lesson, say Mahalo and go back to work.

Beauty has a healing power all of its own

Smile
Days 2-3

Smile and the whole world smiles with you…

You have a choice each day, to be in a positive or negative state. If you choose negative you will look and feel miserable… try smiling.

It will bring good things to you, be open to the world, to new things, and to inner beauty. Have a positive attitude because good things come to good people. Laughing will give you a little piece of happiness even if it's only for a while. If you laugh and smile, you will start to learn how to be happy and love yourself.

Happiness is the only positive emotion we can show through our face. People aren't good at giving genuine smiles. There seems to be a problem with getting eyes and mouth in harmony. If you smile with just your mouth and not your eyes it gives that "snarling" look.

–James Borg

- *You have a choice each day to be happy or sad, positive or negative.*
- *Smiling puts you in a positive state.*
- *Feeling more positive helps you achieve more positive outcomes.*
- *It costs you nothing but the payback is fantastic.*
- *It increases blood flow to the brain.*
- *It releases hormones that make you feel better.*
- *Your stress levels go down.*
- *You become more relaxed.*
- *People become more attracted to you.*
- *People become more willing to listen to your point of view.*

You will leave a trail of goodwill behind you…

> **Affirmation:**
> *I am brightness and I will shine my light on the world.*

Pre-action:

Take one item, any item, for your love list – close your eyes and think of the item, really think of it and smile.

Take a deep breath in through your nose, sucking the happy feeling deep into your stomach area; switch your attention to your head as you breathe out through your mouth.

Repeat three times.

Little Action:

1. Smile at a stranger, notice if you get one back.
2. Try to get five return smiles or more over the next two days.
3. When someone cuts you up on the road, takes your seat on the train, or gets in your way, just smile.

Big Action: ★★★

Learn the smile poem, (below) it will make you smile – forever more.

> **Reflection:**
> *Before you go to sleep reflect on your day and how this exercise made you feel.*

Everyone knows that smiling is infectious
~ you catch it like the flu
Someone smiled at me~ and I started too
I looked around the room~ and someone saw me grin
And when he smiled I realized~ I'd passed it on to him
I've thought about my smile a lot~ and
realized all it's worth
A single smile like mine or yours~ could
travel around the earth
So if you feel a smile begin~ don't leave it undetected
Start an epidemic quick~ and get the world infected!
A wave of aloha starts~ with a single smile…

Found at London Heathrow

Gratitude
Days 4-6

Fill your life with words of love and gratitude…

Look at people in your life as a gift and appreciate them along with the experiences they bring. Do not judge the experience as good or bad but simply as a gift of personal growth. Be grateful and kindness will follow.

*Part Two - **Shine like a star** … the aloha way*

- *Be grateful for all that you are.*
- *Flow with an attitude of serendipity through all kinds of experiences.*
- *Be grateful for your body and bless every part of your body.*
- *Develop an attitude of gratitude.*
- *Be grateful for what you have, don't dwell on what you don't have.*

Always pay forward gratitude; for someone's kindness often makes us want to reciprocate, weaving a web of aloha.

Affirmation:
I am so grateful for all the goodness in my life.

Pre-action:

Make a gratitude list – a list of all the good, helpful, supporting things, places and people you have in your life.

Start by heading up a piece of paper with titles such as: people, pets, places, food, movies, music. In fact you can add absolutely anything as long as you really like/love it and are grateful that it exists in your life.

You can even have a list of people or events that you may not like but nevertheless are grateful that they/it was a part of your life – for example, a teacher who may have been hard on you but you now appreciate why.

You can make the list even more special by adding drawings, photos or any other reminder of a person or object on the list.

Little Action:

- *Write down the top ten from your list, it can be a mixture of anything on the list.*
- *Start at number one from your love list – close your eyes and think of the item, really think of it and smile.*
- *Take a deep breath in through your nose, sucking the happy feeling deep into your stomach area.*
- *Say quietly or out loud: I am so grateful that you are in my life; I thank you for the happiness you bring me… bless you.*
- *Switch your attention to your head as you breathe out through your mouth.*
- *Repeat the process for each item in your top ten.*
- *Gradually work your way through the rest of your list over the three days.*

Big Action:

- *Choose one person on your gratitude list and write a thank you card to them, and tell them how they have inspired and influenced your life.*
- *Send the card to them.*
- *If you are brave enough, hand deliver the card and read it out to them (this will really test your comfort zone).*

Reflection:
Before you go to sleep reflect on your day and how this exercise made you feel.

Part Two - **Shine like a star**… *the aloha way*

Self- Acceptance
Days 7-8

Don't change for anyone...

Love yourself for you, for your great attitude toward the world, for your caring about others not just yourself, and for being you. Be grateful for who you are.

> ***To be beautiful means to be yourself. You don't need to be accepted by others. You need to accept yourself.***
> –Thich Nhat Hanh

Your inner critic will flood you with thoughts of I'm not enough, I don't have enough, and I don't do enough. Feeling worthy requires you to see yourself with fresh eyes of self-awareness and love. Acceptance and love must come from within. You don't have to be different to be worthy. Your worth is in your true nature, a core of love and inner goodness. You are a beautiful light. You are love. We can bury our magnificence, but it's impossible to destroy...

- *Learn to love and accept yourself exactly as you are.*
- *Breathe in and radiate love/aloha every day.*
- *You are more than good enough and get better every day.*
- *Give up the right to criticize yourself.*
- *Adopt the mindset to praise yourself.*
- *Fully approve of who you are.*
- *Be both good and great at all times of day and night.*
- *Let go of fears and worries that drain your energy for no good return.*
- *Let go of blame and speak your truth authentically and without judgment.*

Dance in the body you have, and live the life you have, with no excuses and no regrets.

STARDANCE - Flow with Energy

Affirmation:
*I see perfection in all my flaws
and all my goodness.*

Pre-action:

- Make a "what I love about me" list – a list of all the good, helpful and supporting things you do in your life.
- This will range from jobs to family to volunteer groups; here you list the things you do that you can be proud of.
- Try finding things you have never noticed about yourself, like a great personality or maybe your warm smile.
- Now we get personal.
- Continue with all the things you like about yourself, your attitude, your willingness to help, your kindness, if need be add quotes, identify an incident.
- Finally list all the things you like about your body, even if it's only one thing. The secret here is not to focus on what you don't like but simply to focus on the bits that you do like/love.
- You can make the list even more special by adding drawings, photos or any other reminder of a person or object on the list.

Little Action:

- Look at a mirror.
- Look into your eyes.
- Choose the one eye you are drawn to (this may change each time).
- Look deep into your eye, with the intention of connecting to your spirit being (the body of light inside).
- Say thank you and I love you to your spirit for letting you have this human experience.
- Say thank you to your body for housing your spirit during this experience.
- Promise to look after it, say I love you.
- Carry on with your day.

*Part Two - **Shine like a star**… the aloha way*

Big Action: ★★★

- *Put some time aside for yourself.*
- *Accept and love yourself – how?*
- *Acknowledge that we are spiritual beings, beings of light, beings of love, here to have the human experience.*
- *Therefore we consist of a physical entity and a spiritual entity.*
- *Our physical human body/mind is limited to existence here on earth.*
- *Thank it by repeating the little action.*
- *Our spiritual body consists of soul/spirit and is the eternal you, the part that lives on forever*
- *Thank it by saying I am sorry for ignoring you, please forgive me, I love you… I love me!*
- *Look in a mirror and say out loud: I forgive me.*
- *Show yourself love through a hug by hugging the real you.*
- *Take a deep breath, say to yourself it is done, Mahalo, and breathe out through your mouth with a deep sigh like haa sound.*
- *Be who you really are: express yourself, laugh, play, or sing. Be crazy. Don't be afraid of what others think.*

Now reward yourself with a treat, do something nice, something special that you enjoy.

Reflection:
Before you go to sleep reflect on your day and how this exercise made you feel.

Aloha
Days 9-10

Aloha is cherishing the incredible miracle that you are...

Try to find beauty around you.

Now we put all three elements together: smile; have gratitude and love yourself; then share and radiate that love.

A true beautiful person will be able to smile and get through any problems. Don't be mean to people, try to find the good in them. Remember not to judge; if you love yourself you will be able to love anyone for who they are.

Aloha is the essence of relationships in which each person is important to every other person for collective existence.

Living aloha is the coordination of mind and heart within each person. It brings each person to the self. Each person must think and express good feelings to others.

> *We hope you will embrace the spirit of aloha in your everyday.*
> – Queen Lili'uokalani

- *Every cell in my body is full of aloha and radiates love.*
- *Throughout the day I am full of energy.*
- *Your thoughts are your reality, think of a bright new day.*
- *Fill this day with hope and face it with joy.*
- *Surround yourself with friends who treat you well.*
- *Take a power break.*

Aloha is saying love in Hawaiian, it's something we do without even trying.

Affirmation:
I live each day with happiness and joy trusting that good things will come to me.

Pre-action:

- *Think of a pet or person that you love, one that puts a smile on your face; close your eyes and think of them, really think of them and smile.*
- *Take a deep breath in through your nose, sucking the happy feeling deep into your stomach area; switch your attention to your head as you breathe out through your mouth.*
- *Repeat three times.*
- *Now you are ready for the next step.*

Little Action:

- *Today is aloha day.*
- *You have been given the gift of aloha/love to share with the world.*
- *Today when someone says hello or good morning you respond with aloha instead.*

Big Action:

- *Buy some flowers and hand them out in the street, wishing everyone a happy day.*
- *Or pick some flowers and hand them to a stranger, or any elderly person.*

Reflection:
Before you go to sleep reflect on your day and how this exercise made you feel.

STARDANCE - Flow with Energy

Compliments
Days 11-13

Compliments are little gifts of aloha...

Take a look at the person and see what you like about them. Pay attention to the details and make a mental note of how it makes you feel.

Now let the magic begin...

And yes this is the hard part.

Go up to the person and give them the compliment, be sincere, be specific, be genuine and be warm.

"I like (or I love) the way you have..." is a good introduction.

They are powerful gifts. But compliments only work if they are sincere reflections of what we think and if they are given freely and not coerced.

- ◆ *Be Genuine:*
  A genuine compliment is given without the expectation of getting anything in return. You are simply saying what needs to be said at that moment.

- ◆ *Be Specific:*
  Giving a general compliment is good, but being specific is always better, it turns good to great.

- ◆ *Be Unique:*
  This requires an extreme amount of attention to detail and a genuine interest in the other person. Being unique is a challenge, but it will set your compliment apart and give it far more impact.

- ◆ *Acknowledge their effort:*
  People will like the compliment even more if you acknowledge their effort. It shows that you appreciate what was going on behind the scenes to make it happen.

- ◆ *State how it makes you feel:*
  People like hearing about how they affect others. If you let them know that they have positively impacted you in some way, it will make them feel better.

*Part Two - **Shine like a star**... the aloha way*

You will leave a trail of sunshine behind you...

> **Affirmation:**
> *I love sharing my light with others.*

Pre-action: ★★★

A smile is a compliment, it suggests that we are worthy of attention and/or someone's appreciation. Now we are going to take this one step further with a verbal compliment.

Day 11

- *Look at someone you know and notice something you like about them. It needs to be something they have done, not something they were born with. Pay attention to the details and make a mental note of how it makes you feel.*
- *Go up to the person and give them the compliment, be sincere, be specific, be genuine and be warm.*
- *If they respond back with a thank you, just say you're welcome.*
- *If they respond back with a compliment, smile and say thank you.*
- *Your target today is three people that you know; keep at least two-hour gaps between actions.*

Little Action: ★★★

Day 12

- *Look at someone you don't know and notice something you like about them. It needs to be something they have done, not something they were born with. Pay attention to the details and make a mental note of how it makes you feel.*
- *Go up to the person and give them the compliment, be sincere, be specific, be genuine and be warm.*
- *If they respond back with a thank you, just say you're welcome.*

- *If they respond back with a compliment, smile and say thank you.*
- *Your target today is two people that you don't know; keep at least two-hour gaps between actions.*

Big Action: ★★★
Day 13

- *Look at someone you know but don't like or don't get on with and notice something you like about them. It needs to be something they have done, not something they were born with. Pay attention to the details and make a mental note of how it makes you feel.*
- **There is always something you can find that is good.**
- *Go up to the person and give them the compliment, be sincere, be specific, be genuine and be warm.*
- *If they respond back with a thank you, just say you're welcome.*
- *If they respond back with a compliment, smile and say thank you.*
- *Your target today is just one person.*

This is a difficult and challenging test. To compliment someone you don't like or don't usually get on with is a great personality growth indicator.

You need to be what you desire to become.

Maybe, if you and a friend/work colleague had a falling out a few months ago, and you see them wearing something that you think looks good on them, it doesn't hurt to tell them. Whether or not they publicly accept the compliment, inside they will probably be happy you complimented them.

And you will boost your confidence and self-esteem a little.

Reflection:
Before you go to sleep reflect on your day and how this exercise made you feel.

All creatures great and small
Days 14-16

Know the kind of joy that animals can bring...

When I come home after a long day at the hospital or the studio, the greeting I get from my black Labrador Rosie – her whole body wiggling with happiness – always makes me smile, no matter how exhausted I feel. In our household, animals outnumber humans: we also have a rabbit, five hamsters, three cats (who spend a great deal of their time peering inquisitively at the hamsters), and two tropical fish. I admit I sometimes feel like a zookeeper. But even when the litter box needs cleaning or I have to coax my son Oliver to go outside and walk Rosie before bedtime, I can honestly say I'm happy to share my home with all 12 creatures.

> *If you've ever loved a pet, you know the kind of joy animals can bring.* – Dr. Mehmet Oz

Pet owners know how much their furry friend improves their quality of life. But it's not all about unconditional love, although that actually provides a wellness boost, too. On an emotional level, owning a pet can reduce depression, stress and anxiety; health-wise, it can lower your blood pressure, improve your immunity and even reduce your risk of heart attack and stroke. But the positives don't stop there:

- *Reduces stress*
- *Lowers blood pressure*
- *Eases pain*
- *Lowers cholesterol*
- *Improves mood*
- *Helps people socialize*
- *Prevents strokes*
- *Helps children develop*

> **Affirmation:**
> *I am so grateful for the joy
> my pets bring into my life.*

Pre-action:

- Animal interaction is what this step is all about; if you have pets this will be easy, see it as a reward for your hard work up to this stage.

- If you don't have any animal contact then wow, you are in for a treat! If you don't like animals or you are frightened of them this will stretch your boundaries.

- Take extra care and attention of your own animals; give them a treat.

- If you are frightened of animals watch a few pet videos on YouTube.

- If you have no pets, walk round a pet shop, stop and look at the animals, imagine communicating with them.

Little Action:

- Animal communication is our most natural form of communication. It is a feeling-based instinct that all living beings are connected to.

- Take oats, seed or grapes to a pond and feed the ducks or wild birds; take time out and watch them feed.

- Focus on them for two minutes, really focus and imagine touching their soft feathers and silky body. Using all your expanded senses try to take in every little detail of their being as though you were capturing an image in order to draw them at a later date.

- You can swap birds for any other local animal, but it should not be one of your own pets.

*Part Two - **Shine like a star** … the aloha way*

Big Action: ★★★

- *The big action requires you to do at least one of the following suggestions, please feel free to add your own:*
- *Offer to walk your neighbor's dog or keep them company while they walk together.*
- *Offer to help brush the animal (dog/horse) for someone.*
- *Offer to help clean/feed the animals in a pet store.*
- *Offer your time to a zoo/vets/animal hospital/animal rescue charity for half a day or more.*
- *Adopt or buy a new pet and love it.*
- *The importance here is to experience new animal interaction. It will help develop unity and compassion which we most definitely need to make our lives more fulfilled with expanded awareness.*

–Dr. Mehmet Oz

Reflection:
Before you go to sleep reflect on your day and how this exercise made you feel.

Hugs
Days 17-18

Aloha is embracing the spiritual embodiment of another...

Try to find beauty around you.

We live in such a busy, crowded world yet it's so easy for many of us to go days, even weeks or months without touching or being touched by others.

While you might not notice the effects of not being touched right away, it can negatively affect your mood, your confidence and your health. Modern science is only beginning to understand the holistic way our bodies work and the relationship between our emotional well-being and our physical health.

The human needs are really simple: people want to be loved, touched, fed and to feel safe. If you were raised in a home where this was normal, you will not be able to understand how some people actually crave the human touch.

- *Hugging releases oxytocin (the cuddle hormone).*
- *Hugging builds stronger bonds.*
- *Hugging lowers stress.*
- *Hugging lowers blood pressure.*
- *Hugging feels good.*
- *Hugging can turn a bad mood upside down.*
- *Hugging reconnects the mind with the body.*
- *Hugging spreads aloha.*

Handshakes are for strangers… give me a hug!

Affirmation:
I love to give hugs and to be hugged every day.

Pre-action:

- *Practice "the hug."*
- *Put your arms around yourself, squeeze and cuddle, say I love you to yourself.*
- *Now find your nearest and dearest and do the same to them.*

Little Action:

- *Find a minimum of ten people that you know and give them a hug.*
- *Just tell them that you need a hug.*
- *If they are close, tell them that you love them, even if you haven't done so for years. Sometimes we can forget to say I love you to those closest to us.*

Big Action: ★★★

- *The big challenge is to approach a stranger and ask for a hug.*
- *Approach someone with your arms open wide and ask them for a hug.*
- *Smile, say thank you, and then move on knowing that you just might have made their day also.*
- *When you have expanded your comfort zone and feel good about your achievement, try it again.*

> **Reflection**
> *Before you go to sleep reflect on your day and how this exercise made you feel.*

Forgiveness
Days 19-21

The children of the rainbow forgive you~ aloha...

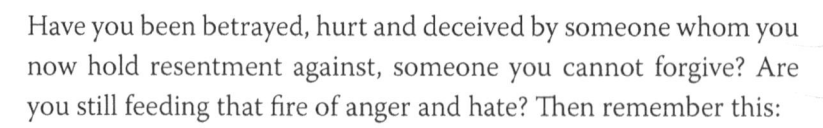

Have you been betrayed, hurt and deceived by someone whom you now hold resentment against, someone you cannot forgive? Are you still feeding that fire of anger and hate? Then remember this:

You can't be angry and hateful and at the same time be in a state of love and bliss.

When you produce the toxins of hate and anger you don't hurt the perpetrator, you just poison yourself – they win!

Kala-kala means to be released. Let go of all the psychic energy you're holding around being wronged so that it will let go of you,

For those non-perfect humans among us here is a little trick: how to forgive without letting them off the hook (if you can forgive unconditionally, do that instead).

Step 1 - *first you need to get to a place where forgiveness is possible. Ask yourself what would need to happen for you to be able to forgive. No matter how implausible that might be, we are not looking for reality, we are looking for possibility.*

Most of us want recognition that we have been wronged, followed by a sincere request for forgiveness.

Some of you may want punishment – that's fine, at this stage we are simply trying to get to a place (after a number of conditions have been met) where you find that you could forgive the trespass against you.

Step 2 - *once you have arrived and accepted that forgiveness is possible (subject to conditions), I want you to feel the emotion of forgiveness; don't forget we are now in a place where all of your conditions have been met, so really feel the emotion of forgiving, feel the emotional release of being told that you are right and were wronged. Feel the power of being asked to forgive the perpetrator who with all their heart wants your blessing.*

Now capture this emotion and place it in a small helium-filled balloon, tie it with a very fine, unbreakable thread of light and connect it to the shoulder of the person you are willing to forgive (if they request it).

Ask for forgiveness from them for any wrong, either real or perceived, that they feel you have done, this may even be feeding the fire of resentment. When you have done this you will feel a lot lighter.

This person now has your full forgiveness attached to them for life, all they have to do is request forgiveness from you, even if it's on their death bed, they just have to ask with sincerity and they will receive it. You in turn have requested forgiveness from them for any wrongs, real or perceived, against them. This is important as we all have a different view of reality; you are not giving them any power, just simply wiping the slate clean, for after this exercise there will be no future contact, either physical or energetic.

Part Two - *Shine like a star… the aloha way*

Step 3 - *the final step is to sever the energy attachment to this person, in Huna these energy cords are called Aka cords. The more energy you have sent down the cord (positive or negative), the thicker the cord and your connection to that person will be.*

Imagine an intense bright light above your head, breathe in the light, deep into your stomach, and fill your body with each breath. Once you have this bright light energy in every part of your body, put a silk tourniquet around the cord at your end and cut the cord so no energy can ever return. Now, with a deep out breath, release a generous blast of light down the cord (just like dragon's fire-breath), watch it burn and consume the cord starting at your end and traveling all the way down until it is detached and gone. Breathe more light energy into yourself and replace the energy that was used to burn the cord. If the cord was thick and the connection very strong you may need to repeat the ritual whenever you feel a possible re-growth; once or twice is usually enough to cut the other person completely out of your life.

If you feel vulnerable, breathe out and surround yourself with a protective firewall; this will burn up and destroy any attempt of reattachment from the other person. Wish them well and let them go on their way – complete with your forgiveness balloon.

You may not be able to stop people hurting you, but you do have a choice as to how long you will allow that hurt to survive. (extracted from Starlite ~ the Secret Lomi)

Why would you swap one moment of love and happiness for the fire of hate and anger?

Affirmation:
The past has no power and no hold over me anymore.

Pre-action:

Forgive yourself for holding on to anger and resentment. Say to your inner spirit: please forgive me, I love you, thank you and know with absolute certainty that you have been forgiven.

Little Action:

- *Make a list of those who have wronged you.*
- *Place them in order with the worst offender at the top and the least at the bottom.*
- *Next to their name state the wrong they have done you.*
- *Start at the bottom of the list working upward.*
- *To those that you can forgive unconditionally say I forgive you for what you did and I forgive me for holding resentment, and then let them go.*
- *Keep going until you reach the person you cannot forgive unconditionally.*
- *Cut off the bottom of the list (those you have forgiven) and burn it, severing any connection to the events.*
- *Allow a night's sleep before returning to the list.*

Big Action:

- *Starting at the top of the list (the worst offender), use the forgiveness balloon technique above and work at it until you find a way of forgiving this person.*
- *Once the worst one is done the others get easier.*
- *Work your way down the list until you have dealt with everyone and every event.*
- *Now burn the list!*
- *Take a deep breath and smile.*

Reflection:

Before you go to sleep reflect on your day and how this exercise made you feel.

*Part Two - **Shine like a star**... the aloha way*

Kindness
Days 22-23

> *You cannot do a kindness too soon for you never know how soon it will be too late.* –Ralph Waldo Emerson

Random acts of kindness

> *When you do random acts of kindness, some magic appears. Some people call it social capital. If I were Austin Powers I'd call it mojo. It's that magic substance that makes things happen.* –Ole Kassow

Love and kindness is not just about that warm fuzzy feeling that could essentially be described as an insular, self-centered, private emotion. It could be defined, even in a business context, as "an unselfish concern for the well-being of others." When done right, it engenders an infectious sense of happiness.

My neighbor did me a kindness when he cut my grass. Now I am always happy to have the opportunity of doing someone a kindness.

> *A lot of people will tell me love is sacred, it can't be genuine in a business context. Nothing could be further from the truth. Love can be both a feeling and an attitude and actions. It can be virtues of human kindness and compassion – words we can incorporate in business, and particularly in a startup, weaving it in from the start.* –Ole Kassow

Pay a kindness forward. If someone does something kind for you, do something kind for someone else, to carry that kindness forward.

- ◆ *When you do kindness, happiness ensues automatically.*
- ◆ *Speak nicely, it's free.*
- ◆ *Love and kindness is the food of aloha.*
- ◆ *Aloha should be the cornerstone of every business.*

> **Affirmation:**
> *I am a kind and considerate being of light.*

*Try to complete **at least one action** from this section.*

Pre-action:

- Start small, keep it simple.
- Hold the door open for someone.
- Help someone cross the road.
- Carry someone's shopping/books/anything.

*Try to complete **at least one action** from this section.*

Little Action:

- Offer to do some shopping for someone.
- Offer to do a chore for someone that you know they dislike doing.
- Offer to tidy an elderly neighbor's garden or home.

*Try to complete **at least one action** from this section.*

Big Action:

- Do something kind anonymously; the rule here is that no one can ever know that it was you who was kind.
- Stretch your imagination, you simply can't get this one wrong!

> **Reflection:**
> *Before you go to sleep reflect on your day and how this exercise made you feel.*

Observation of Beauty
Days 24-25

And I think to myself what a wonderful world...

Try to find beauty around you

Attention is the cognitive process of selectively concentrating on one aspect of the environment while ignoring other things. By selecting to spend a little time consciously focusing on appreciating beauty, this will help you have a more positive outlook on the future.

Beauty is in the eye of the beholder and you are the beholder. Things judged as beautiful set off two different processes in the brain: one based on triggers intrinsic to the stimuli (objective beauty) and one based on the individual's emotional responses to the stimuli (subjective beauty). In the end, beauty probably consists of both objective and subjective components. You are entitled to your own opinions on what is and isn't beautiful to you.

We think of great design as art, not science, a mysterious gift from the gods. When you appreciate beauty, you form a connection with the larger universe, allowing you to feel the emotions of awe and wonder.

- *Only focus on one thing at a time.*
- *Filter out any distractions by narrowing your field of focus.*
- *Focused attention is a key to success.*
- *When you appreciate beauty more, you also experience more happiness.*
- *Learning to appreciate beauty will help you grow as a person.*

May we both give and receive such beautiful things as ideas...

Affirmation:
I will try to see the beauty in all things.

Pre-action: ★

- *Find an image of a building, plane, car, train, ship or any other inanimate object, and study it for a full two minutes with fully focused attention.*
- *Note all the things you like about it, the lines, the curves, imagine what it would feel like and how it would smell.*
- *Now go outside and find any **one** of the above objects in its real form and study it with fully focused attention for five minutes; notice every minute detail and preserve that detail to memory so precisely that you could recreate it if required.*

Little Action: ★★

- *Find an image of any plant, bird, fish or animal, and study it for a full two minutes with fully focused attention.*
- *Note all the things that you like about it, the lines, the curves, imagine what it would feel like and how it would smell; look for the beauty.*
- *Now go outside and find any one of the above in its real form and study it with fully focused attention for five minutes; notice every minute detail and preserve that detail to memory so precisely that you could recreate it if required.*

Big Action: ★★★

- *Find an image of a baby, a child, a man, a woman both young and old and study each one for a full two minutes with fully focused attention.*
- *Note all the things that you like about it, the lines, the curves, imagine what it would feel like and how it would smell; look for the beauty.*
- *Now go outside and find any **two** of the above in their real form and study them with fully focused attention for five minutes; notice every minute detail and preserve that detail to memory so precisely that you could recreate it if required.*
- *Don't forget to look for the beauty in everyone.*

Reflection:
Before you go to sleep reflect on your day and how this exercise made you feel.

Acting
Days 26-28

To be – or not to be...

Get out of your own way

You are more than capable of pushing through whatever barriers are stopping you from achieving your goals. Nothing will ever happen if you continue to play safe and stay in your comfort zone.

Take the leap and go for it.

Whatever you're looking for will be waiting for you once you push through your fears.

- *Loosen up and just go for it.*
- *Don't worry about looking stupid, it's only ego.*
- *Act as if you are an expert.*
- *Work your courage muscles.*
- *Feeling uncomfortable is good.*
- *Feel the fear, but do it anyway.*
- *Never give up!*

Improvise, adapt and overcome in any situation...

> **Affirmation:**
> *I can muster up hope and courage from deep inside me.*

Pre-action:

- *Say Mahalo instead of thank you for one day.*
- *Go outside and shout at the top of your voice: Good morning world, it's a brand new day.*

Little Action:

- *Learn your lines.*
- *Find any paragraph in any book or a poem that inspires you. Read it out loud to yourself (in private). Now repeat it but with feeling. Memorize it if you can. Now act it out as though you were delivering a scene on stage.*
- *Finally go outside into a public space and repeat your performance. Take a friend for support if need be and deliver the speech to them.*

Big Action:

- *Choose a character from a movie, TV program or in your own life (someone of the same gender as you, and someone who inspires you).*
- *Imagine that you have been asked to portray this person in a movie.*
- *You need to study their character, their voice, their body language, their mannerisms, their habits, their viewpoint and their beliefs.*
- *Put aside one to two hours.*
- *Spend some time getting into character, dress up if it helps. Become that person (as an actor), walk around your home talking as you imagine that person would talk, act as if you were that person.*
- *Now go outside, go shopping, go for a coffee, and go for a walk – but stay in character.*

Reflection:
Before you go to sleep reflect on your day and how this exercise made you feel.

When you push through your fears, you'll always find some sort of reward for your bravery.

Dream
Days 29-30

Dream your greatest dream for anything is possible...

What does the future hold?

Many people feel as if they're adrift in the world. They work hard, but they don't seem to get anywhere worthwhile.

But when asked where they want to go, they don't know because they haven't thought about it. Would you get on a train and go for a ride not knowing where you were going to? Of course not – you choose a destination first then plan your route which may include many places of interest on the way. Yet many of us are traveling life's journey without any clear destination; at best we may have chosen one or two places of interest.

| Home | Family | Partner | Car | Job | Money | Travel |

- ◆ Make a few columns and head them up with the important things in your life. There are a few ideas shown above, but feel free to add your own.
- ◆ Under each heading make a bucket list of things you want to achieve in this life. Some can be short term and others long-term targets.
- ◆ Now choose one to three of the most important items on the page.

| START | ——————— | DESTINATION |

- ◆ Now put each target/goal/desire into its own destination box.
- ◆ Look at **every** bucket list and ask yourself if any of these goals/items/targets can be visited while on the way to any of the three destinations, then put them into a holding box next to the relevant destination.

You now have an idea of where you want to go, what you want to achieve. List the three in order of preference; if you can't decide what is most important then start from number three. When you have two left, ask yourself: if I can only do one before I die which one would I want to do? This will identify your number one choice.

This gives your target real purpose and depth; you even have a timeline and can work backwards to the starting point, which in turn will identify the first step forward. It will also help to keep you on the right track if the going gets tough.

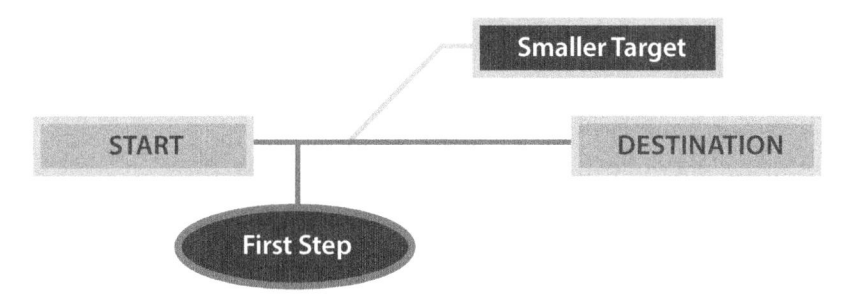

```
                        Smaller Target
  START ─────────────────────────── DESTINATION
                    │
                First Step
```

Now you have an outline plan and can add in smaller targets/goals/desires and bucket list items, the things you want to achieve along the way.

Mission Statement	Vision Statement

Write a short statement in each box.
- **Mission statement** – *This defines your purpose. It's what you ultimately want to achieve in your life or career, expressed in a specific, measurable way.*
- **Vision statement** – *This is a bit more emotional. Here, you define your core values, and how you'll apply those values to your mission.*

Part Two - *Shine like a star* ... *the aloha way*

For example: if your destination target is to learn to drive, your mission statement could be something like: I am going to learn to drive and aim to pass my test by next summer. Your vision might read: I love the countryside and will take a drive out on my own when I pass.

Duration: two days

> **Affirmation:**
> *I am a great, powerful spiritual being and can achieve anything I put my mind to.*

Pre-action:

- *Carry out the exercise as above.*
- *Do this for as many of your dreams as need be.*
- *Choose one, it does not have to be a big one.*

Little Action:

- *The first step toward your desire begins here.*
- *Make contact, get more information, and arrange a visit.*

Big Action:

- *Wow! You have taken a giant stride with that small step toward your future.*
- *Well done – doesn't that feel great?!*
- *Go back to the questionnaire and fill in the second column, then reflect on the difference between the two columns, see just how far you have traveled in just 30 days.*
- *Now decide what you want to do next, pursue your desire with all your heart – it's your future!*

Written by **Kevin England DC.DD.** / Sponsored by:

azura
spirit of aloha ~ in action

STARDANCE - Flow with Energy

STARDUST

Learn how to become **a star** *in* **30 days**

Notes by **Kora**

Flow with Energy
Shine like a star…the aloha way

2:76 Stardust

About me

I suppose I should tell you a little bit about me and why I think my notes can help you.

Well my name is Kora and six months ago I was living in a squat near Regent's Park in London and selling the Big Issue for some cash. Then last night I spent an hour with Tom Cruise on a red carpet in Leicester Square, I was interviewing him for a London magazine.

My first ever job and I loved it!

So how did that happen?

Well I found a radio in a dumpster.

That's right, a radio in a bloody dumpster and it changed my life!

I'm going to tell you why and how, because my life's been sh*t and now it's changed...

So if you want you can use my notes and change yours as well, if you think it's a load of cr*p then don't do it...

I'm not bothered.

But it worked for me!

So here goes for what it's worth... as I said, six months ago I was living in a house near Regent's Park, it must have been worth millions, but it was empty and me and my mates set up home there, I even had my own room and a carpet under my sleeping bag, I've never had a carpet before, life was good.

How I ended up in London is another story for another day.

One day I was talking to a builder working next door, he had bought a copy of the Big Issue from me and gave me a sandwich and a cup of tea as we laughed and joked during his lunch break. I had made friends with the guys over the few months that they had been

Notes by Kora

on the job and even did a bit of cleaning up after them, anything for cash!

Well this day I saw an old radio in the dumpster, it was a small transistor type that looked as though it belonged in the 1950s. It was a little bit broken, had no batteries and did not work, but for me it was like gold dust.

Why?

Because my Mom and Dad had one like it and it brought back memories. Memories of a life I had left behind when I was only four years old and they were both killed in a car accident and my life changed forever.

I remember the radio well, it was a 1950s art deco type of design, light blue, and it had the word Stardust in chrome blazed across the top. My Mom had bought it at the Stardust Hotel in Las Vegas during her honeymoon, we simply called it Dusty and every day Dusty would sing the tunes of a bright summer. I loved that time and I loved my Mom and Dad. Then one day I lost everything, even Dusty.

They said I was too young to understand, they said that I would get over it as I grew up.

They were wrong!

Now I had a little bit of home, okay it was not the same and did not work, but it triggered my memories, memories long buried under a mountain of pain.

How I loved that radio.

I cleaned it up and I even wrote the word Dusty on the top with a bit of black paint that Ben the builder gave me.

Now this is where the story gets a little bit weird. But stay with me and let me explain.

Every night I would talk to Dusty and even sing a song, one of my Mom's favorites, and then I would fall asleep happy.

Then one night I had a dream. I don't know if it was a dream or if it was real. No, it must have been a dream.

However, whatever it was, Dusty talked to me, his knobs turned to eyes and the dial turned into a smiling mouth. "Hi Kora, welcome to the Starlite zone."

"The what?"

"The Starlite zone - the zone of magic. I am going to take you back in time, back to your home on the islands," said Dusty.

Now don't get me wrong. I am a level-headed streetwise 21-year-old who has traveled the world in the most appalling circumstances, and I stand on my own two feet and don't take no sh*t from no one. But dreams are dreams, aren't they?

Well for one hour each night me and Dusty had our own little world and he made me smile, so what's wrong with that?

After a few weeks Dusty started asking questions, sometimes deep penetrating questions: what did I want to do with my life, was I going to get a job, did I want a partner, children, things like that. He was becoming a pain and I considered chucking him out. But I reckon that he must have read my thoughts because that night he gave it to me, lock, stock and barrel.

"Loosen up, change your attitude, get over yourself and get on with it.

"What have you got to lose? Your life is already sh*t. You won't change your life if you won't change.

"When you are down in the muck you are going to get dirty, first thing you have to do is stop wallowing in your own sh*t (self-pity).

"Take a deep breath, decide to do something about it and stand up.

Forget about looking cool. Forget about feeling stupid. That is all ego feeding on your fear, only you can change your life. Take a leap and go for it.

"- Just do it!"

The message was clear, things had to change, I couldn't keep bumping along the rock bottom end of society.

"OK! I hear you... now clever clogs, if it's that easy, tell me how."

"I didn't say it was easy... it's pretty simple, but it's not easy," said Dusty.

"Give me 30 days, commit to 30 days, fully commit and I will show you how to become a star in your own life, how to let your light really shine on your world. Make your Mom proud."

"Okay little guy, that's pretty low..."

I looked at the only thing I had left from Mom, it was an old tattered postcard from the Stardust Hotel.

Okay Mom! I tell you what - I'll give it a go. After all, what have I got to lose?

For 30 days I listened to Dusty, and carried out his instructions to the best of my ability. It was not easy: every day I was challenged and often had to fight with my ego as I confronted parts of myself I had either avoided most of my life or had never encountered before. Each week was a scary battle to face my fears and I was pushed to the limits: I struggled, I felt uncomfortable, I felt like quitting and giving up.

But I'll tell you what: when you face those fears and realize that nothing awful happens afterward it strengthens your courage muscles and you feel elated.

So stay with me if you want, and day by day I will show you what I did, and you too can do it - as Dusty said:

~ Just do it!

Learn how to become a star in 30 days
Notes by Kora

The Rules

"Here are the rules," said Dusty.

"What the fu*k, I don't do rules, you said nothing about rules!"

"Will you shut up and listen, Kora, these are not rules, they are more like guidelines. But you have to follow them otherwise we can't see you grow into that bright star you want to be."

"Okay! Guidelines are okay!"

So Dusty explained...

1. There are a number of steps for you to take over the next 30 days.
2. Complete each step before moving on to the next, even if it takes longer than the allotted time.
3. The first step is a powerful key to unlock your mind and open it up to new ideas.
4. You will be given a reason why and how, maybe a when and where, but don't question~ just do it!
5. If you want or need to know more of the Ws then I will give you a list of books etc. at the end.
6. There is an affirmation related to the step at hand and should be repeated several times every day for the duration of that step.
7. Each step will have a number of tasks (1-3) ranging from simple to hard, complete each task in order.
8. Don't even look at the next step until you have completed the one you are on.
9. You will be pushed out of your comfort zone, embrace everything even if you feel stupid, get brave, do it and grow beyond all expectations.
10. Finally, at the end of each step write down your thoughts and feelings.

As I said 'simple but not easy'."

Questionnaire

Answering the questions is a process that can be valuable in itself. It gives you the opportunity to look at many aspects of your values, beliefs and life skills. It gives you the opportunity to think about what is important to you and what aspects of yourself you would like to improve.

Mark yourself between 0-10: zero is low and ten is high; five is average. You are only comparing against yourself, no one else needs to see this questionnaire. Be honest.

Question	Before	After
I get anxious meeting new people		
I find it difficult to take criticism		
I fear being made to look stupid		
I fear making a speech		
I am easily embarrassed		
I feel interior to others		
I get defensive quickly		
I find it difficult to focus on one thing		
I do not set goals for the future		

Question	Before	After
I spend most of my time in a happy mood		
I spend most of my time in an unhappy mood		
I am grateful for the good things in my life		
I focus on the things I don't have in my life		
I find it hard to forgive people		
I often do random acts of kindness		
I often tell those closest to me that I love them		
I am happy about my future		
I find it hard to share my emotions		

STARDANCE - Flow with Energy

How

"I know that I am expecting you to follow my lead without any great explanation of why. So to redress the balance before we start I am going to tell you a little bit of how this works, then hopefully you will stop moaning when asked to do something a bit challenging",
said Dusty.

"Me moan! Sometimes I wish I could just switch you off."

"You know that this room is full of energy waves even if you can't see them. Just imagine that you have all these songs vibrating around the room from many different radio stations, all at the same time, yet you can't hear any of them. Why? Because your hearing is not tuned into the frequency that any of the stations are broadcasting on.

"In order to hear them you purchase a radio, or pick one up out of the trash."

"Ha, ha, get on with it."

"When you turn the radio on you have to move the dial and tune into a station by corresponding your antenna with the frequency of the broadcast. As you start to get near to the station you pick up a weak signal, which then gets stronger and stronger until you receive a perfect sound. That perfect sound is on a very narrow wave and if you go too far it will start to get weaker again until you eventually lose it. Are you with me so far?"

"Boring! I have better things to do than to listen to you talking about how to use a radio."

"Really? You're lying there in a sleeping bag at six o'clock in the evening because you want to keep warm, and I am trying to help you change your life's situation, so what better things have you got to do, then?"

"Okay, okay, I'm sorry, just make it more interesting, please..."

Notes by Kora

"Now where was I? Ah yes, imagine if everything you can see and hear was an energy wave just like that sound wave on the radio. Things you can see will be resonating at a slow deep vibration with many waves pushed close together so that they appear solid. Then you have energy waves that resonate at a slightly faster and slightly higher vibration, you see these as light, light in many colors, various shades of the rainbow.

"Are you still with me?"

"Yeah and it's getting more interesting, keep going."

"As we carry on tuning into the higher frequencies, we reach wave bands that we can only see in certain circumstances, energy waves like infra-red, x-rays and ultraviolet. If we keep going up the scale we meet waves that we know exist through science, but we can't see them – sound waves for example. These are measurable in the physical sense and understood by most of us.

"Now it starts to get more exciting as we leave the physical world and start tuning into the world of non-physical existence.

"What do I mean?

"Well we've established that everything, absolutely everything is a wave of energy; as we start to tune into the higher frequencies we're into the realms of thoughts and ideas, spirituality and universal intelligence; things that exist in a metaphysical world. We may not yet have the tools and skills to measure these energy waves, but nevertheless they exist, and what's more they can be used to enhance all our lives by taking an idea formed in the higher frequencies to produce a result in the low frequencies."

"You have now got my attention; what you are trying to say is if we can think of something, we can make it happen."

"That's right."

"Even if that something is a change in your circumstances, a change in your life, a change in your beliefs, a change in your **attitude**; notice that I left that one till last," said Dusty.

STARDANCE - Flow with Energy

"Oh, you are sooo funny. But seriously it's fascinating to think that I can change my physical reality by just thinking of a different existence."

"I wish it was that easy. But you're on the right line you see, for a non-physical thing to appear in the physical world requires action.

"Think about it, if you have an idea, it's something we can't see because…"

"It's vibrating at a higher frequency; it's an energy wave that lives higher up the scale."

"I think you are beginning to understand," said Dusty.

"So am I correct in thinking that if I want to make that idea real all I have to do is change its vibration by bringing it lower down the scale?"

"That's right, just like we can change ice into water and water into vapor simply by changing the density of the vibration; we can create a manifestation of an idea through the process of action. But it has to be the right method and the right action in order to get the right result.

"Not so boring now is it?"

"Okay, let's see if I have got this correct. You are going to show me how to tune into a frequency where my thoughts and my desires can become a reality in my life through a series of actions that I have to complete."

"Brilliant! That is exactly what I can offer you, if you are up for it."

"'Bring it on, when do we start?"

"We can start tomorrow, but first I must explain the method we are going to be using.

"As I said earlier, between the physical and the metaphysical lies an area where all things become possible, a magical zone where change takes place- the Starlite zone.

Notes by Kora

"This zone is the frequency occupied by the cosmic wave of Starlite energy. And I am going to give you a method and show you a way of tuning into that zone. At first the signal will be weak, but as you progress day by day the signal will get stronger and stronger, your confidence will grow along with your ability to manifest your desires and dreams.

"All I ask is that for the next 30 days you leave behind any preconceived ideas, beliefs and prejudices, keep an open mind and as Nike say ~ Just do it..."

The Start
Day 1

This is great, I am ready for anything. Last night I went to bed and just as I was going off to sleep Dusty came alive and he explained to me that the Starlite zone (the zone) is found in a place between awake and asleep, it's that dreamtime when you are not sure if you are still awake or if you are dreaming in your sleep.

He said that when you are awake you use your conscious mind to think and take control, and when you are asleep your subconscious mind takes over control and dreams.

However, the in-between, the zone, is where we find the superconscious mind and it is by stimulating the superconscious that we can make things happen. He said imagine the superconscious mind as a muscle, and if we want that muscle to lift the weight of the world from our shoulders we need to make it strong. And we make it strong by using it, using it every day, pushing it to new limits.

We do this by tuning into the zone and getting energy to flow between the conscious and the subconscious states. Sounds complicated but he promised me that each baby step is doable.

Well~ I kept this note pad next to my sleeping bag so that I could write down everything during the night before I forgot it and this was my first task:

Today we are going to start to learn how to tune into the energy wave in the zone.

Each day for 30 days you must do three exercises: one at the start and one at the end of the day, then one more at any time in the day.

First thing in the morning (within the first two hours) do this:

Good Day exercise

1. Take three deep breaths into your stomach, breathe in through your nose and out through your mouth - make a loud HAA sound.
2. Say to yourself I'm going to tune into the zone and today is going to be a good day - it's raining (change the weather to match the day) but I love it - I must keep my eyes open for the lessons, gifts and opportunities that the day has to offer, no matter how small.
3. And when I notice these things a little spark of Starlite energy will radiate from me and I will feel good.
4. Take another deep breath and say bring it on.
5. Step out into the world and start your day.

Power exercise

This can be done any time in the day when you need a power boost.

1. Stop whatever you are doing for a minute or two.
2. Take one deep breath into your stomach, breathe in through your nose and out through your mouth - make a loud HAA sound.
3. Look around and find something that you like: it could be a cup of coffee or donut, a car, a jacket in a shop window, anything at all, just don't make it too big to start with.

Notes by Kora

4. Now really focus on it, imagine touching it, what does it feel like? What does it smell like? Look closely at the finer detail, really burn it into your memory and appreciate its beauty.

Evening exercise

Just before you go to sleep do this exercise, it will tune you into the zone ready to stimulate the superconscious for more help and assistance:

1. Clear your mind by taking two deep breaths into your stomach, breathe in through your nose and out through your mouth.
2. Think about what happened today, find one thing that you were grateful for and say thank you in your mind. Find one lesson that you learned today and say thank you in your mind.
3. If someone has done something wrong or pissed you off, say forget about it and let it go. Hold no emotion, no anger when you go to sleep.
4. If you have done something wrong or pissed someone off, just say sorry, I didn't mean anything, and let it go. Hold no emotion, no guilt when you go to sleep.
5. Finally think of something good you have done today, something you are proud of, or a simple act of kindness.
6. Say there you go, Dusty, I can do it, smile, be proud of yourself and go to sleep.

Now this may feel like a lot to start with, but it's not. After two days I did it without having to think too much. Sometimes I would forget to do one or the other, if you also forget don't beat yourself up, just carry on as though you have done it.

I felt a bit silly to start with, but no one was watching and I must admit it did make me feel good.

Days 2-3

Did you remember to do the Good Day exercise? I did.

Last night Dusty told me the next step is to smile... really! Don't say anything but this isn't as hard as he made out it is! I think I am going to have a lot of fun with this one - smile and laugh, but he did say that I have to get it right.

Apparently smiling with your mouth only is wrong because it looks like you are snarling or posing - yah, I've seen lots of pics on Facebook like that.

He said the right way is to smile with your eyes, like you do when you really like someone, and to do that you have to be in a good mood. Now I get it, that's where the Good Day exercise comes in.

Okay - here it is for the next two days.

Laugh and Smile

1. Look at yourself in the mirror and smile, does it look false? Now think of something or someone that you love, really think of them and smile, does that look better?
2. That's the smile you need during this task.
3. When things happen you can feel good or bad, happy or sad, you choose. So for two days smile and laugh no matter what happens, even if it's at yourself.
4. Smile at a stranger and notice if you get one back. Try to get at least five back in two days. If you get good at this try it with different types of people from builders to judges, cops to joggers.
5. When someone cuts you up on the road, takes your seat on the train, or gets in your way, just smile.
6. Sit in a public place, coffee shop, park, on a bus, be happy, smile and pass it on. If you get a smile back notice if they pass it on to someone else.

Notes by Kora

7 You might even change one small part of the world for a moment or two. You may change someone's mood or their entire day with your smile.

8 Don't just smile, mean it and notice its effect.

I liked this one, did you?

This morning I was sitting on the subway here in London looking at the miserable face of a man opposite. He looked like he was going to work in an office; he was dressed in a pinstripe suit and was reading a newspaper. Well I made him my target, I wanted to see if he would smile back. So I stared at him (be careful who you choose): well he must have felt me looking, like you do sometimes. He looked up from his paper and we had a moment's eye contact, and I smiled... Guess what! He didn't blink an eye, he just looked back down at his paper. We arrived at St. Paul's station and as he got up to leave I smiled again, he looked confused, turned around and got off the train.

Oh well, you can't win them all.

Then it happened: as the train started to pull away he turned around on the platform, looked at me through the window, and smiled.

Yes! I got the miserable bugger!

Made my day - and probably his as well.

Days 4-6

Well I had a lot of fun over the last couple of days, did you?

I think it's about to get a little harder now, I'm not too comfortable thinking about myself or even thinking too deeply, and the next task seems to be a lot of thinking...

I hope you've got a pen and notepad as you are going to need one.

Attitude of gratitude

1. Take three deep breaths into your stomach, breathe in through your nose and out through your mouth – make a loud HAA sound.
2. Look at people in your life as a gift and appreciate the experiences they bring.
3. Do not judge the experience as good or bad but simply as a gift of personal growth.
4. Make a gratitude list – a list of all the good, helpful, supporting, things, events, places and people you have in your life.
5. Start with people at the head of a list. Then write down the names of people whom you are grateful for, for their support, their help, even their love. It doesn't matter if the list is short as long as it is heartfelt.
6. Repeat the exercise with different headings.
7. Now write the numbers 1-10 and choose a top ten on a love list – this can be any item from any list. For example I have my Mom, my Dad, my dog Smudgy and yes... my radio Dusty.
8. Start at number one on your love list, close your eyes and think about them, really think about them and get the emotional feelings working.
9. Take a deep breath in through your nose, sucking in that happy feeling deep into your stomach.
10. Say quietly or out loud: I am so grateful that you are in my life, I thank you for the happiness you bring me... thank you.
11. Gradually work your way through all your list over the three days.

Finally: choose one person from your gratitude list and write them a thank you card or note, telling them how much they have helped or inspired you, or influenced your life. Now give or sent it to them. If they are no longer alive, simply read it out loud and post it or burn it, but do it with gratitude.

Notes by Kora

Well I don't know about you but I found that really hard. I began by thinking I can't do this, my life is sh*t, and the people in it are not much better.

Then I thought about the title of the task "an attitude of gratitude" which got me thinking it doesn't matter how bad life is, there is always something that makes you laugh. I realized that if I stopped thinking about myself and my problems and started thinking about what makes me laugh, what makes me happy, then I can be grateful for those things.

It got a lot easier after that and made me look at my life in a different way. I think I need to spend more time with the things or people on my list, and that will help develop my attitude of gratitude.

What do you think – any other ideas?

Days 7-8

I was hoping that it would get easier after yesterday, but this is even worse - more thinking but this time it's all about ourselves.

Dusty told me that the two days are a minimum and if I needed an extra day then that's okay, I can just start the next step when I am ready.

You know what? I'm going to do it. I'm going to take one little bite at a time and see how I get on. Like I said, this is all about us, all about accepting and loving ourselves for who and what we are. If you're like me I can give you a long list of the things I hate or don't like about myself, my life or my body, that's easy... but loving me... f**k!

Dusty said that he loved me for my great attitude toward embracing this task, well that's a start anyway. Anything else? He said to have got this far shows that we care about others not just ourselves, we have changed someone else's day, made them happy, we've given thanks for those who helped and supported us, which is a good thing to do and only can be done from a loving heart, which in turn means that we are worthy of praise. I haven't heard that word since I was four years old.

Accept and love yourself:

1. Look at a mirror.
2. Look into your eyes.
3. Choose the one eye you are drawn to (this may change each time).
4. Look deep into your eye, with the intention of connecting to your spirit inside. (Your spirit is that little light that you know lives inside, it is more than your body and will live on after the body is gone.)
5. Say thank you and I love you to your spirit for letting you have this human experience.
6. Say thank you to your body for housing your spirit during this experience.
7. Promise to look after it, say I love you.

What I like about me

1. Make a "what I love about me" list – a list of all the good, helpful and supporting things you do in your life.
2. This will range from jobs to family to volunteer groups; here you list the things you do that you can be proud of.
3. Try finding things you never noticed about yourself, like a great personality or maybe your warm smile.
4. Now we get personal.
5. Continue with all the things you like about yourself: your attitude, your willingness to help, your kindness, if need be add quotes, identify an incident.
6. Finally, list all the things you like about your body, even if it's only one thing. The secret here is not to focus on what you don't like but simply to focus on the bits that you do like/love.

Notes by Kora

7 Take three deep breaths into your stomach, breathe in through your nose and out through your mouth – make a loud HAA sound.

8 Now go through all the items on your list one by one and say I am grateful that you (state the item or body part) are in my life and I thank you for being a part of me. Thank you.

9 When you have finished the list take a deep breath and say I am special because there is no one else like me in the world, I am unique and I will sing my praise and shine my light, and no one has the right to stop me.

10 Be who you really are, express yourself, laugh, play, sing, and be crazy. Don't be afraid of what others think.

Now reward yourself with a treat, do something nice, something special that you enjoy.

Did you have the same problem as I did? Every time I thought of something good to put on the list, I thought of ten bad things to add.

In the end I thought f**k it, everyone deserves a chance, that's why they queue up for the X-factor and shows like Britain's got Talent and America's got Talent – for that chance. Well this is my chance and I'm going to grab it by the b*lls.

I think this has helped me to kick the monkey off my back, the little sh*t who keeps nagging in my ear, telling me that I am not good enough, I don't have enough, I don't do enough.

Well you little bugger, let me tell you something...

I am going to stand up tall and shout out loud that I love me, I love what I do for others and I deserve a chance, I deserve my time in the spotlight.

Hold my hand and let's walk this road together because you and I are going to claim the life we deserve.

Days 9-10

What treat did you have?

Did you go out for a drink, have a meal, or get your nails done?

You know what I did? I went for a swim at the local pool, I have been sweeping the building site next door to our squat, selling the Big Issue, handing out leaflets for pizzas and even doing a bit of busking around Covent Garden for tourists. I'm keeping the money well hidden because otherwise it will disappear. Well last night I spent a little of it at the Cally pool near Kings Cross. I had a long beautiful swim and it reminded me of home and made me happy, today I'm going to treat myself to a new pair of jeans, I have had my eye on a pair, they have a little bit of glitter on the back pocket and I love them, they are in a vintage shop in the fashionable Camden Market and now I have the money to buy them, and why not? As Dusty said, I deserve a treat, because like you I'm worth it!

Today is a happy day, all we have to do is put the three elements together: smile; have gratitude; accept and love ourselves; and share that with others.

Don't judge people, don't be mean to people, have a happy day. Don't forget to start and finish the day in the proper way and have a power-boosting break when you need one.

Happy Days

1. Think of a pet or person that you love, one that puts a smile on your face, close your eyes and think of them, really think of them and smile.
2. Take a deep breath in through your nose, sucking the happy feeling deep into your stomach area; switch your attention to your head as you breathe out through your mouth.

Notes by Kora

3. Repeat three times.
4. Now you are ready for the next step.
5. Today is aloha day.
6. In Hawaii the word aloha means hello with happiness.
7. Today when someone says hello or good morning you respond with aloha instead.
8. Buy some flowers and hand them out in the street, wishing everyone a happy day.
9. Or pick some flowers and hand them to a stranger, or any elderly person.

How many alohas did you give? It was great to see the surprised look on people's faces and then the smile that followed. To be honest I found this very easy, I was born on Oahu and used the term for 12 years before I ran away, but it was great to use it again, and I think I just may carry on using it, thank you Dusty.

Okay, the flower thing was not so easy: early this morning I went down to The Cut at Waterloo and met a flower seller called Jimmy who I sometimes help and he gave me a nice box of mixed flowers left over from yesterday, they were good but not as fresh as today's, still beggars can't be choosers. I spent most of the day handing these out to tourists and saying aloha, have a nice day, in return they would take my picture and even give me a few coins.

I had enough to buy a McDonald's and some fresh flowers for my friend, at CityLit in Convent Garden who has managed to get me on a subsidized teaching course at the adult education college, my life is beginning to change, I can feel it in my bones.

Days 11-13

I've enjoyed the last two days, but it looks like we have some more work to do that's way outside my comfort zone. This step is all about giving compliments, genuine and sincere compliments.

Do you know that receiving a smile is a compliment, as it suggests that we are worthy of attention and appreciation. Has someone smiled at you recently? Then know that you are worth it. Now it's your turn to give, but we are going to take it one step further by giving a verbal compliment.

There are some guidelines in giving great compliments:

1. Notice something you like or appreciate about someone, pay attention about the detail and make a mental note about how it makes you feel.
2. Now go up to the person and start by saying, "You know that I love/like the way you have..."
3. Make the compliment genuine, sincere, specific and warm.
4. Turn a good compliment into a great compliment by paying attention to detail, acknowledging effort and stating how it made you feel.

A compliment a day

Task A:

1. Look at someone you know and notice something you like about them. It needs to be something they have done, not something they were born with. Pay attention to the details and make a mental note of how it makes you feel.
2. Go up to the person and give them the compliment, be sincere, be specific, be genuine and be warm.

Notes by Kora

3. If they respond back with a thank you, just say you're welcome.
4. If they respond back with a compliment, smile and say thank you.
5. Your target today is three people that you know; keep at least two-hour gaps between actions.

Task B.

1. Look at someone you don't know and notice something you like about them. It needs to be something they have done, not something they were born with. Pay attention to the details and make a mental note of how it makes you feel.
2. Go up to the person and give them the compliment, be sincere, be specific, be genuine and be warm.
3. If they respond back with a thank you, just say you're welcome.
4. If they respond back with a compliment, smile and say thank you.
5. Your target today is two people that you don't know; keep at least two-hour gaps between actions.

Task C.

1. Look at someone you know but don't like or don't get on with and notice something you like about them. It needs to be something they have done, not something they were born with. Pay attention to the details and make a mental note of how it makes you feel.
2. There is always something you can find that is good.
3. Go up to the person and give them the compliment, be sincere, be specific, be genuine and be warm.
4. If they respond back with a thank you, just say you're welcome.
5. If they respond back with a compliment, smile and say thank you.
6. Your target today is just one person; keep at least two-hour gaps between actions.

This is a difficult and challenging test.

To compliment someone you don't like or don't usually get on with is a great personality growth indicator.

You need to be what you desire to become.

Maybe, if you and a friend/work colleague had a falling out a few months ago, and you see them wearing something that you think looks good on them, it doesn't hurt to tell them. Whether or not they publicly accept the compliment, inside they will probably be happy you complimented them.

And you will boost your confidence and self-esteem a little.

I don't know what's happening to me. I have an internal conflict going on, a war between my confidence, my ego, my defense and my fears. Are you feeling the same? The first task wasn't too bad because I knew and liked the people even if they were a little surprised, because I don't give compliments. The second task was easy; I'm used to talking to strangers in the street and there is always someone with something I like.

But that last one, holy sh*t that was difficult to say the least. I try to avoid people I don't like, to give one of them a compliment was hard enough, but to give a genuine compliment meant I had to spend time looking at them -without them noticing- and find something I liked about them, not easy...

Looking for something I liked about them actually meant looking at them completely differently, which if I was honest with you, I didn't want to do. I think I wanted to keep the bad things going because that justified my viewpoint. Looking for something good meant questioning my own beliefs.

I think this woman, who is one of my tutors, looks down her nose at me, talks down to me and has an air of superiority about her. My fear in giving her a compliment is that it will be seen as a "brown nose" act, or worse still it will be rebuffed and used against me to reinforce her feelings of superiority. I spent some time looking at her in class so it wasn't obvious; what did I like about her personality? Nothing! What did I like about her teaching? Nothing! What did I like about her dress sense? Noth... wait a minute, today she has a very fashionable Hermes scarf, it probably cost more than my entire year's wardrobe spend, if I had a wardrobe that is, but I did like it on her.

So I waited for the break and thought here goes, and taking a deep breath, I said, "Mrs B, I really like your Hermes scarf, I can see you spent some time choosing the right color as it complements your hair perfectly." She responded in a way that I didn't expect by saying something like, "Well thank you Kora, it was nice of you to say so."

You know it really pisses me off when Dusty's right – he can be such a pain rubbing it in. But I have to say that it made me feel good and I am absolutely sure that it made Mrs B feel good too.

Days 14-16

Well can you believe it, we're at the halfway mark already!

Last night Dusty asked me if I felt more confident, if I had more self-worth, and did I feel I had made improvements in my outlook. You know, as much as it pains me to admit it, things are changing, very slowly, but I do really feel different. I hope that you have also noticed a little change for the better. The next two days should be fun.

I hope you like animals because this step is all about animal interaction and the experience of unconditional love that goes with it.

Apparently there are many benefits of owning or interacting with animals. On an emotional level, owning a pet can reduce depression, stress and anxiety; health-wise, it can lower your blood pressure, improve your immunity and even reduce your risk of heart attack and stroke.

Animal interaction

1. Animal interaction is what this step is all about, if you have pets this will be easy; see it as a reward for your hard work up to this stage.
2. If you don't have any animal contact then wow you are in for a treat! If you don't like animals or you are frightened of them this will stretch your boundaries.
3. Take extra care and attention of your own animals; give them a treat.
4. If you are frightened of animals watch a few pet videos on YouTube.
5. If you have no pets walk round a pet shop, stop and look at the animals, imagine communicating with them.

Task A:

6. Animal communication is our most natural form of communication. It is a feeling-based instinct that all living beings are connected to.
7. Take some oats, seed or grapes to a pond and feed the ducks or wild birds – take time out and watch them feed.
8. Focus on them for two minutes, really focus, imagine touching their soft feathers and silky body. Using all your expanded senses try to take in every little detail of their being as though you were capturing an image in order to draw them at a later date.
9. You can swap birds for any other local animal, but it should not be one of your own pets.

Task B.

10. This task requires you to do at least one of the following suggestions, please feel free to add your own:
11. Offer to walk your neighbor's dog or keep them company while they walk together.
12. Offer to help brush the animal (dog/horse) for someone.
13. Offer to help clean/feed the animals in a pet store.

Notes by Kora

14 Offer your time to a zoo/vets/animal hospital/animal rescue charity for half a day or more.
15 Adopt or buy a new pet and love it.
16 The importance here is to experience new animal interaction. It will help develop unity and compassion which we most definitely need to make our lives more fulfilled with expanded awareness.

I loved this, I hope you did too. When I was a little girl living at home I had a puppy called Smudgy, he was a ball of blond fur, black eyes, red tongue and a wet nose, and I loved him. I always felt safe around animals as they gave unconditional love, something I've not had since my Mom and Dad died when I was four. At birth I was given the name Kona because I was born on the Kona cost of Oahu; when I ran away at 12 I changed it to Kora because I was now Born Free just like the lions in the film of the same name who lived at a free place called Kora. So you see me and animals are happy together. When I get somewhere more suitable to live I will get another puppy, that's for sure!

Days 17-18

Get in there; it's another one of those challenging exercises, but I'll let you into a secret: I'm beginning to enjoy them now.

This one is all about touching others, in particular hugging others. At the moment I am doing a massage course and I was really surprised how many people go for so long without being touched by others.

Our human needs are really simple: people want to be loved, touched, fed and to feel safe. If you were raised in a home where this was normal, you will not be able to understand how some people actually crave the human touch. While you might not notice the effects of not being touched right away, it can negatively affect your mood, your confidence and your health. Hugging is a great way to meet many of these needs.

*I always say to people I know handshakes are for strangers...
Give me a hug!*

Task A.
1. Practice "the hug."
2. Put your arms around yourself, squeeze and cuddle, say I love you to yourself.
3. Now find your nearest and dearest partner or friend and do the same to them.
4. Find a minimum of ten people that you know and give them a hug.
5. Just tell them that you need a hug.
6. If they are close, tell them that you love them, even if you haven't done so for years. Sometimes we can forget to say I love you to those closest to us.

Task B.
7. The big challenge is to approach a stranger and ask for a hug.
8. Approach someone with your arms open wide and ask them for a hug.
9. Smile, say thank you, and then move on knowing that you just might have made their day also.
10. When you have expanded your comfort zone and feel good about your achievement, try it again.

You know, I am beginning to love this course – is it a course? No, I don't think it is a course~ just 30 days to discover how to become a star. Anyway, whatever it is I am enjoying it. I hope you are still with me, facing your own challenges and beating your own fears. Keep going girl (or boy).

Notes by Kora

Days 19-21

Ho no!

Just when I thought I was enjoying it, we get another one of those thinking challenges again - this time it's all about forgiveness.

What the fu*k is Dusty doing to me? He knows the abusive sh*t I've been through. I've escaped it, and looked after myself for years. Why the fu*k do I want to go back and think about those days? I sure as hell don't want to forgive the ba**ard!

You know I'm really thinking about not doing this- and I told him that. Do you know what he said?

Something about the toxins of hate I was producing did not hurt that ba**ard at all, they were just poisoning me. Got me thinking, that did.

Then he said that you can't be happy and Sad at the same time, and you can't feel love and hate at the same time. And I have the choice at any time in any day to choose which ones I want, but whatever I choose is at the expense of the other. I think he said something about not getting love in my life until I deal with my feelings of hatred.

You know, between you and me I think he might have something. I don't seem to trust people enough to let them get close to me. I'm only 21 but would like to find a loving partner one day. Maybe I should just look at what's on the table.

Stay with me, I might need your help and support here, support me by doing it with me... please.

Forgiveness task (easy part)

1. Make a list of those who have wronged you.
2. Place them in order with the worst offender at the top and the least at the bottom.
3. Next to their name state the wrong they have done you.
4. Start at the bottom of the list working upward.

5. To those that you can forgive unconditionally say I forgive you for what you did and I forgive me for holding resentment, and then let them go.
6. Keep going until you reach the person you cannot forgive unconditionally.
7. Cut off the bottom of the list (those you have forgiven) and burn it, severing any connection to the events.
8. Allow a night's sleep before returning to the list.

A bubble of forgiveness

Have you been betrayed, hurt and deceived by someone whom you now hold resentment against, someone you cannot forgive?

Then here is a little trick: how to get rid of the poison of hate without letting them off the hook.

a.) Step 1 - Ask yourself what would need to happen for you to be able to forgive that person. Make a list of all the things that would need to happen, even if it includes a groveling apology, a sincere request for forgiveness, being told that you are right and they are wrong, a public announcement of what they did, punishment, even the death penalty if you feel that is what you need to be able to forgive them.

b.) Now feel the weight lift when you know you can have what you want: no hatred, no desired revenge, just relief, and a sense of happiness.

c.) Step 2 - Imagine that these conditions have been met, now I want you to feel the emotion of forgiveness: really feel the emotion of forgiving, feel the emotional release of being told that you are right and were wronged. Feel the power of being asked to forgive the perpetrator who with all their heart wants your forgiveness.

Notes by Kora

d) Now capture this emotion in your imagination and place it in a small helium-filled balloon, tie it with a very fine, unbreakable thread of light and connect it to the shoulder of the person you are willing to forgive (if they request it).

e) This person now has your full forgiveness attached to them for life, all they have to do is request forgiveness from you, even if it's on their death bed, they just have to ask with sincerity and they will receive it.

f) The final step is to sever the energy attachment to this person. Don't forget everything has an energy wave, even your hatred. The more (hate) energy you have sent down the wave to the person, the thicker your connection to that person will be.

g) Now imagine that you have the strength and power of a dragon, think of the burning fire of the sun, breathe a deep breath in through your nose taking the fire deep into your belly, now breathe out a breath of fire, burn to cinders any energetic or emotional attachment you have with this person. Repeat this if necessary knowing that all connections will be burned forever and you no longer have to feed the fire of hate. Let it go and move on. They now have to deal with the consequences of their actions while you are free to enjoy all that life has to offer.

Forgiveness task (hard part)

1. Starting at the top of the list (the worst offender), use the forgiveness bubble technique above and work at it until you find a way of forgiving this person.
2. Once the worst one is done the others get easier.
3. Work your way down the list until you have dealt with everyone and every event.
4. Now burn the list!
5. Take a deep breath and smile.

Well how hard was that?

I didn't think I could face that task, but I did and you know what? It feels great!

I feel like I've dumped a lot of sh*t. I feel lighter, happier, less stressed – less, dare I say it... hateful.

And you won't believe this but some of my friends have said that my face seems softer, more beautiful...

What a result!

I hope, I really, really hope that this exercise has worked for you as well.

Thank you for being there for me; if you were here in person I would give you a big hug!

But promise me... you won't tell Dusty!

Days 22-23

After the last few days I really want to get out and do something.

And guess what! I can, great, fantastic, let's go...

Oops! Forgot to say what the task is.

This task is about doing random acts of kindness. Doing a good deed just for the hell of doing it.

When you help someone by doing a kindness you are rewarded with a happy feeling.

Don't forget if someone does something kind for you, always pay it forward and do something nice for someone else.

Listed below are three different levels of kindness. Do at least one from each level, and feel free to add your own.

Notes by Kora

Helping others

Level A:
1. Start small, keep it simple.
2. Hold the door open for someone.
3. Help someone cross the road.
4. Carry someone's shopping/books/anything.

Level B:
1. Offer to do some shopping for someone.
2. Offer to do a chore for someone that you know they dislike doing.
3. Offer to tidy an elderly neighbor's garden or home.

Level C:
1. Do something kind anonymously: the rule here is that no one can ever know that it was you who was kind.
2. Stretch your imagination: you simply can't get this one wrong!

For two days I've had a lot of fun and done all sorts of kind deeds: just holding the door open and smiling is an easy way to make people happy. I helped Jimmy out on his flower stall so that he could attend his daughter's school play. I've helped serving in the Pizza Hut to give the manager a lunch break when he was on his own. I even washed a posh car outside the squat because it was covered in builder's dust and left a flower under his windshield wipers.

And yes I feel great!

So tell me, what have you been up to?

Days 24-25

Today's task should be okay because it's all about observation, looking at beautiful things — how easy is that?

Dusty said that I need to spend a little time focusing on and appreciating beauty as it will help me to have a more positive outlook on the future.

I was thinking that what looks beautiful to me maybe won't be seen as beautiful by someone else. Apparently that doesn't matter — as long as I think it looks beautiful, that's all that counts.

Anyway, what we are supposed to do is to look at things around us as a piece of art, appreciate the design and yeh, that's right... the beauty.

He said that I should focus on one thing at a time, filter out any distractions by narrowing my field of focus. I think he means that if I was looking at a painting in an art gallery — okay, let's get real, maybe a poster of my favorite rock band — I would look at the detail and the good-looking guys in the photo and wouldn't notice who was walking past; yeh I think I can do that!

He also said that by appreciating its beauty I will experience more happiness. I think he's right — I'm smiling just thinking of my favorite rock stars.

Let's do it...

Looking for beauty

Task A.

1. Find an image of a building, plane, car, train, ship or any other inanimate object, and study it for a full two minutes with fully focused attention.
2. Note all the things you like about it, the lines, the curves, imagine what it would feel like and how it would smell.

Notes by Kora

3. Now go outside and find any one of the above objects in its real form and study it with fully focused attention for five minutes; notice every minute detail and preserve that detail to memory so precisely that you could recreate it if required.

Task B:

1. Find an image of any plant, bird, fish or animal, and study it for a full two minutes with fully focused attention.

2. Note all the things that you like about it, the lines, the curves, imagine what it would feel like and how it would smell; look for the beauty.

3. Now go outside and find any one of the above in its real form and study it with fully focused attention for five minutes; notice every minute detail and preserve that detail to memory so precisely that you could recreate it if required.

Task C:

1. Find an image of a baby, a child, a man, a woman both young and old and study each one for a full two minutes with fully focused attention.

2. Note all the things that you like about it, the lines, the curves, imagine what it would feel like and how it would smell; look for the beauty.

3. Now go outside and find any two of the above in their real form and study them with fully focused attention for five minutes; notice every minute detail and preserve that detail to memory so precisely that you could recreate it if required.

4. Don't forget to look for the beauty in everyone.

I like that one. I found it easy doing the things I already liked. So I thought it would be fun to look at something that I thought was bad and then try to see the beauty in it. Well I chose this pile of garbage behind Victoria coach station, only because I was standing around having a can of coke. So I though why not? There were a few pizza boxes, black sacks, and just general mess, nothing nice about it at all. Then one of the bags moved, I swear it moved and I thought rats! Then there was a furry head, and I quickly took a couple of steps back. I was about to run fast and scream even louder when I saw a cat emerge from the garbage with food in its mouth. I can tell you it gave me a laugh; you know it may not be beautiful, but something good came as a result of that garbage. Makes you think doesn't it? It's not what is going on around us that's good or bad but more the way we choose to see it.

I think it's opened my eyes a little bit, maybe I won't be so judgmental from now on, or at least I will try not to be.

I found this quote the other day in a basketball mag that someone threw away, I tore it out and I've got it in my pocket:

> *If people around you aren't going anywhere, if their dreams are no bigger than hanging out on the corner, or if they're dragging you down, get rid of them.*
>
> *Negative people can sap your energy so fast, and they can take your dreams from you, too.*
>
> –Earvin 'Magic' Johnson

Part Two - **Shine like a star**… *the aloha way*

Days 26-28

"If you truly want to become a star then you need to get over yourself," said Dusty. "If you are going to be the star of your life, then you need to dump the ego and the attitude that is holding you back. The world owes you nothing; if you want it, if you really want it, stand up and claim it by your authenticity, be yourself... be you. Then become everyone else."

What does he mean now? I think that I'm beginning to know the way he works. He means that I should be me and not pretend to be what I'm not, but also try to see things from other people's point of view by looking at life from their direction.

See, I've got it!

Just like a good actor can become many people and play many parts by studying the characters of each person before becoming that person in front of our eyes. But he still remains who he is ~ the actor.

So, Dusty, what part do you want me to play?

He then told me that this may be the hardest test so far, and that we will have to summon up deep strength from inside to face our fears, push through any barriers that are preventing us from achieving our goals.

This is a point of no return, for nothing will ever happen if you continue to play safe and stay in your comfort zone.

You want to be in the starlight - then take a leap and go for it!

Guess what!

Whatever you're looking for will be waiting for you once you push through your fears.

Remember:

- Loosen up and just go for it.
- Don't worry about looking stupid, it's only ego.
- Act as if you are an expert.
- Work your courage muscles.
- Feeling uncomfortable is good.
- Feel the fear, but do it anyway.
- Never give up!

You can improvise, adapt and overcome in any situation...

Act as if.... You can!

Task A:

1. Say Mahalo instead of thank you for one day.
2. Go outside and shout at the top of your voice: Good morning world, it's a brand new day.
3. Learn your lines.
4. Find any paragraph in any book or a poem that inspires you. Read it out load to yourself (in private). Now repeat it but with feeling. Memorize it if you can. Now act it out as though you were delivering a scene on stage.
5. Finally go outside into a public space and repeat your performance. Take a friend for support if need be and deliver the speech to them.

Task B:

1. Choose a character from any movie, TV program or someone in your own life (someone of the same sex as you, and someone who inspires you).
2. Imagine that you have been asked to portray this person in a movie.

Notes by Kora

3. You need to study their character, their voice, their body language, their mannerisms, their habits, their viewpoint and their beliefs.

4. Put aside one to two hours.

5. Spend some time getting into character, dress up if it helps. Become that person (as an actor/actress), walk around your home talking as you imagine that person would talk, act as if you were that person.

6. Now go outside, go shopping, go for a coffee, and go for a walk - but stay in character, walk the walk and talk the talk of that character.

7. Before you start this last task write down your fears. Once completed write down your feelings.

Task C:

Check out the Starlite children's charity at www.starlight.org.uk - they put on pantomimes to entertain children with life limiting illness, find out who the famous actor is who acts as their ambassador. You are not being asked to help or donate, just read about how young kids deal with their life limiting problems and then ask yourself if you can adopt part of that attitude with your problems. Be brave, give it a go.

"When you push through your fears, you'll always find some sort of reward for your bravery," said Dusty.

How scary was that?

I have to tell you, I took four days to do that. Every time I went to go outside I froze. In the end I visited a drama group practicing in the local church hall, told them what I wanted to do and asked them for help.

I never ask anyone for help.

STARDANCE - Flow with Energy

Anyone who knows me will be so surprised, me asking for help. You know what, thinking about it? That was probably the hardest thing I had to do; getting over myself and asking for help.

Well they not only helped me learn how to act, but they even walked over to Regent's Park with me, in costume and in character. I can't remember the last time anybody has supported me like that, unconditionally!

In return I committed to help the drama group with their charity panto this year, raising funds for the Starlight children's foundation, which somehow just seems right.

I'll tell you another secret: that night I cried! Real tears, but they were happy ones. I was happy, felt good, and felt brave, I felt like a star!

And to top it all James the producer also writes for a London magazine and has invited me along to assist him interviewing Tom Cruise at a movie premiere next week.

How cool is that!

Days 29-30

Dream your greatest dream for anything is possible...

What does the future hold? Who knows? But the only place you will get to without a map is lost.

Therefore this final task is to help you map out your next journey on the pathway to the stars!

"Good luck and good night from the Starlite zone."

Signing off:

Dusty

Notes by Kora

The formal bit

Many people feel as if they're adrift in the world. They work hard, but they don't seem to get anywhere worthwhile.

But when asked where they want to go, they don't know because they haven't thought about it. Would you get on a train and go for a ride not knowing where you were going to? Of course not – you choose a destination first then plan your route which may include many places of interest on the way. Yet many of us are traveling life's journey without any clear destination; at best we may have chosen one or two places of interest.

| Home | Family | Partner | Car | Job | Money | Travel |

- *Make a few columns and head them up with the important things in your life. There are a few ideas shown above, but feel free to add your own.*
- *Under each heading make a bucket list of things you want to achieve in this life. Some can be short term and others long-term targets.*
- *Now choose one to three of the most important items on the page.*

| START —————————————— DESTINATION |

- *Now put each target/goal/desire into its own destination box.*
- *Look at **every** bucket list and ask yourself if any of these goals/items/targets can be visited while on the way to any of the three destinations, then put them into a holding box next to the relevant destination.*

You now have an idea of where you want to go, what you want to achieve. List the three in order of preference; if you can't decide what is most important then start from number three. When you have two left, ask yourself: if I can only do one before I die which one would I want to do? This will identify your number one choice.

STARDANCE - Flow with Energy

This gives your target real purpose and depth; you even have a timeline and can work backwards to the starting point, which in turn will identify the first step forward. It will also help to keep you on the right track if the going gets tough.

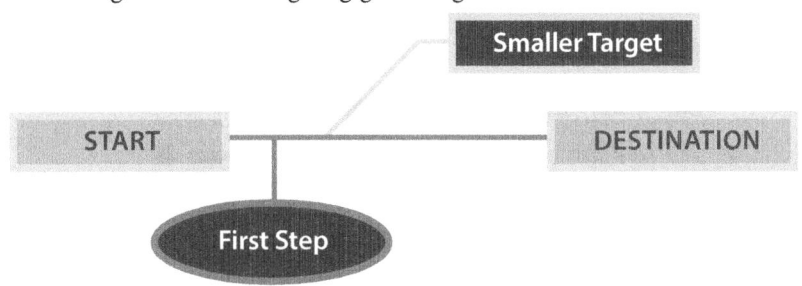

```
                    Smaller Target
START ─────────────────────── DESTINATION
          First Step
```

Now you have an outline plan and can add in smaller targets/goals/desires and bucket list items, the things you want to achieve along the way.

Mission Statement	Vision Statement

Write a short statement in each box.

- **Mission statement** – *This defines your purpose. It's what you ultimately want to achieve in your life or career, expressed in a specific, measurable way.*
- **Vision statement** – *This is a bit more emotional. Here, you define your core values, and how you'll apply those values to your mission.*

For example: if your destination target is to learn to drive, your mission statement could be something like: I am going to learn to drive and aim to pass my test by next summer. Your vision might read: I love the countryside and will take a drive out on my own when I pass.

Now you have an outline plan and can add in smaller targets/ goals/ desires and bucket list items, the things you want to achieve along the way.

The next step

I am a great, beautiful and powerful being and can achieve anything I put my mind to.

Task A:

1. Carry out the exercise as above.
2. Do this for as many of your dreams as need be.
3. Choose one, it does not have to be a big one.
4. The first step toward your desire begins here.
5. Make contact, get more information, and arrange a visit.

Task B:

Wow~ you have taken a giant stride with that small step toward your future.

Well done~ doesn't that feel great?

Go back to the questionnaire and fill in the second column, then reflect on the difference between the two columns, see just how far you have traveled in just
30 days.

Now you know what it takes to become the star of your life. You have the ability to light up the world with your kindness, your personality, and the beautiful you that lives inside. Don't hold back anymore, go out there and let your light shine.

Well I know my next move, do you?

By the way I found this site yesterday www.kevinengland.london

There's some free bits, lots of help and advice, check it out.

Till we meet again.

Warm wishes

Kora xx

Decide what you want to do next, pursue your desire with all your heart and remember... it's your future!

Sponsored by:

azura
spirit of aloha ~ in action

Raising funds for:

STARLIGHT
Brightening the lives of seriously and terminally ill children

Charity Registration Number: 296058

Notes by Kora

2:77 Turning dreams into reality

Everyone has, or at least at one time had, dreams about what their life would be like. Dreaming can be healthy: dreams can inspire, compelling us to look forward in our lives, rather than being stuck in the past. Dreaming is entirely a mental and emotional process, limited only by the imagination. Dreaming requires little energy and no action.

Dreaming is easy, but translating those dreams into reality is not.

This is precisely what the Starlite method does: it turns metaphysical energy into physical energy for use in our daily lives.

In order to turn dreams into reality we need energy, strategy, programing, and a very special set of skills and knowledge. We begin by turning your dreams into goals, for it is goals, and not dreams, that you can effectively pursue and capture.

Setting goals

> *Goals should be set using the ubiquitous SMART objectives as defined by Paul J. Meyer. They should be Specific, Measurable, Achievable, Realistic and Timed.*

Specific – goals should be straightforward and emphasize what you want to happen. Specifics help you to focus your efforts and clearly define what you are going to do.

Measurable – if you can't measure it you can't manage it. Choose a goal with measurable progress, so you can see the change occur.

Achievable – all your goals should be achievable, which means they should be within the bounds of possibility.

Realistic – this provides the check on achievable. Realistic, in this case, means do-able.

Timed – set a clear time frame for the goal. Putting an end point on your goal gives you a clear target to work toward.

–Lindsey Agness

Seven steps to acquiring your goals

#1 Express your goal in terms of specific events or behaviors. In order for a dream to become a goal it needs to be specifically defined. In order for a goal to be attainable, it must be operationally defined. Identify what steps are required to achieve the goal and in what order they need to be taken.

- *How will you recognize the goal when you have it?*
- *What will you be doing when you have it?*
- *How will you feel when you have it?*

#2 Express your goal in terms that can be measured. Unlike dreams, goals must be expressed in terms of outcomes that are measurable, observable, and quantifiable. You need to know when the goal has been reached.

- *Where will I be?*
- *What will I have?*
- *Who will be with me?*

#3 Assign a timeline to your goal. Goals require a particular schedule or date for their achievement. You will achieve your goal once you have determined precisely what it is you want and the time frame for having it.

#4 Choose a goal you can control. Dreams allow you to fantasize about events over which you have no control; goals have to do with aspects of your existence that you can control.

#5 Plan and program a strategy that will get you to your goal. Dreams are longed for but goals involve a strategic plan for getting there. To pursue a goal seriously requires that you realistically assess the obstacles and resources involved.

Make a plan and work your plan, rely on your strategy, planning and programing, not your willpower, and you will attain your goal.
- *Identify time required.*
- *Places to be.*
- *Things to do.*
- *People to meet.*

#6 Define your goal in terms of steps. Goals are carefully broken down into measurable steps that lead, ultimately, to the desired outcome.

Steady progress, through well-chosen, realistic, interval steps, produces results in the end. Know what those steps are before you set out. Have a map of where you want to go.

#7 Create accountability for your progress toward your goal. Know precisely what you want, when you want it by, and the time and place are scheduled and protected. Set up some form of accountability, real consequences for not doing the work; this will make it impossible for you not to achieve your goal. –Dr. Phillip McGraw

> *All the flowers of all the tomorrows
> are in the seeds of today.*
>
> -Hawaiian proverb

2: 78 Faith, trust and stardust

Congratulations, well done for getting this far and completing 30 days on the "pathway to the stars" – are you ready to shine your light on the world yet?

You now have your dream and your first taste of stardom, what next?

Did you know that Stardust and the Aloha Diet are the first 30 days of a 90-day Shine Your Light program known as the Starlite experience?

The way is clear; all you have to do is keep moving in the right direction until you reach your dream.

Turning your dreams into reality – that has been my vision statement, my goal, for as long as I can remember. Native Americans use something called a dream catcher; my mission in this book has been to help you see and catch your dream and now it's to help you turn that dream into a reality. Wow! Big ha! Some might say impossible...

But we know differently, don't we?!

> *The ancients call them miracles, but
> they are not miracles. They are the
> produce of someone's dream.*
>
> -Whoopi Goldberg

*Part Two - **Shine like a star**... the aloha way*

> *Life is what happens while you are dreaming of doing something else.*
>
> –John Lennon

2:79 If only…

Many moons ago there was a man who had a dream, a dream to live in Provence in France. Year after year he would say if only life was kind to him he could move to Provence, if only he had this, if only he had that, then he could live in Provence.

Then one day we went away for the weekend and he said if only he was made redundant he would have the money to move to Provence. "This is my real wish, my dream, I hate my job," he said.

Well, within three months his wish was granted: not only was he made redundant but he was given a financial package you would give your right arm for; what a lucky guy. So what did he do? Realize his dream, move to Provence and have a happy life? No, he put the money in the bank and said, "If only my life was different I would be living in Provence now."

The old saying that you can lead a horse to water but you can't make him drink comes to mind.

So what happened?

He was scared, scared to grasp life by the horns, scared to take a chance. What happens if it doesn't work out? Scared to take a step out of the mist in the gray zone, he adopted the "at least I know what I've got is okay" approach to life.

I fear that when it is his time to leave this earthly plane behind his last words said with regret will be, "If only…"

Don't be an "if only" person.

There is no point spending your life hoping that your boat will come in just to see it sail on past because you are afraid to get on board for the journey of your life.

Dare to dream.

Know what your dream is, grasp the opportunity when it comes along, and sail into a beautiful new dawn...

2:80 Starlite is:

Starlite system is a way of tuning in, connecting to universal energy and then using that energy to inspire, empower and encourage balance, harmony and healing in the world.

Starlite zone is a zone of energy found betwixt and between spirit and matter. It's a creative environment where attitudes can change and beliefs can shift, where wishes are granted and dreams come true.

Stardance is a way of living with this enchanting interaction of spirit and science. This inspirational and transformational cosmic wave infused with aloha can be used to encourage metaphysical energy into physical manifestation.

Starlite Lomi is the divine energy of aloha, being infused into the healing arts.

Principle 1: We are spirit beings, beings of light, here to have the human experience.

Principle 2: We live in a Star-lite Universe-ity of life, where everything is energy and anything is possible.

Starlite is an inspirational and transformational wave of cosmic energy that transcends the spiritual and the physical, creating a cosmic interface~ in and around the body. An entanglement of cosmic energy, swaying to the vibration of creation, transmuting metaphysical energy into a physical existence, and turning dreams into reality.

Surfing this wave is to develop a deep understanding of the process of living, thinking with your whole body and dancing with your whole mind.

In the enchanting interaction between science and spirit, the light forces of the cosmos and the dense frequencies of matter, vibrating, circulating and resonating to the movement of beauty, love and aloha, it is a galaxy of wonder, gracefully gliding effortlessly to the tune of the universe, and creating a dance... a stardance!

Kevin England DD, DC

azura © 2014

www.kevinengland.london

2:81 Mahalo

The living expression of aloha is love of the highest ideal that by pursuing love as aloha at its highest level of excellence is a celebration of life, and from its union come the blossoms of everlasting love, a family, a new generation of aloha.

Touching and caring is the natural and Hawaiian way to love... aloha.

-Patrick Ka'ano'i

Testimonials

"I really love your book content. Spiritually your journey visits places I have only dreamt of. Your book fills me with warmth, light and hope."

-Michael Inns, *Creative Designer*

"The author has managed to mix, the principles of urban living, Huna, Quantum Physics and Shamanism with the spirit of aloha into a magical cake, I employ you to take a bite and taste.... a new future."

–Susan O'Hannon, *Angel Therapist*

"Wow! Science, philosophy, spiritualism, all served up on a plate of realism."

–Bailey King PhD

"I have always felt that there was something very special about Kevin; he is a great presenter, very personable, humble and modest."

-Theresa White, *singer and song writer*

"This book is a real treasure trove for those who are looking for that elusive 'something.' The author introduces us to a 'star- lit Universe –ity' of life where anything is possible. The lessons and wisdom found in this book should really be taught to every student at high school, the world would be a far better place for it."

–S. Davis, retired school teacher

"Kevin brings a breath of fresh air to the world of complementary therapy."

–Keion Connor

"Energy is the fuel of excellence. The higher your energy level the better you feel, and the better you feel the more astounding your results will be."

–Lindsay Agness

Bibliography

Agness, L. (2008). **Change Your Life with NLP.** Harlow: Pearson.

Arledge, H. U. (2007). **Wise Secrets of Aloha.** San Francisco: Weiser Books.

Borg, J. (2004). **Persuasion.** Harlow: Pearson.

Borg, J. (2010). **Mind Power.** Harlow: Pearson.

Braden, G. (2007). **The Divine Matrix.** London: Hay House.

Brinkley, D. & Brinkley, K. (2008). **Secrets of the Light.** US: Harperone.

Britten, R. (2001). **Fearless Living.** London: Hodder & Stoughton.

Byrne, R. (2010). **The Power.** London: Simon & Schuster.

Cabane, F. (2012). **The Charisma Myth.** Penguin.

Campbell, E. (1991). **A Dancing Star.** London: Harper Collins.

Chopra, D. (1989). **Quantum Healing.** London: Bantam Books.

Courtney, E. A. (1999). **The Essentials of McTimoney Chiropractic.** London: Thorsons.

Cowan, T. (1996). **Shamanism.** Berkeley: Ten Speed Press.

England, K. (2013). **Starlite - The Secret Lomi.** St. Albans: Panoma Press.

Exley, H. (1997). **In Beauty May I Walk.** Watford: Exley.

Gawain, S. (1986). **Living in the Light.** London: Eden Grove.

Goodard, N. (n.d.). **Power of Awareness.**

Gregg, B. (2007). **The Divine Matrix.** London: Hay House.

Hamilton, D. R. (2010). **Why Kindness is Good For You.** London: Hay House.

Hatty Uhane Jim, G. A. (2007). **Wise Secrets of Aloha.** San Francisco: Weiser Books.

Huang, C. A. & Lynch, J. (1992). **Thinking Body, Dancing Mind.** New York: Bantam Books.

Ingerman, S. (2001). **Medicine of the Earth.** Random House.

Ingerman, S. (2010). **How to Thrive in Changing Times.** Weiser.

Ka'ano'i, P. (1988). **Kamalamalama.** Honolulu: Ka'ano'i Publishing.

King, S. K. (2008). **Huna Ancient Hawaiian Secrets for Modern Living.** New York: Atria books.

Kos, K. H. (2000). **From Ecstasy To Success.** Kilauea: Gamma Group.

Lauterstein, D. (1985). **Putting the Soul Back in the Body.** Austin, Texas: Lauterstein & Conway.

Lipton, B. H. (2013). **The Honeymoon Effect.** London: Hay House.

McGraw, P. C. (1998). **Life Strategies.** London: Vermilion.

McGree, P. (2010). **Self-Confidence.** Chichester: Capstone.

Melville, L. (1969). **Children of the Rainbow.** Wheaton: Quest.

Millman, D. (1995). **The Laws of Spirit.** Tiburon: HJ Kramer.

Myers, J. E. (2010). **Fascial Release for Structural Balance.** Berkeley: North Atlantic Books.

Provenzano, R. (2001). **A Little Book of Aloha.** Honolulu: Mutual.

Ramtha. (1999). **The Whit Book.** Yelm. Washington: JZK Publishing.

Ramtha. (2003). **That Elixir Called Love.** Washington: JZK Publishing.

Roger, J. & McWilliams, P. (1991). **Do It!** London: Thorsons.

Rohr, C. H. (2003). **Chicken Soup from the Soul of Hawaii.** Florida: Health Communications Inc.

Samet, R. (September 2004). **Massage World Magazine.**

Sanderson, M. (1998). **Soft Tissue Release.** Chichester: Corpus.

Say, R. (n.d.). **Managing with Aloha.**

Weinman, R. A. (1988). **Your Hands Can Heal.** London: Harper Collins.

Wesselman, H. (1995). **Spiritwalker.** New York: Bantam.

Wesselman, H. (2011). **The Bowl of Light.** Boulder, Colorado: Sounds True.

Williamson, M. (2003). **Everyday Grace.** London: Bantam Books.

Wood, J. M. (2002). **Easy-to-use Shamanism.** London: Vega.

Song Lyrics:

Coolidge, P & R. (1997). **Circle of light.** Walela.

Crowley, D.K. & Keala, A. & Kua, C. & Ioane, M. (1976). **Hawaii 78.** Israel Kamakawiwo'Ole.

Gerome, R. & Rado, J. (1969). **Good Morning Starshine.** Oliver.

Gilmore. Mason. Waters & Wright. (1973) **Dark Side of the Moon.** Pink Floyd.

Knopflier, M. (2013). **Oldest Surfer on the Beach.** Jimmy Buffet.

Marley, B. (1979). **Redemption Song.** Bob Marley.

Leonard, P. & Robertson, R. (1994) **Skinwalker.** Robbie Robertson.

Love, M. & Wilson, B. (1966) **Good Vibrations.** Beach Boys.

Savigar, K. & Stewart, R. (2013). **Can't stop me now.** Rod Stewart.

Lightning Source UK Ltd.
Milton Keynes UK
UKOW07f0821141214

243095UK00002B/15/P